D1190905

Lightning
Over
Bougainville

The Yamamoto Mission Reconsidered

Lightning Over Bougainville

Edited and with an Introduction by
R. Cargill Hall

Smithsonian Institution Press

Washington and London

This book was edited by Therese Boyd and designed by Janice Wheeler.
∞ The paper used in this publication meets the minimum requirements
of the American National Standard for Permanence of Paper for Printed
Library Materials Z39.48-1984.
This book is part of the Smithsonian History of Aviation Series. Published in
the United States by the Smithsonian Institution Press, this series of books is
distributed in the United Kingdom, Europe, the Middle East, and Africa by
Airlife Publishing Ltd.
Library of Congress Cataloging in Publication Data
Lightning over Bougainville: the Yamamoto mission reconsidered /
R. Cargill Hall, editor.
p.   cm.—(Smithsonian history of aviation series)
Includes bibliographical references (p.) and index.
ISBN 1-56098-012-5
1. World War, 1939-1945—Aerial operations, American—Congresses.
2. World War, 1939-1945—Campaigns—Bougainville Island—Congresses.
3. Yamamoto, Isoroku, 1884-1943—Death and burial—Congresses.
4. Bougainville Island—History—Congresses. I. Hall, R. Cargill. II. Series.
D790.L49 1991
940.54′4973—dc20   90-9950
Printed in the United States of America
10 9 8 7 6 5 4 3 2 1
   99 98 97 96 95 94 93 92 91

To friend and foe alike, who, in 1942-1943 during the Guadalcanal and northern Solomons campaigns in the South Pacific, contended for their countries so savagely on land, at sea, and in the sky:

> From this day to the ending of the world,
> But we in it shall be remembered,—
> We few, we happy few, we band of brothers;
> For he to-day that sheds his blood with me
> Shall be my brother; be he ne'er so vile,
> This day shall gentle his condition:
> And gentlemen in England now a-bed
> Shall think themselves accurs'd they were not here
>
> William Shakespeare
> *King Henry V*
> Act IV, Scene 3

Contents

Foreword

Tom D. Crouch

Just after 9:30 on the morning of 18 April 1943, a tight formation of sixteen Lockheed P-38s roared across a beach some 30 miles northwest of Buin, on Bougainville, in the northern Solomon Islands. Led by Major John W. Mitchell, commanding officer of the 339th Fighter Squadron, they had departed Fighter Two, a rough airstrip near Kukum, Guadalcanal, some two hours before. Staying well to the west of the Japanese island strongholds at Rendova, Vella Lavella, Treasury, and Shortland, the big Lightnings had flown over 430 miles, skimming the waves of the Solomon Sea to avoid detection.

First Lt. Douglas Canning, a twenty-three-year-old Nebraskan, was the first to sight the quarry. He broke the long radio silence at precisely 9:34, calling out, "Bogeys, 11 o'clock high." Three miles away a flight of eight aircraft, six Mitsubishi A6M3 Type 32 Zeros and a pair of G4M1 Betty medium bombers, was approaching its destination, Ballale Island, off the southern tip of Bougainville. Spotting the Americans, the pilots of the Zeros jettisoned their drop tanks and turned to meet the attack. The two bombers dove for the safety of a nearby fighter airstrip at Buin, Bougainville.

It was over in less than ten minutes. The Zeros claimed a single victim. Lieutenant Ray Hine would not be going home to Indianapolis. But the Japanese had paid a far heavier price. The returning Lightning pilots reported three Zeros destroyed. One of the Bettys had splashed down in the ocean just off Moila Point, within sight of a Japanese army station. A patrol boat fished three survivors, including Vice Adm. Matome Ugaki and Rear Adm. Kitamura, out of the water.

A column of black smoke rising above the jungle canopy marked the spot where the second Betty had come to earth. A search party led by Lt. Tsuyoshi Hamasuna reached the crash site a day later. They found no survivors. The body of Adm. Isoroku Yamamoto, commander-in-chief of the Japanese Combined Fleet, had been thrown clear of the aircraft. Dressed in khakis, he still wore one white glove, and clutched a dress sword in his hand.

The Yamamoto mission is the best-known and most thoroughly studied fighter engagement of the Pacific War. It may well be the most celebrated sortie ever flown by American fighter pilots. The participants, American and Japanese, have been interviewed repeatedly and at length. The action has been dissected from every possible angle. Futile attempts have been made to reduce the chaotic movement of the twenty-four assorted Lightnings, Zeros, and Bettys to a series of neat lines on paper. Yet for all of that effort we have still not satisfied our curiosity as to precisely what occurred in the air over Bougainville on that morning almost half a century ago.

It seems only reasonable to inquire as to the reason for our fascination with this single aerial encounter. The sheer narrative quality of the story is part of the explanation. From the interception of the coded message announcing the admiral's itinerary, through the high-level discussions of the wisdom and the morality of the venture, to the meeting of American and Japanese aircraft at the precise time and place predicted, this is a whopping good yarn.

Like all good stories, this tale is built around a powerful and intriguing central character. The citizens of wartime America regarded Isoroku Yamamoto as a fiend incarnate. They knew him as the man who masterminded the attack on Pearl Harbor, the warlord who boasted that he would dictate the terms of the peace in the White House. Writing in the *New York Times* in 1945, Thomas Lanphier, the P-38 pilot credited with having destroyed Yamamoto, described his victim as "a conceited and arrogant man . . . with a face like a frog":

"Yamamoto! All the cunning and power-madness of his race embodied in one man, the epitome of every brutal, strutting little savage he commanded. From infancy a hater of all things American, he lived out every day of his vengeful life . . . in anticipation of that moment when he would stand with his foot upon the throat of the United States, and lay down the Emperor's dictates for its bondage. The same Emperor to whom, with tongue in cheek, he rendered such homage as suited his ambitious purpose, and whom he and Tojo used as a front for their insane program for world conquest.

Lanphier regarded Yamamoto as "an easy man to hate. . . . And one it would be an honor to destroy. For in his malevolent person he contained such power for evil that he was a walking and talking military target of first priority."

The article serves to remind modern readers of the extent to which deep-seated racial hatred on both sides fueled the savage fighting in the Pacific. Virulent prejudice did not disappear after 1945, but the opportunity to study Japanese records in the immediate postwar years did lead to a dramatic reassessment of the role and character of Isoroku Yamamoto. It became clear that, far from being an extreme militarist or a rabid anti-American, the admiral had been a force for caution and restraint. His much-publicized threat to dictate peace in Washington, D.C., had actually been an attempt to warn his countrymen of the difficulties they would face in a war with the United States.

Americans came to recognize Yamamoto as a brilliant commander and a stern but honorable foe. Rex T. Barber, the other claimant to the Yamamoto victory credit, summed the matter up in a letter written to a student of the Yamamoto mission in 1984. "The more I study and read about Admiral Yamamoto, the more I respect and admire him." Barber was convinced that the mission had shortened the war, but regretted that "the world did lose a great man."

The unique quality of Yamamoto's genius lends an additional element of fascination to the story of his death. The temptation to wonder what might have been is irresistible. Obviously, the events of 18 April 1943 did not alter the final outcome of the Pacific War. By the spring of 1943, Japan faced inevitable defeat. The length of time and the number of lives required to achieve the final Allied victory was still very much at issue, however. Thousands of American and Japanese soldiers, sailors, and airmen who survived to enjoy the fruits of peace should, perhaps, be grateful that Isoroku Yamamoto was not present at the Battle of the Philippine Sea.

Finally, like all good stories, the tale of the Yamamoto mission includes an element of mystery. Who did kill Yamamoto? There are those who believe that the controversy over the victory credit is of little consequence, and somehow tarnishes the essential heroism of all the participants. Others argue that simple justice demands a firm and final answer. Of one thing we can be certain. Like the debate over the circumstances of the death of Baron Manfred von Richthofen, it is a question that will probably be argued for a long time to come.

For those who care about the debate, this book offers a definitive summary of the evidence on which to base a decision. Serious students of the Pacific War will appreciate the volume for the new light that it sheds on an important incident of that conflict. But the armchair aviator in all of us also owes a considerable debt to the editor and authors. For, in addition to its other sterling qualities, this book is nothing less than an open invitation to imagine yourself in the cockpit of a Lightning, flying low over the Solomon Sea toward Bougainville, your eyes peeled for the first glint of sunlight on a flight of Zeros and Bettys headed for Ballale.

Preface

In the South Pacific, early on the morning of 18 April 1943, Admiral Isoroku Yamamoto, commander-in-chief of the Japanese Combined Fleet, waved to those nearby at Lakunai Airfield, Rabaul, New Britain Island. Then he turned and entered a Mitsubishi G4M1 "Betty" bomber. Moments later, the twin-engine naval aircraft took off and, with its occupants, flew into history.

The flight planned for this day was to bring the Japanese leader southeast from New Britain to frontline bases on Ballale and Bougainville islands. There he would meet the emperor's soldiers and sailors who faced Allied forces, confer with their commanders, and return in the afternoon to naval headquarters at Rabaul. Instead, about 0940 local time, the flight ended in the jungle of Bougainville's south coast, with Yamamoto and his subalterns dead amidst the bomber's burned-out wreckage. A companion "Betty" bomber carrying other members of the admiral's staff crashed into the Solomon Sea with the loss of all save three on board. United States Army Air Forces pilots had intercepted the admiral's flight and, in one blow, decapitated Japanese military leadership in the Pacific. That blow, like the failed invasion and loss of aircraft carriers at Midway Island ten months earlier, was one from which wartime Japan would never fully recover.

The near-miraculous interception and subsequent shooting down of Admiral Yamamoto's plane in April 1943 provoked immediate controversy among British and American leaders, for it involved the use of "broken" Japanese naval codes and threatened to alert an implacable enemy to this most secret of Allied secrets in World War II. In the years after the war, the Yamamoto mission also provoked controversy among those who argued the morality and military value of targeting enemy leaders for death. And the Americans who flew on the mission would eventually contest claim to the aerial victory credit for the admiral's bomber.

Forty-five years later, in April 1988, the Admiral Nimitz Museum in Fredericksburg, Texas, sponsored a "Yamamoto Mission Retrospective." Scholars and surviving American and Japanese aviators attended the symposium and addressed the military, political, ethical, and historical issues of that famous wartime operation. Recollections were marshalled and surviving records assayed in an attempt to fully explain the mission as it was planned and executed. This volume contains the proceedings of that symposium—the papers presented and recollections offered, along with related documents and interviews. It brings together for the first time in one work all of the key information currently known about the Yamamoto mission. The leader of the American attacking element, Thomas G. Lanphier, died in November 1987, a few months before the retrospective convened in Fredericksburg. Because his recollections of the engagement differed substantially from those of his wingman, Rex Barber, I have introduced them directly in the narrative—instead of placing them in an appendix— along with the statements of his colleagues in attendance. Lanphier's account of the Yamamoto mission is excerpted from a lecture he delivered at the National Air and Space Museum in 1985 and appears with the permission of his widow and the Smithsonian Institution. Because I have used the current spellings of place-names throughout the text, they do not always correspond to spellings used in World War II. In these instances, the contemporary spelling of the place-name appears in brackets at the first mention.

On 22 June 1990, Hisashi Takahashi, of the National Institute for Defense Studies, and Jay Hines, Fifth Air Force historian, conducted a taped interview with the one remaining Japanese survivor of the

Yamamoto mission, Hiroshi Hayashi. Pilot of the second Betty bomber shot down in the Solomon Sea, Hayashi observed the entire engagement from the moment it began until Admiral Yamamoto's bomber crashed in the jungle. A translation of the interview appears in this volume, and Hayashi's recollection emphatically underscores the sage counsel General James Doolittle offered Lanphier in December 1984 (see p. 30).

Hayashi's recollection also added to this story one final, ironic footnote. Both he and the surviving Zero pilot, Kenji Yanagiya, received flight instructions in different places on the evening of 17 April 1943. Both unequivocally declare their destination was Buin, not Ballale. At the last minute, Admiral Yamamoto altered his itinerary, but not his time of departure. Because the two airfields were close by one another, John Mitchell's aerial encounter succeeded. Had the interception been planned for land or sea, it doubtless would have failed.

I am indebted to numerous individuals who made possible the compiling and editing of these proceedings. Bruce Smith and Helen Springall of the Nimitz Museum furnished audiotapes of the panel sessions and numerous photographs from the museum collection. Dr. Jerry R. Kelly and Joann Vasco transcribed the panel and question-and-answer sessions, while George Chandler and Rex Barber provided questions for an initial transcription of the Yanagiya interview. Roger Pineau, Douglas Canning, Terry Gwynn-Jones, Charles Darby, and Rollins Snelling furnished other photographs that appear in this volume. Julius Jacobson identified the squadrons to which American pilots were assigned. A special debt of gratitude is owed Roger Pineau, David Chenoweth, and Shirley Crawford for their editorial assistance, and Capt. George Cully, USAF, who compiled the comprehensive bibliography that appears at the end of this volume. Finally, we are all indebted to Therese Boyd, who admirably edited our work for the Smithsonian Institution Press. The interpretation of acts and events in chapter 1 is my own and does not represent the official view of the Nimitz Foundation or the departments of the Navy or Air Force.

R.C.H.

Chapter 1

The Yamamoto Mission: A Retrospective

R. Cargill Hall

Few Americans knew of Admiral Isoroku Yamamoto, commander-in-chief of the Japanese Combined Fleet, before 7 December 1941. A few months later, there were few who did not judge him among all Axis leaders the most treacherous. For Yamamoto had planned the Japanese surprise attack on Pearl Harbor, an attack that took the lives of 2,400 American servicemen, an attack that all but eliminated the Pacific Fleet, an attack that catapulted the United States into a world-wide conflict. Fanning American hatred in the first days afterward, Tokyo Radio broadcast for propaganda purposes a vainglorious de-claration attributed to the admiral: "I am looking forward to dictating peace to the United States in the White House in Washington." The animosity toward Japanese military leaders and their countrymen culminated in the incarceration during World War II of virtually all West Coast Japanese-American citizens. It also turned the Pacific Theater into a war with racial overtones, one that provoked military atrocities, one where combatants seldom asked for quarter, and even less frequently gave any.

The Man

Events such as these could hardly have been imagined by the parents who, on 4 April 1884, welcomed into the world the future Japanese admiral. Born to Sadayoshi Takano and his second wife, Mineko, this

1

seventh child in their family at first went unnamed. Pressed for a name, Sadayoshi settled on his age at the time of the baby's birth: fifty-six, or, in Japanese characters, Isoroku. Isoroku's father served as headmaster of the primary school in the town of Nagaoka. Situated in the rugged Kiso Mountains above the bleak west coast of Honshu, two hundred miles northwest of Tokyo, the town was especially remote in the late nineteenth century. The snows from Siberia usually fell in the Kisos in late October and stayed until March. The precocious Isoroku would be raised in a spartan environment.

The Emperor Meiji, meanwhile, labored to bring Japan into the select circle of nineteenth-century world powers. The country needed a modern military establishment and in 1873, at Japan's invitation, Britain built and staffed a naval academy on the island of Eta Jima, near Hiroshima, to train the leaders of a modern navy. About the same time, France built a dockyard for the Imperial Navy near Yokohama, and for ten years French engineers taught their Japanese counterparts all they knew about building modern warships. With the dockyard under construction, Japan purchased battleships and cruisers from Britain, France, Germany, and the United States. By the turn of the century, Japan possessed a growing fleet of warships that compared favorably with those of the western powers, and the state encouraged the best among its youth to apply for naval training. In 1900, at sixteen years of age, Isoroku took the examination for the naval academy and finished second in the nation. Four years later, standing seventh in the 1904 graduation class, the new ensign was posted on board the cruiser *Nisshin* in the fleet of Adm. Heihachiro Togo.

The Russo-Japanese War, provoked by Japan primarily to gain hegemony over Korea, had already begun. To secure the Korean peninsula, the Japanese acted to eliminate the Russian Far East Fleet and capture its base, Port Arthur, on the tip of Manchuria's Liaotung Peninsula astride Korea Bay. Hostilities commenced suddenly on 8 February 1904, when Japanese torpedo boats staged a surprise attack on the Russian fleet at anchor in Port Arthur, while Togo's fleet simultaneously imposed a naval blockade. The next day, with the Russians reeling from the blow, Japanese forces landed in Korea. Japan formally declared war two days later, on 10 February. While the struggle for Port Arthur intensified during the summer and fall, the Russian Baltic Fleet on 15 October 1904 set sail for the Orient to lift the siege. Admiral Zinovy Rozhdestvenski commanded the armada of eight battleships, eight cruisers, nine destroyers, and some smaller craft that made its way through the English Channel and turned south. But the Baltic Fleet, beset with command and logistic problems, proceeded around the world at a snail's pace. Long before it even reached the Yellow Sea, Port Arthur and the remnants of the Far East Fleet had capitulated, on 2 January 1905.

With the New Year, and without Port Arthur, Rozhdestvenski elected to sail onward, past Korea and Japan, to the Russian port of Vladivostok. On the morning of 27 May 1905, eight months after putting to sea, the Baltic Fleet entered the strait between Korea and Japan. Ensign Isoroku Takano, just five feet three inches in height, numbered among those manning Togo's fleet of four battleships, eight cruisers, twenty-one destroyers, and sixty torpedo boats that awaited the Russians. The engagement began early in the afternoon, near Tsushima Island, which divides the strait, and raged into the night. By next morning, Admiral Togo could claim victory in the greatest naval battle since Trafalgar. Except for one Russian cruiser and five destroyers that managed to escape, the entire Baltic Fleet was sunk or captured. Togo's fleet, though battle-damaged, counted only three torpedo boats missing.

The Battle of Tsushima Strait marked a turning point in history. It brought the Russians to the peace table, and it brought to Japan all the territory for which it had fought, and more. More important, perhaps, Japan emerged a recognized world power. The crushing naval victory most emphatically dispelled any notion of "European invincibility"—at least among the Japanese, if not yet among the western nations. In the fray, Ensign Takano was injured by shrapnel, which badly scarred his legs and severed the middle and index fingers of his left hand. Togo's victory, however, ensured that the Imperial Navy would remain the premier service in the insular Land of the Rising Sun.

In the years that followed, Takano sailed with his squadron on training cruises throughout the Pacific. He visited ports in Korea, China, the west coast of America, and Australia as he perfected the skills of a gunnery officer, completed the advanced course at naval gunnery school in 1911, and gained the rank of lieutenant. In 1914, shortly before Europe plunged into World War I, he entered the Navy Staff College, and in 1915 was promoted to lieutenant commander. Solemn, taciturn, and unconventional in social settings (he was known to stand on his head or perform a plate-balancing dance on occasion), Takano could now be counted among the most promising of the young men in Echigo Prefecture. His father and mother had both died two years earlier and, following Japanese custom, the locally prominent family of Tatewaki Yamamoto, in Nagaoka, offered to adopt him. Isoroku accepted. In a Buddhist ceremony he renounced the name Takano and took in its place Yamamoto, the surname registered when he graduated from the Navy Staff College in 1916.

Two years later, when Lieutenant Commander Yamamoto was thirty-four, he married the daughter of a dairy farmer from his home province, Reiko Mihashi. This union produced two sons and two daughters. Though it met all requirements of Japanese social convention, the marriage was not a close one, for Yamamoto would spend over half his career away from home. Indeed, the first separation began just eight months later, in April 1919, when he was posted to America for two years of language study at Harvard University in Cambridge, Massachusetts.

While enrolled at Harvard, Yamamoto was promoted to commander. He was listed as a "special student in English" and took up residence in Cambridge, but never attended a class. Instead, he devoted all of his efforts to the study of petroleum production and refining. The era of coal-burning navies was nearing an end, and Yamamoto perceived oil to be the logical choice to replace coal in firing the boilers of steam turbines. The commander traveled widely and assessed first-hand the techniques of American mass production and petroleum technology in visits to automobile plants in Detroit and oil fields and refineries in Texas and Mexico. During this period he also read widely among military articles and books published in English, especially those written by members of the U.S. Army and Navy's fledgling air arms.

The period 1919-21 was indeed one of considerable ferment in American military circles. Brigadier General William Mitchell, who returned from France in March 1919, began his campaign for a separate, independent air force made up of both army and navy aerial components, modeled after the combined arms of Great Britain's Royal Air Force. Testifying before Congress in the months that followed, Mitchell came down hard in favor of aircraft carriers that could provide command of the air in operations at sea. In June 1919, the Navy General Board directed to a sympathetic secretary of the navy an aviation policy statement that declared air operations at sea to be a preserve of its own. "A Naval air service," the board asserted, "must be established, capable of accompanying and operating with the fleet in all waters of the globe."* Ten months later, in March 1920, the naval collier *Jupiter* entered Norfolk to be converted to an aircraft carrier, later commissioned as USS *Langley* (CV-1). Finally, in July 1921, the Navy Department formally recognized fleet aviation by establishing the Bureau of Aeronautics, and, in the same month, its aviators participated with their army counterparts in the test-bombing of captured German ships off the Virginia Capes.

Yamamoto was unquestionably well acquainted with these events and the tensions existing within the United States defense establishment. To be sure, when he returned to Japan in the summer of 1921, this lifelong gunnery officer began to expound ideas and concepts about naval aviation that must have seemed "foreign" to those Japanese who represented, guided, and protected classic naval tradition—the commanders of battleships and battle cruisers of the line. Named an instructor at the Navy Staff College from which he had

*Quoted in Melhorn, *Two-Block Fox*, 26.

graduated five years before, Yamamoto offered students a novel view of naval operations that turned on two key points. First, he asserted, no future navy could exist without oil. Second, he affirmed that military airplanes were of much greater potential than was generally supposed, that control of the air would determine the outcome of naval engagements, and that navy leaders must plan for air armament. These were strong views in 1921-22, when Japanese naval expenditures accounted for one-third of the national budget, almost all of which went to procure and support coal-fired capital ships fitted with the naval long rifle.

Not all of the naval expenditures, however, were so directed. With an eye on Great Britain and the United States, the Japanese navy had already begun building its first aircraft carrier, *Hosho,* which would enter service in 1923. Whether Yamamoto's views of naval aviation were judged heretical or prescient by his superiors is not recorded. But at age thirty-nine he was promoted to captain and, about the time *Hosho* began sea trials, Yamamoto accompanied Adm. Kenji Ide on a nine-month tour of America and Europe. On his return to Japan, Yamamoto was, reportedly at his own request, appointed to the naval air station at Lake Kasumigaura, effective 1 September 1924. At this station, founded just two years earlier about forty miles northeast of Tokyo, he served as the second-in-command and director of studies. Here, he guided the early planning of tactics and training practices of Japanese naval aviation.

He might have preferred naval aviation and exploring the tactical role of aircraft carriers in warfare at sea, but Yamamoto's knowledge of the United States and proficiency in the English language soon brought him once more to America. Named the naval attaché at the Japanese embassy in Washington, D.C., he spent 1926-28 acquiring information about U.S. defense, shipbuilding, and aeronautical programs. It was during this time that Yamamoto's skills as a card player became widely recognized among the American naval officers with whom he associated. To the game of poker, learned during his first stay in the United States, he added the more complicated game of bridge. "Anticipation, bluff and luck appealed to his temperament,"

Roger Pineau has observed,* and he had a remarkable ability to remember the cards already played. Poker and bridge became his "passions." Judged by many to be a world-class player at both games in the years that followed, few had the pleasure of besting him at either one.

Shortly after returning again to Japan in March 1928, Yamamoto was given his first command, light cruiser *Isuzu*. Four months later, in December, he was named commander of *Akagi*, one of Japan's largest and newest aircraft carriers. Promoted to rear admiral in 1929, he accompanied the Japanese delegation to the London Naval Disarmament Conference later that year. In London, though the ratio of capital ships established among the major powers in the Washington Naval Treaty of 1922 remained unaltered (5 : 5 : 3 for the United States, Britain, and Japan respectively), Yamamoto helped secure parity for Japan in submarines and light cruisers. Meanwhile, participants of the naval arms limitation agreements planned for another conference in 1935, one year before the Washington treaty was scheduled to expire.

Returning from London in June 1930, Yamamoto became chief of the Technical Division of the Aeronautics Department in the Navy Ministry, followed in 1933 by eight months at sea as commander of the First Carrier Division. Afterward, he returned to the Naval General Staff for briefings prior to his departure as Japan's chief delegate to the London Naval Conference that began in December 1934. In the 1930s, the Japanese navy, like the army, was divided by serious internal rivalries, and officials of the Navy Ministry and Naval General Staff contested for influence within government circles. The ministry was responsible for naval policy, the budget, weapons procurement—including aviation—ship construction, personnel, and relations with the Diet and cabinet. The general staff directed fleet operations, prepared war plans, and had historically occupied a subsidiary role in

---

*Pineau, "Admiral Isoroku Yamamoto," 392.

the councils of power. Now, however, leaders of the Naval General Staff who largely opposed naval arms limitations found ready support among army leaders. Known as the "Fleet Faction," they succeeded in markedly reducing the influence of the admirals in the Navy Ministry who favored continued cooperation with the United States, France, and Great Britain.

Isoroku Yamamoto numbered most prominently among those in the Navy Ministry who sought cooperation with the western powers. But he had his orders and, promoted to vice admiral as Japan's delegate to the 1934-35 London Naval Conference, Yamamoto firmly rejected continuance of the 5 : 5 : 3 ratio in capital ships. Attempts to sway him otherwise came to naught. Trading on the words of western leaders, the imperial plenipotentiary demanded national self-determination of armaments as a sovereign right. He gained notoriety with an aphorism offered in defense of this position. Asked about Japan's adamancy at a British dinner party, Yamamoto retorted that, although smaller than his hosts, he was not expected to eat only three-fifths as much.[*]

The vice admiral was named chief of the Aeronautics Department when he returned to Japan in 1935. There he would supervise work that led to the production of the Japanese A6M3 Zero fighter. By this time, Yamamoto held no doubts whatever about the importance of military aircraft employed at sea. Aircraft, he averred, would play the decisive role in any future naval battles. Aircraft carriers, therefore, should become the core of Japan's naval task forces. This proposition, hardly obvious in the absence of any historical support, the aeronautics chief advanced as self-evident. It brought him into sharp conflict with admirals in the fleet faction who, almost without exception, favored capital ships and the naval long rifle.

When the naval disarmament treaties expired in 1936, plans were already made to begin building two enormous battleships, each displacing 73,000 tons and mounting batteries of 18.1-inch guns. Yamamoto vigorously opposed this plan and the diversion of resources

---

[*]Cited in Potter, *Yamamoto: The Man Who Menaced America,* 39.

to build what he derisively termed "white elephants." Indeed, the factional dispute became so heated that a prince of the royal family was called to mediate. Ultimately, however, the fleet faction prevailed, and in 1937 work began in secret on the largest battleships ever built, *Yamato* and *Musashi*. But just as Yamamoto perceived, aircraft carriers would soon become the naval weapons of choice; shells from the immense guns of *Yamato* and *Musashi* would never sink a ship in combat. And both of these behemoths would be sunk during World War II, victims of American military aircraft.

However disappointed Yamamoto must have been on failing to make more of his associates air-minded, at his insistence navy admirals did agree to build two new aircraft carriers. The 30,000-ton, 34-knot *Shokaku* and *Zuikaku* slid down the ways a few years later. They carried more airplanes and were faster than Japan's other big carriers, *Akagi* and *Kaga*. Meanwhile, at the request of the navy minister, Adm. Osami Nagano, on 1 December 1936 Yamamoto assumed the duties of vice-minister of the navy, while remaining head of the Aeronautics Department.

During his tenure as vice-minister, Yamamoto pressed hard for his weapon of choice: air power. At the same time he viewed with concern the growing threat of war with the western powers. But the July 1937 incident at the Marco Polo Bridge near Peiping, in which Chinese and Japanese infantry clashed, became the excuse for a full-scale invasion of China. As Japanese forces moved up the Yangtze River in December after seizing Shanghai, naval aircraft attacked and sank the American gunboat *Panay* moored near Nanking. It fell to the vice-minister to arrange payment of an indemnity and to pen the note of apology to the U.S. government. "That the incident has been solved despite distorted reports and propaganda," his note observed, "is due mainly to the fair judgment of the American government and people."

Yamamoto's intimate knowledge of America, its people, culture, geography, and industrial capacity, made the vice-minister a hardcore opponent of those forces in Japan that in 1938 sought a defense pact with the Axis powers, Germany and Italy. Moreover, on pragmatic grounds alone, he judged the German and Italian navies insufficient to successfully challenge the western powers at sea, and, in 1938 the Imperial Navy certainly was unprepared to challenge the combined Dutch, British, French, and American navies. But as pressure increased from the army and rightwing extremists who approved of the Axis defense pact, Yamamoto found himself the target of numerous death threats and letters demanding his resignation. The atmosphere became so charged that tanks and machine guns were positioned about the Navy Ministry, and Yamamoto, against his wishes, was assigned a bodyguard.

Although Navy Ministry opposition to the tripartite defense pact caused the Japanese government to shelve the matter, it did not deter those who favored war to achieve Japanese objectives in Asia and the Pacific. In Germany, meanwhile, Adolf Hitler made other plans. On 21 August 1939, the Nazi government abruptly announced it would sign a nonaggression treaty with the Soviet Union. Thrown into confusion by this turn of events, the Japanese cabinet resigned and the navy minister and vice-minister were replaced. On 1 September, as German and Soviet forces stormed into Poland, Vice Admiral Yamamoto was named commander-in-chief of the Combined Fleet and, perhaps to remove him from proximity with ultra-nationalist Japanese, ordered to sea.

In the months that followed, Yamamoto led the fleet in training exercises, preparing it for all emergencies, and rarely returned to the Japanese home islands. Meanwhile, the political situation continued to deteriorate, with one cabinet replacing another. Ultimately, in September 1940, after the continent of Europe fell to the Axis, the Japanese government signed the Tripartite Pact with Germany and Italy. In solemn but ambiguous language, it pledged to enter the European war on the Axis side if America should join Great Britain in the conflict. Yamamoto, now promoted to admiral, knew well that Japan, despite an intensive shipbuilding program, could not sustain a war against the United States for more than a year or two. Back in January 1940, the fleet had possessed only 3,500 naval aviators. Eighteen months later, in August 1941, that number had scarcely increased, and a decision made at that time to begin training annually 15,000 military pilots came too late.

With the Tripartite Pact signed, however, Yamamoto began in late 1940 and early 1941 to consider plans that might even the military odds with the United States in the event war became unavoidable. The plan he chose to pursue was an attack on the Pacific Fleet anchorage at Pearl Harbor, on Oahu, Hawaii. If the Japanese Combined Fleet could severely cripple the U.S. Navy in the Pacific, he reasoned, there might also be a chance for an early, negotiated peace. Even as the pros and cons of attacking Pearl Harbor were argued in the Naval General Staff and in the Navy Ministry in April and May 1941, the admiral continued privately and publicly to oppose war. A talk he gave at a reunion of his Nagaoka schoolmates in Tokyo on 18 September provoked an uproar throughout the government, and was ridiculed by his opponents as representing a "defeatist attitude." Yamamoto told those assembled, "It is a mistake to regard Americans as luxury-loving and weak . . . Lindbergh's solo crossing of the Atlantic Ocean is the sort of valiant act which is characteristic of them . . . Do not forget, American industry is much more developed than ours— and unlike us they have all the oil they want. Japan cannot defeat the United States. Therefore, she should not fight the United States."[*]

Events, nevertheless, had already moved Japan and the United States inexorably toward war. A few months earlier, on 26 July 1941, the Japanese and French governments announced complete agreement on the "joint defense of French Indochina." A Franco-Japanese covenant to that effect, signed in Vichy three days later, allowed immediate occupation of southern French Indochina by units of the Japanese army and navy. Alarmed by Japan's advance to the south, the American government reacted immediately and vigorously, freezing all Japanese assets in the United States and, on 1 August, announcing a ban on almost all exports to that nation, including oil. Given its limited petroleum reserves, and known production and consumption,

---

[*]Potter, *Yamamoto,* 59-60.

without oil from America Japan would be forced within about four months to capitulate—or to seize equivalent supplies in South Asia.

Although the United States and Japan were on the very edge of hostilities, few leaders in the island nation appeared willing to consider any rapprochement that involved political compromise in Asia. One politician willing to do so, however, was a cultivated member of the royal family, Prime Minister Fumimaro Konoye. During August and September 1941, he conferred with numerous parties, including Isoroku Yamamoto, to explore ways out of the impasse. On 12 September the prime minister and the navy admiral met secretly in Tokyo to discuss a proposed Japanese-American summit conference in Honolulu, one at which Prime Minister Konoye would hold direct talks with President Franklin Roosevelt. During the conversation, Konoye asked Yamamoto, "What about the navy in the event negotiations come to nothing?" The admiral replied, "If you insist on my going ahead, we can run wild for six months or a year, but I can guarantee nothing as to what will happen after that."*

Indeed, in succeeding weeks a summit conference, much less a negotiated compromise with the United States, failed to materialize. On 25 November 1941, Yamamoto received instructions to "go ahead," and he issued orders to the Pearl Harbor task force. The next day, on 26 November, the fleet set sail for Hawaii; the attack on Pearl Harbor that followed on 7 December began the war that Yamamoto had for so long sought to avoid. Though brilliantly planned and executed, the Japanese strike was not thorough. Shore installations and oil-tank farms were not destroyed, permitting the surviving American ships to begin combat operations immediately—albeit momentarily on the defensive. Moreover, to the admiral's dismay, the attack transpired before Japan formally severed relations with the United States, rather than afterward, as planned. Instead of encouraging a negotiated peace as he had hoped, the "surprise" attack neutralized isolationist sentiment and unified American resolve to defeat Japan at any cost. In London, British Prime Minister Winston Churchill

---

*Cited in Agawa, *The Reluctant Admiral,* 232.

immediately judged Pearl Harbor to be the decisive battle of World War II, for it brought a united America into the conflict. And that, he was sure, inevitably doomed the Axis powers.

Few, however, understood these ramifications at the close of 1941—certainly not the sailors and aviators of a victorious Japanese fleet that returned triumphant to the home islands. Pilots volunteered for combat in hopes of seeing action before the United States capitulated. To be sure, within the next four months Japanese naval and ground forces swept throughout the East Indies and the western Pacific, occupying territory that it would take the Allies three years to recapture. As these initial military operations drew to a close in early 1942, Japan's military leaders considered four alternatives: an attack on the Soviet Union, an attack on Australia, an advance westward into the Indian Ocean, and, finally, an advance eastward through Midway Island and simultaneously northward into the Aleutians, with the aim of drawing out the remainder of the U.S. Pacific Fleet for a final battle in the manner of Tsushima Strait. Despite its complexity, Yamamoto favored the latter plan, and, given his reputation, it was adopted.

The Japanese navy in 1942 thus set out on a course that led to the disaster at Midway in early June, with the loss of four first-line aircraft carriers out of the eleven with which it entered the war. Afterward, navy and army leaders fell back on a plan to isolate Australia from the United States by advancing through the Solomon Islands to New Caledonia, Fiji, and Samoa; this would prevent Allied reinforcements needed for a counteroffensive in the South Pacific from reaching Australia. But this plan, too, was improperly executed.

The Mission

Guadalcanal, an island strategically located near the southern end of the Solomons, was key to Japanese plans for an advance on New Caledonia. On 4 July 1942 aerial reconnaissance revealed Japanese construction teams hurrying to complete a large airfield on the island. The purpose of this activity was not lost on Adm. Ernest J. King, Commander-in-Chief, United States Fleet. In a surprise amphibious assault on 7 August 1942, the American 1st Marine Division landed at Lunga Point on Guadalcanal's north shore, and on the south coast of Tulagi and Florida islands, just across Sealark Channel, heralding the start of the Allied counteroffensive in the South Pacific. Once ashore on Guadalcanal, the marines quickly scattered Japanese defenders and secured a half-moon, shoreline perimeter around the airfield.

Plans called for the navy task force that supported the landing to remain on station until 11 August, to complete unloading all of the supply transports. But Guadalcanal lay within easy range of Japanese air and naval forces that controlled the Solomons from New Britain and Bougainville islands. Japanese aerial counterattacks began immediately. On 8 August, Vice Adm. Frank Jack Fletcher, who commanded the task force, decided it best to withdraw his three aircraft carriers. Near midnight that night, Rear Adm. Richmond Kelly Turner, who directed amphibious operations, called the marine commander on board his flagship. Without air cover, Turner told Maj. Gen. Alexander A. Vandegrift, he would have to withdraw the transports the next day.

Whatever Vandegrift's terse reply may have been to this disquieting piece of news, two hours later Japanese naval forces struck Turner's fleet in a nighttime engagement in Sealark Channel near Savo Island. Four Allied cruisers were sunk and one more badly damaged in one of the worst defeats ever suffered by the U.S. Navy. Hours later, in the afternoon of 9 August 1942, the remnants of Admiral Turner's warships and the transports departed. With them sailed half of the supplies and equipment of the 1st Marine Division. In the days that followed, the Marines ashore on Guadalcanal, completely isolated, absorbed round-the-clock aerial attacks, ate Japanese rations, fought to hold their defensive perimeter against newly landed Japanese troops, and rushed the airfield to completion. The first American airplanes to arrive on 20 August were Grumman F4F Wildcats of VMF-223, led by Capt. John Lucian Smith. The exhausted marines at least could hope for some respite from the daytime aerial attacks.

Two days later, the first five Army Air Forces P-400s of the 67th

Fighter Squadron, shepherded by two B-17 bombers, completed a 640-mile flight over water from Espiritu Santo to Guadalcanal. They too landed on the bumpy crushed coral of Henderson Field, named after Maj. Lofton Henderson, commander of the Midway-based marine dive bombers in the Battle of Midway. The besieged marines, bitter over their treatment by the navy, waved to and cheered the flight leader, Capt. Dale D. Brannon, from their foxholes: "The army has come!" The sleek P-400 fighters were the British export version of the Bell P-39 Airacobra, and the marines could hardly know how these machines, far racier in appearance than the stubby-winged marine Wildcats, had come to Guadalcanal. In fact, this fighter performed so poorly in the air that the Royal Air Force, after flying one combat mission with them, declared the P-400 to be non-combat-capable, withdrew them from service, and refused to accept any more. Those not yet delivered, as well as many of those already delivered, were sent to the Soviet Union or the Pacific, and were there, in the Pacific Theater, consigned to the Army Air Forces. Because bottled oxygen for the British system was unavailable, the P-400s could fly no higher than 14,000 feet without risking pilot blackout. And the standard P-39s that soon appeared on Guadalcanal, even with oxygen, could struggle up to only 25,000 feet. Neither was a match for the Japanese A6M3 Zero, a fact made plain in the first aerial engagement on 30 August. Only six of ten P-400s returned to Henderson Field, and all of those that made it back were badly shot up.*

Beginning on 1 September 1942, the P-400 was pressed into service almost exclusively as a ground-support fighter bomber to assist the hardpressed marines. For this task it was eminently suited, mounting a 20-mm Hispano MK1 cannon in its nose, two .303-caliber machine guns in the top side of the nose cowling, and two more .303-caliber machine guns on each wing. Moreover, it could carry a 500-pound bomb. While the Grumman fighters fought Japanese aircraft overhead, the P-400s bombed and strafed Japanese forces on the ground. On

---

Ed. note: Army pilots that flew them on Guadalcanal wryly defined the P-400 as "a P-40 with a Zero on its tail."

14 September the last three P-400s remaining in service helped repulse a concentrated Japanese attack against Henderson Field in the Battle of Bloody Ridge. Around and around the field they flew, dipping behind the ridge where their chattering machine guns cut into the massed troops. Afterward, a bulldozer buried the six hundred Japanese that lay dead before the marine positions.

Unbeknownst to those on Guadalcanal, the Battle of Bloody Ridge marked a turning point in the campaign to take the island. Although savage fighting would continue for another four months, the Japanese would never again so seriously threaten to retake Henderson Field. In the weeks that followed, the P-400s supported the infantry. They strafed and dropped demolition bombs, fragmentation bombs, incendiaries, and even depth charges as called for by the marines. Armorers also devised a bomb of their own, called a "Rube Goldberg"—a belly tank filled with a mixture of gasoline and oil, with an incendiary to set it ablaze on impact. The gasoline firebomb had been born.

Meanwhile, more marine and army aircraft joined the VMF-223 and 67th Fighter Squadron on Guadalcanal. The first contingent of the 68th Fighter Squadron, flying P-40s from Noumea, landed on 12 November 1942, followed that same day by twelve P-38s of the 339th Fighter Squadron. The 12th and 70th Fighter Squadrons flying P-39s arrived on 19 and 22 December respectively. To accommodate the growing number of aircraft, including B-17s of the 11th Bombardment Group, in October the marines carved out a small strip near Henderson for the fighters, eventually known as Fighter One. A second strip, also for fighters and known as Fighter Two, opened in late November. The army fighters moved to it, leaving most of the marine and naval aircraft at Fighter One (except for a few naval aircraft that used Fighter Two from time to time), while the bombers used Henderson Field exclusively. The bombers and longer-range fighters now began to strike targets in the northern Solomons, and personnel at Japanese military installations found themselves on the receiving end of offensive aerial attacks. Though the American toehold on Guadalcanal had appeared questionable in late August and September 1942, by year's end officials in Washington, D.C., could no longer doubt that their ground forces were in the Solomons to stay.

Back on 17 August 1942, when it became apparent that Americans had landed in force on Guadalcanal and not simply put ashore a raiding party, as first reported, Adm. Isoroku Yamamoto left Japan on board the battleship *Yamato* and sailed south with a destroyer escort toward the Solomons. When *Yamato* dropped anchor at Japan's naval center at Truk atoll on 26 August, the Battle of the Eastern Solomons had already been fought. The Imperial Navy had lost aircraft carrier *Ryujo*, while the Japanese army's crack Ichiki detachment, dispatched for a counterlanding on Guadalcanal and the recapture of Henderson Field, would be eventually annihilated. Between September and year's end, when the preliminary decision to withdraw Japanese forces from Guadalcanal was made, a succession of intense sea and air battles found Japan in the position that Yamamoto most feared—a war of attrition. One year had elapsed since Pearl Harbor; intelligence reports told the admiral that Allied forces grew in strength daily while his own forces diminished. The initiative was lost and no reasonable military alternatives remained. At the close of 1942 Yamamoto must have recognized that his prophesy would be fulfilled: the military situation was beyond his control. He now presided over a long, losing struggle.

By January 1943, Allied forces operating from Henderson Field could claim control of the air over the southern Solomons, aerial supremacy that brought with it control of the sea. Clearly on the defensive, Japan began withdrawing its remaining troops from Guadalcanal on 1 February. On 11 February, headquarters of the Combined Fleet was transferred from *Yamato* to sistership *Musashi,* also at anchor in Truk Harbor. There, Yamamoto directed operations for the next six weeks. But the deteriorating military situation in the Solomons and the aircraft carriers already lost in combat forced increasing numbers of his surviving naval aircraft to withdraw to land bases at and near Rabaul, on New Britain Island. On 3 April 1943, the admiral temporarily shifted his headquarters from *Musashi*, at Truk, to Rabaul, to oversee Operation "I."

Operation "I," an all-out aerial attack on Guadalcanal and Allied vessels in the vicinity, was scheduled to begin on Yamamoto's fifty-ninth birthday, 4 April 1943. Inclement weather intervened, however, and the operation did not commence until 7 April. During four separate days, through 14 April, 680 fighters and bombers, some operating from forward bases in the Bougainville and Shortland islands, were hurled against the Americans on Guadalcanal. Each day when the aircraft took off from Rabaul, Yamamoto appeared in white dress uniform and waved his cap in salute. The military results of the operation, though reported most optimistically by his returning pilots, ultimately proved a disappointment—the Allied advance through the Solomons continued.

Most of the American combat aircraft that engaged the Japanese in Operation "I" flew from "Cactus," as Guadalcanal was called in classified messages. They were directed by the Commander Air, Solomon Islands, or COMAIRSOLS, and in April 1943 that man was Rear Adm. Marc A. Mitscher. The army squadrons reported to the XIII Fighter Command detachment on Guadalcanal, led by Lt. Col. Henry Viccellio, who reported in turn to Mitscher's Fighter Command. The army pilots served a six- to eight-week combat tour, and then rotated to Australia (and later New Zealand), for a week or ten days of rest. Afterward, following a few weeks of training in New Caledonia or Fiji, they returned to Guadalcanal for another tour of combat. The army pilots were frequently reassigned from one squadron to another, or temporarily assigned or detached to another squadron, and most of those who arrived in late 1942 knew one another. For example, Capt. (later Maj.) John W. Mitchell of the 70th Fighter Squadron took a cadre of fourteen pilots from Fiji to join the 67th Fighter Squadron in New Caledonia in September, and members of the 67th and former 70th personnel subsequently manned the 339th Fighter Squadron when it was formed on 3 October 1942, at Tontouta Field, New Caledonia, specifically to fly the Lockheed P-38 Lightning. And pilots from the 70th were commonly attached to the 68th Fighter Squadron while at Cactus. As a result, on Guadalcanal more than one squadron might claim the same pilot as its own.

Before March 1943, the newer Army Air Forces P-38 Lightning twin-engine fighters, which had turbo-superchargers and could operate above 30,000 feet, were employed primarily to escort bombers, conduct sweeps and patrols, and provide high cover for the other navy and army fighters. During these missions, one seldom found a P-38 below 12,000 feet. Beginning in March 1943, however, XIII Fighter Command and COMAIRSOLS began using the P-38Gs at high and low levels, and the twin-boom fighter with a tricycle landing gear soon made its mark as an effective engine of war. Mounting a 20-mm Hispano cannon and four .50-caliber machine guns in the nose of the gondola, it matched the firepower of the P-39—and it could outclimb and outdive (though not outturn) the Japanese Zero.

On 29 March 1943, Capt. Thomas Lanphier and his wingman, 1st Lt. Rex Barber, along with Lts. George Topol, Joseph Moore, and Robert Petit, P-38 pilots of the 339th, flew a circuitous low-level route just above the water from Guadalcanal northwest, around the Solomons, to strike the Japanese naval base on Shortland Island. A destroyer in the harbor engaged the P-38s, and Lanphier and Barber attacked and sank the vessel with gunfire. So close did Barber press home the attack that he left a few feet of one wingtip in the ship's superstructure. That kind of aggressiveness impressed staff officers of COMAIRSOLS on Guadalcanal, who earnestly hoped the air corps pilots scheduled to replace Lanphier and Barber in rotation on 17 April would be near their equal.

Meanwhile, back in Rabaul, before the disappointing outcome of Operation "I" became obvious to those at Japanese naval head-quarters, Admiral Yamamoto decided to visit his forward bases in the Bougainville-Shortland Island area that had experienced increasing aerial attacks. A coded message of his itinerary was radioed to the field on the afternoon of 13 April 1943, and American communications intelligence listening posts promptly intercepted it. Because of the variety of addressees, the message drew the immediate attention of cryptanalysts. At Pearl Harbor on Wednesday, 14 April, Adm. Chester W. Nimitz, Commander-in-Chief, Pacific Ocean Area, was advised of the message contents and the possibility of striking down the Japanese commander when he arrived at his first stop, Ballale Island, early on Sunday morning, 18 April. On Thursday, Nimitz notified Vice Adm. William F. Halsey, Commander, South Pacific Area, in Noumea, New Caledonia, to proceed with the interception, adding a personal fillip: "Good luck and good hunting." Although various reports suggest that Nimitz at least consulted Secretary of the Navy Frank Knox in Washington before proceeding, no documentary evidence of it has ever been uncovered.

Whether approved or not by officials in Washington, Halsey's headquarters relayed the execute order to Rear Admiral Mitscher on Guadalcanal on 16 April. Mitscher gathered his staff, including Marine Col. Edward Pugh, commander of Fighter Command, who directed all navy, marine, and army fighter operations. After discussion, these officers decided that only Army Air Forces P-38 fighters had the necessary range to perform the special operation. The fuel drop tanks needed to give them a range of some one thousand miles were immediately ordered from the Fifth Air Force, and these tanks arrived late the next day. They also agreed that the route flown to the Bougainville-Shortland Island area should be patterned after the 29 March mission: low-level, over water, away from the other Solomon Islands where coast watchers or ships might provide advance warning of the flight. Finally, they decided to recommend to the mission flight leader elected, Maj. John W. Mitchell, that Thomas Lanphier and Rex Barber be designated as two of the shooters on this mission, which meant they would be held over and not rotated to New Zealand for "rest and relaxation" as planned.

On Saturday, 17 April, Rear Admiral Mitscher summoned to his operations room Captain Lanphier, Lt. Col. Henry Viccellio, commander of the XIII Fighter Command detachment, and Major Mitchell, commander of the 339th Fighter Squadron. The army pilots were apprised of the mission and conferred with Mitscher's staff. After considering the parameters and prospects at some length, Admiral Mitscher agreed with Major Mitchell that the intercept should be made in the air, and not on land or sea after Admiral Yamamoto landed at Ballale. Afterward, the pilots in attendance adjourned to the Fighter Command

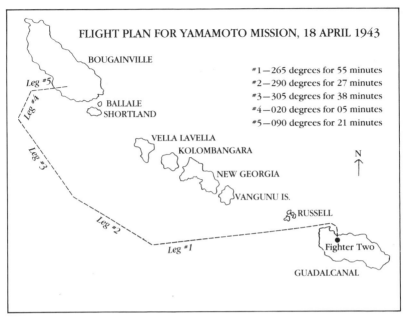

FLIGHT PLAN FOR YAMAMOTO MISSION, 18 APRIL 1943

BOUGAINVILLE

Leg #5

Leg #4

BALLALE
SHORTLAND

Leg #3

VELLA LAVELLA
KOLOMBANGARA

NEW GEORGIA

VANGUNU IS.

Leg #2

Leg #1

RUSSELL

Fighter Two

GUADALCANAL

N

#1—265 degrees for 55 minutes
#2—290 degrees for 27 minutes
#3—305 degrees for 38 minutes
#4—020 degrees for 05 minutes
#5—090 degrees for 21 minutes

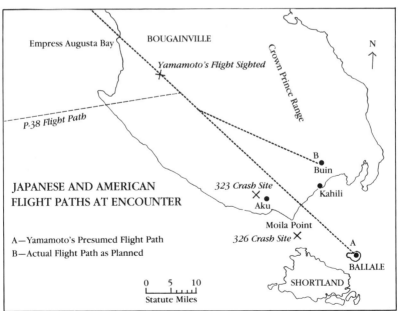

Empress Augusta Bay

BOUGAINVILLE

N

Yamamoto's Flight Sighted

Crown Prince Range

P-38 Flight Path

B
Buin

JAPANESE AND AMERICAN
FLIGHT PATHS AT ENCOUNTER

323 Crash Site

Kahili

Aku

Moila Point

326 Crash Site

A

A—Yamamoto's Presumed Flight Path
B—Actual Flight Path as Planned

BALLALE

SHORTLAND

0   5   10

Statute Miles

dugout, called "the opium den." Mitchell selected an intercept point along Yamamoto's flight path on Bougainville Island just south of Empress Augusta Bay. Colonel Pugh's operations officer, Marine Maj. John Condon, sat down after the others departed and plotted the course headings and airspeeds needed to meet the intercept point selected, checked the plot with his colleagues, and sent it over to Major Mitchell at Fighter Two, who still had to determine how surface winds and power settings would affect his true course and airspeed.

Early Sunday morning, 18 April 1943, Adm. Isoroku Yamamoto climbed on board a Mitsubishi G4M1 "Betty" bomber at Lakunai Airfield, Rabaul, New Britain Island. Moments later, the twin-engine naval aircraft and a companion bomber carrying the admiral's staff took off. At about the same time, on Guadalcanal, Mitchell led eighteen P-38s into the air from Fighter Two. He had designated four men as shooters to engage Yamamoto's flight: Captain Lanphier and First Lieutenants Barber, James McLanahan, and Joseph Moore. The remaining pilots, led by Mitchell, were to ascend and fly topcover to engage any fighters sent from Bougainville to meet the Japanese admiral. McLanahan's P-38, however, blew a tire on takeoff, and Moore found he could not draw fuel from his drop tanks. The flight was thus reduced to sixteen, with 1st Lts. Besby Holmes and Ray Hine replacing McLanahan and Moore as shooters. After an uneventful but remarkably navigated two-and-one-half-hour flight of some four hundred miles out of sight of land, just above the waves, the P-38s made landfall at the designated intercept point just south of Empress Augusta Bay on Bougainville and began to climb. Breaking radio silence for the first time, 1st Lt. Douglas Canning called out, "Bogeys, 11 o'clock high."

Right on schedule, far above and to the left of them, the admiral's flight consisted of two Betty bombers cruising at 4,500 feet altitude, proceeding southeast along the coast over the jungle. Above and slightly behind the bombers at 6,000 feet, flying cover, were six Type 32 naval Zeros. The flight, now descending slowly toward Ballale, was only ten or twelve minutes from landing, with the nearby Japanese

Table 1   USAAF Pilots on the Yamamoto Mission

Name	Unit/Transferred From
John Mitchell	339th/70th/67th
Roger Ames	12th
Everett Anglin	12th
Rex Barber*	339th/70th
Douglas Canning	339th/70th/67th
Delton Goerke	339th/67th
Lawrence Graebner	12th
Ray Hine	339th/68th
Besby Holmes	339th/67th
Julius Jacobson	339th/70th/67th
Louis Kittel	12th
Thomas Lanphier*	339th/70th
Albert Long	12th
James McLanahan*	339th/70th/67th
Joseph Moore*	339th/70th
William Smith	12th
Eldon Stratton	12th
Gordon Whittaker	12th

*Designated shooters.

airfields of Buin and Kahili clearly in sight. Mitchell and his eleven companions dropped their fuel tanks and pushed their P-38s at full power to climb rapidly upward. Lanphier and his three shooters, also at full power and rising, crossed the beach at about 1,000 feet and headed directly for the bombers above the jungle. But the fuel tank remaining on Holmes's P-38 failed to drop, and he turned southeast along the coast performing violent maneuvers to shake it free, accompanied by his wingman, Ray Hine.

Lanphier and Barber rose to meet the bombers, paralleling their course on an oblique intercept. They had closed to within one mile of their quarry before the Zero pilots spotted the P-38s beneath them, dropped their fuel tanks, and dove to repel the American fighters. Realizing that the Zeros would reach them before he and Barber reached the bombers, which had begun to dive at full power toward the jungle, Lanphier pulled left up into and fired on the first flight of three Zeros, breaking up their attack. Moments later, Barber swung in behind a bomber and raked it from the rear with his guns. In the debriefing afterward, he reported the tail disintegrated and the bomber plunged to earth. Lanphier, meanwhile, rolled over at 6,000 feet and dove under full power back toward the bombers' line of flight over the jungle. He observed a second bomber fleeing due south, across his own line of flight, just above the treetops toward the beach. Approaching the bomber perpendicularly, from nearly a 3-o'clock position, Lanphier told debriefers that he fired on it from a distance, observed the starboard engine burst into flame and, moments later, watched the right wing separate just as it plunged into the jungle.

Further down the coast, Holmes had by now shed his drop tank. He and Hine encountered a third Betty bomber just above the surface of the ocean, flying southeast toward Ballale. Now joined by Barber, the three attacked and watched the Betty bomber explode into the Solomon Sea. After further tangles with Japanese Zeros as they attempted to leave the area, the American aviators returned to Guadalcanal. Of those on the mission, only Ray Hine was lost, doubtless the victim of a Japanese Zero.

During the debriefings of Mitchell, Lanphier, and Barber later that day at Fighter One on Guadalcanal, the P-38 pilots claimed three Betty bombers and three Zeros confirmed destroyed. Whichever bomber carried Yamamoto, they were convinced that the admiral had been killed. This word undoubtedly pleased Rear Admiral Mitscher; 18 April 1943 marked for him a special anniversary. Exactly one year earlier he had commanded the aircraft carrier *Hornet* that launched Col. James Doolittle's B-25 bombers for the first American aerial attack on Japan, an attack that helped shock and provoke Japanese leaders into the ill-fated June 1942 attempt to take Midway Island.

Indeed, the American aviators were right. Tokyo Radio announced the death of Adm. Isoroku Yamamoto in aerial combat at the front lines some four weeks later, on 21 May 1943, after his ashes had been returned to Japan. On page 1 that day, the *New York Times* relayed the word to Americans: "Japanese Admiral Killed in Combat: Commander of Fleet Had Said He Would Dictate Peace in Washington." Political and military leaders on both sides of the Pacific exploited his memory for whatever propaganda purposes they could. Certainly Yamamoto, the man who, by attacking Pearl Harbor, ensured Japan's absolute defeat in World War II, received a state funeral—only the twelfth ever accorded a Japanese commoner. The one other sailor so honored, ironically, was the man who first brought Japan recognition as a world power, the man Yamamoto most admired, victor over the Russians in the Battle of Tsushima Strait, Adm. Heihachiro Togo.

And what of Yamamoto's purported boast about dictating peace terms so widely propagandized on all sides during World War II? If it instilled any confidence among Japanese soldiers and sailors, it unquestionably fueled the antipathy of the American aviators who claimed his life. Hardly boastful, however, were the words in a letter that Yamamoto wrote to a rightwing leader, Ryoichi Sasakawa, just a few months before Pearl Harbor. Sasakawa led the ultra-nationalist All-Japan Labor Class Federation and was the only prominent rightist who openly supported the admiral in the late 1930s. The letter in question, dated 24 January 1941, was reprinted in full on 13 January 1946 in the magazine section of the *New York Times*:

Dear Sir:
I trust that you are in the best of health. I deeply appreciate the trip of inspection you made to the South Seas on the *Uranami*. In this age when armchair arguments are being glibly bandied about in the name of state politics, your sober attitude in going to such trouble to be loyal to your own opinion is to be most highly commended. But it embarrasses me not a little to hear you say that you "feel at ease in the knowledge that Yamamoto is out at sea (with his fleet)." All that I am doing is to devote my utmost both day and night toward building up our strength, ever bearing in mind the Imperial admonition:

Despise not an enemy because he is weak;
Fear him not because he is strong.

I am counting only on the loyalty of the one hundred thousand officers and men who are going about their duties in silence and without boasting.

Should hostilities once break out between Japan and the United States, it is not enough that we take Guam and the Philippines, nor even Hawaii and San Francisco. We would have to march into Washington and sign the treaty (i.e., dictate the terms of peace) in the White House. I wonder if our politicians (who speak so lightly of a Japanese-American war) have confidence as to the outcome and are prepared to make the necessary sacrifices.

With best wishes for your good health.

Respectfully yours,
Isoroku Yamamoto

The Aftermath

If the death of Adm. Isoroku Yamamoto changed the conduct of the Japanese war effort, it certainly soured relations between Great Britain and the United States. Prime Minister Winston Churchill reportedly protested directly to President Franklin Roosevelt over America's jeopardizing the security of communications intelligence, upon which so much of the Allied war effort depended, in so venal a pursuit as the killing of an enemy admiral. Negotiations between Great Britain and the United States to exchange Ultra communications intelligence halted. After some British fingerpointing and American reassurances, however, the two countries resumed negotiations and concluded the exchange agreement in late May 1943. During the summer and fall of that year, the United States also adopted new, more secure procedures for disseminating and handling Ultra intelligence in the Pacific Theater. For its part, Admiral Mitscher's Fighter Command on Guadalcanal sent P-38s to the Bougainville-Shortland Island area for the next few weeks at random times, hoping to make it appear that Yamamoto's interception was coincidence, and that Japan's military codes had not been compromised. Fortunately for the Allies, the conceit of Imperial Navy commanders embraced the first explanation and dismissed the second.

The Yamamoto mission also changed the lives of the American aviators who shot him down. Although anyone who willingly risks his life in great events is changed by the experience, the pilots in this instance occupied a special niche: for better or worse, they had changed the course of the war in the Pacific. For the rest of their lives they would be singled out and asked to tell and retell the story. And with the passage of time and memory, the recollections would not converge, but diverge.

Born in Panama, Thomas G. Lanphier came from an Army Air Corps family. His father, Lt. Col. Thomas G. Lanphier, Sr., a West Pointer who, as a Black Knight halfback watched Knute Rockne throw a football over his head for the first passing touchdown in history, had served in the army with distinction in World War I, commanded the 1st Pursuit Group between the wars, and, after a career in industry, during much of World War II was chief of the Air Unit, Intelligence Group, of the Military Intelligence Service, G-2, at Headquarters United States Army in Washington, D.C. The senior Lanphier, who would lose one of his two aviator sons to the Japanese during the war, read the classified message traffic to the South Pacific with a special interest. In April 1943, he doubtless took pride in the knowledge that one son had participated in the Yamamoto mission, and, moreover, had been credited in military dispatches with shooting down one of the Japanese bombers over Bougainville Island. Ten days after the Japanese announced the death of Admiral Yamamoto, *Time* magazine in its issue of 31 May 1943 carried two articles which, if put together, had obviously drawn on intelligence sources. The magazine reported on page 28 the shooting down of the admiral, and confided to its readers: ". . . the U.S. will have a new hero." A glowing biographical sketch of Capt. Thomas G. Lanphier, Jr., the South Pacific aviator, followed on page 66. In it appeared a veiled reference to the death of Yamamoto.

The younger Lanphier, subject of the *Time* biography, could claim a degree from Stanford University, dashing good looks, and Maj. Gen. James Doolittle as his godfather. He could also claim exclusive credit for shooting down the bomber that carried the Japanese admiral. After all, two bombers were gunned down over the jungle, and he was confident that his was the one that carried Yamamoto. In 1945 he chose to make that claim exclusively and publicly. In a three-part article, Lanphier told readers of the *New York Times* on 12-14 September of the action over Bougainville two years before. Essentially a repeat of the XIII Fighter Command debriefing, Lanphier said he shot down the admiral's bomber, though acknowledging that his wingman, Rex Barber, held sole credit for another bomber down in the jungle on that mission. Barber, if he disputed the account, was stationed in California—too far removed from New York to be heard.

In the years that followed, Lanphier was widely recognized as the man who got Yamamoto, despite occasional protests to the contrary from Rex Barber. To those who asked, flight leader John Mitchell declared, "Nobody on God's green earth knows who shot down Yamamoto." But both Barber and Lanphier could take personal satisfaction in the knowledge that the bomber he alone shot down was the one in which the admiral rode. Beginning in the mid 1950s, however, published Japanese wartime records confirmed only two bombers gunned down over Bougainville on 18 April 1943: one in the jungle and another in the sea. Lanphier and Barber, two comrades-in-arms who had depended on each other for life in combat, now had to conclude that the other fabricated his story about shooting down a bomber on that day long ago in the South Pacific.

At about the same time, Headquarters USAF asked historians in the USAF Historical Division, the precursor of the USAF Historical Research Center at Air University, to verify the general and special orders that awarded victory credits to army and air force fighter pilots in the various wars, and confirm which ones could claim to be "aces" —those having five or more aerial victories. This effort led eventually to a computer listing of all fighter pilots who had verified aerial victory credits, whatever the number. As new documents or other conclusive evidence became available, the listings were amended.

During the 1960s, air force historians considered victory credits for the Yamamoto mission. Making the assessment more difficult, in adhering to wartime secrecy surrounding this mission, Thirteenth

Air Force's Fighter Command never issued victory credit orders, orders that might have resolved the discrepancy in the number of bombers the pilots reported shot down. After evaluating the limited primary documentation, historians concluded that two bombers had been destroyed. Of these, the admiral's bomber had been fired on first by Barber and subsequently by Lanphier who watched it crash into the jungle a few moments later. Neither pilot had seen the actions of the other. Under rules applied by the Thirteenth Air Force at that time, if two or more pilots fired on an armed enemy aircraft in flight and destroyed it, they shared credit equally. Thus the credit was shared between the two men. But that finding hardly pleased either pilot, most especially Lanphier, who had since World War II publicly claimed sole credit. Furthermore, it became the subject of debate among numerous military historians and World War II veterans—most of whom, it seemed, chose one side or the other.

Although the entire question can be considered a footnote to the history of the war in the Pacific, the passions it stirred would prompt those who favored Lanphier's claim to petition the U.S. Air Force in early March 1985 for a reevaluation of the original finding. Later that month a board of air force historians was convened for that purpose. Because no new evidence was submitted, board members confined their attention to the available primary documentation and agreed it to be consistent with the finding of a shared credit; the original award remained unaltered. This second opinion, however, failed to satisfy anyone with a presumed stake in the issue.

The Yamamoto Mission Retrospective held in April 1988 at the Nimitz Museum in Fredericksburg, Texas, rekindled the debate, especially among proponents who supported Rex Barber's claim. Photographs of the bomber wreckage furnished to the USAF Historical Research Center in 1987 and put on display at the Texas symposium showed conclusively that the outer left wing of the bomber had separated on impact with the forest canopy, flipped up, and fallen about forty yards behind the bomber's fuselage. It was, to be sure, not the right wing that separated as Lanphier supposed. But in the heat of combat, might not a fighter pilot presume the wing that flew off the bomber as it plunged into the jungle to be the one at which he was firing? An interview of the surviving Zero pilot, Kenji Yanagiya, using questions submitted by Rex Barber and his associates, also failed to settle the question to anyone's satisfaction.

After the Texas symposium, opinion among those who favored one side or the other stiffened into belief. Perhaps conclusive evidence in the case of this famous aerial engagement will yet emerge. Or perhaps the counsel that General Doolittle offered his godson, Thomas Lanphier, in a 27 December 1984 letter concerning the recollection of World War II events sums up the matter best:

The human mind is a very complicated thing. When one thinks over and over a certain event in which he participated, or even watched—particularly if the action is fast—[he is] inclined to change it an infinitesimal amount each time—*always in his own favor.* After a long period of time he may change it 180 degrees and never realize that he has done so. This is one reason why, in recalling an event after a long period, people who all saw it—for example an accident—may later remember it very differently [italics in original].

History does not always furnish hard answers to our questions; it often taunts us with a mystery. What *is* known currently of the Yamamoto mission appears in the following pages.

Chapter 2

The Academic Panel

Dean C. Allard*

We are going to have five presentations this afternoon, each of which
will run about fifteen minutes. We will try to observe that time limit
to ensure an opportunity for a good discussion afterward, including
exchanges on the issues that are going to be raised. The five speakers
include three historians and two philosophers. Two of the three historians will discuss the historical background of attacks upon senior
military leaders in time of war. The third historian will give us the
details of the planning for the Yamamoto mission. At that point I will
turn to the last two speakers on the panel, both of whom are philosophers. They intend to address the ethical issues involved in singling out for attack a senior military commander on the enemy side.

The first of our speakers is Joseph G. Dawson, who is an associate
professor of history at Texas A&M University. He was educated at
Louisiana State University, and his dissertation and first book dealt
with Louisiana during the years of reconstruction. It is a prize-winning
volume entitled *Army Generals of Reconstruction, Louisiana 1862–
1877*. Dr. Dawson has contributed many other books and articles
in the field of military history.

Roger Beaumont is a professor of history, also in the department
of history at Texas A&M University. He undertook his undergraduate

---

*Director, Naval Historical Center, Washington, D.C.

work at the University of Wisconsin in Madison and holds a doctorate from Kansas State University. Dr. Beaumont's publications include *Military Elites, Sword of the Raj,* and more than fifty articles on other aspects of military history and defense affairs.

The third historian is Capt. Roger Pineau, USNR (Ret.). He is a graduate of the University of Michigan and of the George Washington University Law School and served as an intelligence and Japanese language officer in the Pacific during World War II. Between 1947 and 1957, he was the principal assistant to Samuel E. Morison in the preparation of Morison's well-known naval history of World War II. He has coauthored, edited, or translated a number of books, including a recent volume, *And I Was There,* written with Edwin T. Layton and John Costello.

Paul Woodruff is chairman of the philosophy department at the University of Texas at Austin and the first of the philosophers to participate in this panel. He holds graduate degrees from Oxford and Princeton and has published widely in his field. Among his works are two books dealing with the philosophy of Plato, and an article in the *Canadian Journal of Philosophy* entitled "Justification or Excuse: Saving Soldiers at the Expense of Civilians."

The final panelist is a professor of philosophy, Manuel Davenport, of Texas A&M University. He holds degrees from Colorado College and the University of Illinois. Among Dr. Davenport's many publications is an article entitled "Ethics and Military Organizations."

Targeting Military Leaders:
A Historical Review

Joseph G. Dawson, III

Military officers have always understood that being in the service of their country could eventually place them in mortal danger. As Clausewitz observed, "Danger is part of the friction of war."[*] In

---

[*]M. Howard and P. Paret, eds., *On War* (Princeton: Princeton University Press, 1976), 114.

ancient times, military commanders led directly by personal example. In later eras, phrases such as "leading from the front" and "being in the thick of the fight" had special meaning for such figures as Harold II of England, Richard the Lionhearted, Gustavus Adolphus, and Charles XII—all monarchs who died on the battlefield. Subsequent commanders knew that "riding to the sound of guns" could result in personal injury or death.

Before the First World War, top army or navy commanders often found themselves in the midst of combat. Being seen in battle by one's soldiers was important for generals; having one's flagship maintain station and keep firing could inspire an admiral's fleet. Prior to 1900, a commander of an army or a fleet was much more likely to share the immediate dangers of battle with his subordinates than top officers in the twentieth century.

The occasional loss of top commanders was an accepted part of Clausewitz's "friction of war." Edward Braddock was mortally wounded by French and Indian gunfire on the Monongahela in 1755; James Wolfe fell at the hands of the French at Quebec four years later. Mortally wounded, Confederate Gen. Albert Sidney Johnston bled to death on the field at Shiloh in 1862.

Trying to decide whether the loss of a top army or navy commander affected, or might have affected, the outcome of a battle, campaign, or war, has been one of the perennial subjects of discussion among students of military history. Speculation abounds, of course. What of the American Civil War without Grant or Lee? Ulysses S. Grant's victory at Shiloh was a close call; had his army lost, Grant (and probably William T. Sherman as well) might well have been dismissed or sent back to Cairo, Illinois, to count blankets for the quartermaster. What other generals would have used the North's resources so well? Probably the Union would have found others.

But Grant was not killed in battle or otherwise removed. On the other hand, Confederate Gen. Joseph E. Johnston was severely wounded at the Battle of Seven Pines, opening the way for Jefferson Davis to assign Robert E. Lee to the top command of the main Confederate field army in the east. Although Lee has been criticized by Thomas L. Connelly and others, many would say that Lee was a better general than Joe Johnston, and that in this instance the loss of one commander put a better general in his place.

The American Civil War was hard on corps commanders as well. A famous loss was that of Jeb Stuart, Lee's cavalry commander, gunned down by a Yankee sergeant on the field at Yellow Tavern in 1864. Worse for Lee was the accidental killing of Stonewall Jackson by his own men after the Battle of Chancellorsville the year before. Lee's plans never seemed to work as well after Jackson was gone. And another top officer, Gen. A. P. Hill, was killed in the fighting around Petersburg in 1864.

The North suffered its losses among highly regarded corps commanders. John Reynolds was shot dead on the field at Gettysburg after outlining an excellent defense. Shortly after receiving high accolades from General Sherman, Gen. James B. McPherson was killed by rebel fire while commanding the Union's Army of the Tennessee outside Atlanta in July 1864. Back east, Gen. John Sedgwick, while placing artillery units of his corps outside Spotsylvania, Virginia, disdainfully rejected advice to remain low because of rebel sharpshooters. "They couldn't hit an elephant at this distance," Sedgwick is quoted as saying, moments before a rifle bullet shattered his skull.[*]

After the Civil War, two other notable U.S. Army officers were killed on campaign. Lieutenant General George A. Custer, 7th Cavalry, was killed on the battlefield leading one wing of an army expedition against the North Plains tribes in 1876. Earlier, Modoc Indians killed Gen. Edward Canby in 1873 during a council called to negotiate matters between the tribe and the United States. But of these many examples, there is a sharp contrast with the death of Adm. Isoroku Yamamoto in 1943. None of them, perhaps with the exception of Canby, show direct, deliberate singling out of the officers mentioned. The deaths came about through happenstance or pressures of the moment.

Naval officers, like army officers, understood and accepted the dangers of warfare. In the 1700s and 1800s sharpshooters could take

---

[*]Bruce Catton, *Grant Takes Command* (Boston: Little Brown, 1969), p. 217

a terrible toll of enemy officers on the opposite decks as ships closed in for final broadsides. Obviously, those shots were made deliberately, with careful aim. Just such a shot took the life of Adm. Horatio Nelson at Trafalgar in 1805.

We do know that some commanders believed the chance dangers of combat and service life were enough without intentionally directing fire against enemy commanders. The story of the Duke of Wellington at Waterloo is perhaps the most famous example of not firing on an enemy commander, even when the opportunity arose: "Across the field stood Napoleon Bonaparte with his staff. An alert English artilleryman called out to the Duke: There's Bonaparte, Sir; I think I can reach him; may I fire? [Reportedly, the Duke was aghast.] Wellington replied to the gunner: No, no, Generals commanding armies have something else to do than shoot at one another."*

Was it only a matter of what Wellington and some other nineteenth-century commanders may have considered "sporting" or "fair"—or something that "just was not done" to a brother general? It was universally admitted that any officer, no matter how high his rank, might die in combat or campaigning, but here is the prime nineteenth-century example of one senior officer who would not order disciplined troops to fire upon the known location of a senior enemy leader, while simultaneously efforts were underway to kill or maim hundreds or thousands of other enemy soldiers on the same battlefield. Was Wellington not emotional enough to seek revenge against Napoleon for spurring the continental war that had absorbed Europe for two decades?

A number of points of contrast might suggest themselves between Wellington's order not to fire in 1815 and the direct orders to bring down Admiral Yamamoto in 1943. One might be that by 1943 the outlook of "total war," developed over nearly a century after the American Civil War, had changed the attitudes of military men and their civilian superiors. By the 1940s, almost any action would be

---

*E. Longford, *Wellington: The Years of the Sword* (New York: Harper and Row, 1969), p. 472.

taken if it might lead to ultimate victory, or even contribute to that victory in a minor way. Witness Hiroshima and Nagasaki.

Unlike Wellington in 1815, the Americans in 1943 seized the chance to bring down the enemy commander. Today, national protagonists command intercontinental ballistic missiles to be employed in the event of a total nuclear war. Many of them are targeted against command centers, intended expressly to "decapitate" the enemy's political and military leadership at the outset of hostilities.

Targeting Military Leaders: Another View

Roger A. Beaumont

My two main tasks are, first, to provide historical perspective, to set the stage, offering a sense of what historians call *zeitgeist,* the spirit and flavor of the times in which events take place, and, second, to consider the Yamamoto mission as a "special operation."

First, what was the "big picture" that major leaders involved in the decisionmaking behind the Yamamoto mission—Halsey, Nimitz, and perhaps King and Knox—had in view? A good portion of it was visible to the soldiers, sailors, and airmen in the field when they looked at the news in *Stars and Stripes,* after reading "Terry and the Pirates" and "Male Call." In April 1943, the war was moving beyond that uncertain, early, "too little or too late" phase that many of you have doubtless tried to explain, with varying results, to children and grandchildren. In that grim interval between December 1941 and mid-1942, the Allies suffered defeat after defeat. In April 1943, in spite of some major successes—Coral Sea, Midway, Alamein, Stalingrad, Hill 609—the outcome of the war was not yet certain. It had reached a point that Winston Churchill referred to as the "hinge of fate," and major military problems and uncertainties still faced the Allies at every turn.

In the Battle of the Atlantic, sinkings by German U-boats were surging toward the wartime peak of almost a million tons a month. The Anglo-American forces had no foothold on the continent of Europe, and Erwin Rommel was building the Westwall as part of Festung Europa—Fortress Europe. The Second Front, in the form of a major landing in northwest Europe, had been postponed in 1942 and was about to be postponed once again. In the air war, both the U.S. Army Air Forces and the Royal Air Force strategic bombers grappled with inaccurate bombing. American daylight attacks were beginning to suffer from the effects of the "fighter escort gap" as B-17s and B-24s hit targets deep inside the Third Reich, where Albert Speer was about to begin vastly increasing the productivity of the Nazi war machine. One bright spot for the western Allies in April 1943 was North Africa, where American, British, and French forces tightened a fatal noose on German and Italian armies in Tunisia.

The Nazis, however, still held the strategic advantage on the Eastern Front in spite of their defeat at Stalingrad. They were massing tanks near Kursk for the biggest armor battle of the war. The outcome seemed uncertain enough to the Soviets that they reportedly talked secretly with the Nazi representatives in Stockholm, even though the western Allies had issued an "unconditional surrender" proclamation at Casablanca in January 1943.

Atrocities abounded in almost all theaters of the war. The Gestapo was going about its grisly work in occupied Europe. In 1942, the village of Lidice in Czechoslovakia had been obliterated in retaliation for the assassination of Himmler's henchman, Reynard Heydrich. And all across Europe, the trains of the Holocaust were rolling to the death camps day and night, carrying out the Nazis' apocalyptic policy of extermination.

In the Far East, the pattern was similarly grim. Japanese armies massed on the borders of Burma as the British, bracing for an invasion of India, their premier imperial possession, also faced an uprising, having jailed Gandhi and many other prominent Congress Party leaders in 1942. Again, as many of you remember, the Guadalcanal campaign had become a battle of attrition, a grinding away by both sides on the land, in the air, and at sea, not completely resolved until early 1943. The campaign in New Guinea was still a matter of slogging, small gains, and high casualties, as Douglas MacArthur and his air commander, George Kenney, worked out the bypass strategy that would soon accelerate progress in that area. In the North Pacific, Japanese forces held Attu and Kiska in the Aleutians. The Marines had not yet made the first of that series of major amphibious landings that marked the rungs of a bloody climb up the Central Pacific. The U.S. Navy's submarine force had been frustrated by major defects in the fuses of its torpedoes and the problem was not yet fully solved. The only clearcut American strategic naval success had been at Midway almost a year before.

The war in the Pacific had also become savage in the true sense, far beyond the grimy, marginal living conditions. Charles Lindbergh, working as a Lockheed "tech rep," noted this sorrowfully in his diary, describing the use of Japanese skulls as drinking cups. The ferocity ran both ways, as John Dower has observed in his study, *War without Mercy*. Reports of the torture and execution of U.S. fliers from the Doolittle raid captured in China had filtered back through intelligence channels. (The story of the Bataan death march would not be known until mid-1944.) Fury in America over the apparent sneak attack at Pearl Harbor continued unabated until after the war, when more details were released. A perhaps apocryphal report held that President Roosevelt's wife Eleanor, while visiting her son James, the executive officer of Carlson's Raiders (who were far from being Eagle Scouts), had been so shocked at what she saw that she recommended that all Pacific veterans be placed in six months' quarantine before returning to polite society.

Turning from the big picture of the war to a "micro" focus on the Yamamoto mission of April 1943, it is easy to see that it had all the basic elements of a special operations mission: speed, a tight focus, animosity, and a linkage to technical intelligence systems and psychological warfare. It was, of course, not the only special operation carried out by standard forces. There were others: the Dieppe raid, the Hammelburg raid in Europe, and the Cabanatuan and Los Banos raids, which rescued prisoners of war in the Philippines.

As for the matter of precedent, when British commandos had earlier failed to kill Rommel, the Germans treated the captives as regular prisoners of war in spite of Hitler's fury over earlier commando operations. Dr. Dawson has pointed out previous practices and values. The view of targeting enemy commanders, however, changed in the twentieth century, due partly to the dispersal of armies and fleets in space and time, all controlled by webs of electronic communication radiating out from central headquarters. The vulnerabilities of such systems led J.F.C. Fuller, the British military theorist and armored warfare pioneer, to suggest that the object of war was no longer to kill off a foe's privates one by one, but to surprise the enemy generals at the breakfast table. Thus, while headquarters' *chateaux* above division level were generally not targeted deliberately by artillery or air in World War I, by 1940 French G.Q.G. (General Headquarters) used no radios for fear that, in command-and-control parlance, the electromagnetic "signature" would attract enemy air attack.

Although deliberate attacks on enemy commanders in World War II were relatively rare, they did occur. Extensive camouflage was deployed to mask headquarters, and both Hitler and Churchill and their staffs spent much of the war in underground headquarters. The Royal Air Force purportedly tried to "take out" Hitler in Munich on one occasion. Low-level RAF raids against Gestapo headquarters demonstrated a new dimension of "surgical" aerial special operations, and USAAF tactical air units hit what they thought was a major German headquarters during the Normandy campaign. German Army officers tried to kill Hitler at various times, and in the Soviet Union, German intelligence infiltrated at least one agent to try and kill Stalin, who lived under conditions of very tight security. Ukrainian nationalist partisans behind Soviet lines ambushed Red Army Marshal Vatutin in 1944. And, in the Battle of the Bulge later that year, the false belief that Nazi special operations maestro Otto Skorzeny was trying to kill top Allied commanders led to major security measures that paralyzed the high command for several days.

Many years later, the assassination of hostile political and military leaders re-emerged in Washington, D.C., during the 1975 Church Committee hearings, as it examined intelligence policy in the wake of Vietnam and Watergate. A special subhearing led to legislation outlawing assassination in the conduct of American foreign policy. But the collapse of restraint regarding the targeting of military commanders and headquarters is today recognized in both Soviet and British command-and-control networks, which are designed to operate on the basis of surviving nodes, irrespective of rank.

After the American Civil War, commanders at the very highest levels became ever more isolated from battle, compared to "great captains" like Marlborough, Napoleon, Nelson, and Lee who were often under fire. Although centralizing communications at higher levels made headquarters and leaders increasingly important targets in military operations, tactical thinking has rarely aimed at the kind of "decapitation" that nuclear analysts often speak of today, that is, the deliberate attacking of such key nodes. In spite of Fuller's adage, there is a sense that senior commanders should be somehow more immune to danger and risk than those at lower echelons, a paradoxical erosion of their status as fighters.

The Yamamoto mission, then, along with the other raids and missions noted, did mark a fork in the road of warfare. Although not usually described as such, it was a "special op" very much in the spirit of RAF low-level attacks on the Gestapo in World War II and the Libyan raid of 1986.

The Code Break*

Captain Roger Pineau, USN (Ret.)

In February 1943, after a bitter six-month struggle for Guadalcanal, Japanese troops were forced to evacuate that blood-drenched island. In retaliation, Adm. Isoroku Yamamoto, commander-in-chief of the Combined Fleet, ordered vigorous air strikes against Allied bases in the southern Solomons. Yamamoto, the man who originated both the Pearl Harbor attack and the disastrous attempt to take Midway Island, was launching another offensive.

To supervise this operation personally, on Sunday, 3 April 1943, Yamamoto left his flagship, battleship *Musashi,* at Truk, and flew to Rabaul, the Japanese stronghold at the northern tip of New Britain. It was the day before his fifty-ninth birthday. In the next ten days more than six hundred planes were launched from New Britain to attack American forces in the Solomons. Each day Yamamoto appeared in white dress uniform to see them off. At Rabaul he also conferred with his fleet commanders, visited hospitals, and played chess with Comdr. Yasuji Watanabe, his staff administrative officer and friend.

On Tuesday morning, 13 April, Yamamoto decided to personally inspect frontline naval bases in the Shortland area, off the southern tip of Bougainville Island. Watanabe worked out plans for the journey, and that afternoon sent a radio message to the various base commanders involved:

On 18 April Commander in Chief Combined Fleet will inspect Ballale, Shortland, and Buin as follows:
  1. Depart Rabaul 0600 in medium attack plane escorted by six fighters, arrive Ballale 0800. Depart at once in subchaser to arrive Shortland 0840. Depart Shortland 0945 in subchaser to arrive Ballale 1030. Depart Ballale by plane to arrive Buin at 1110. Lunch at Buin. Depart Buin 1400 by plane to arrive Rabaul 1540.

Encoded and enciphered, this message was radioed to its intended recipients, who promptly decoded and deciphered the text. The radio message was also picked up, just as promptly, by unintended recipients: U.S. naval radio stations that regularly intercepted Japanese broadcasts and relayed them to three special processing units known as Negat, Frupac, and Frumel, located in Washington, D.C., Pearl Harbor, and Melbourne, Australia, respectively.

These three stations got the intercept just as promptly as did its Japanese addressees, but the Americans had more difficulty in reading the text. Not having the benefit of current Japanese additives and code books, they relied on a handful of traffic analysts, cryptanalysts, and linguists to render the message intelligible. Via an exclusive radio circuit, the three stations could exchange information instantly, and pool their efforts to produce "comint"—communications intelligence—our most important source of enemy information in World War II.

Watanabe's 13 April 1943 message—because of its great variety of addressees—immediately caught the attention of the American comint units. The message was punched into newfangled IBM cards for processing. They spewed out a Japanese text containing lots of blanks and geographic designators. At Frupac in Pearl Harbor, this "puzzle" first reached the hands of Marine Lt. Col. Alva B. Lasswell, one of the Navy's most experienced cryptanalyst-linguists.

"Red" Lasswell had studied Japanese in Tokyo from 1935 to 1938. After comint duty at Cavite and Shanghai, and seven months in San Diego, he had reported to Pearl Harbor in May 1941. From his very first worksheet on this message, Lasswell knew it was important. Lieutenant Commander John G. Roenigk, another linguist, recalled that Lasswell leapt to his feet and exclaimed, "We've hit the jackpot!" All hands pitched in. Traffic analysts Tom Huckins and Jack Williams reworked the addressee information, cryptanalysts Tommy Dyer and "Ham" Wright worked to recover new additives and code groups, and "Jasper" Holmes's estimates section searched for area designators. Joe Finnegan, Roenigk, and other linguists dug for collateral information in other messages.

At stations Negat and Frumel, too, all hands scrambled to decipher this message. Commander Redfield Mason, in charge of translating at Negat in Washington, saw the raw message the minute it came in. Chief Petty Officer Albert J. Pelletier, who carpooled with him, remembers Mason's shouting, "I want every damned date, time, and place checked and double-checked." Mason poured over every squeaked-out recovery, exclaiming, "Good." And Mason's "Good" was very high praise indeed. Pelletier recalls thinking and saying, "I hope we get the SOB."

In Pearl Harbor, meanwhile, Lasswell, as was his practice when there was a "hot" item, worked all night on this one. At 1008 on Wednesday, 14 April 1943, Frupac issued a preliminary translation:

On 18 April CinC Combined Fleet will [blank, blank] as follows: [blank, blank] Ballale [blank, blank, blank] Frupac comment: This is probably a schedule of inspection by Cinc Combined Fleet. The message lacks additives, but work is being continued on it.

Feverishly, work continued at all three processing stations. At Pearl Harbor, when Lasswell finally had it deciphered completely later that day, he showed it to Jasper Holmes. By secure scrambler telephone, Holmes informed Comdr. Edwin T. Layton, Admiral Nimitz's intelligence officer. Then, to ensure against any possible mistake, Holmes and Lasswell handcarried the translation to Layton's office. Layton took it directly to Admiral Nimitz. In a discussion of the contents, Nimitz asked, "Do we try to get him?" Layton, who knew Yamamoto personally and professionally, offered pros and cons, and concluded, "You know, Admiral Nimitz, it would be just as if they shot you down. There is no one to replace him."

Whether and how to carry out this death warrant were difficult decisions. There were tactical and strategic considerations, including the danger that shooting down Yamamoto's airplane would tip off the Japanese that we were reading their communications.* One had also to consider that assassinating so eminent a person might have political repercussions. Admiral Nimitz, it is said, checked with Washington and received the go-ahead from Secretary of the Navy Frank Knox and President Franklin Roosevelt. Nowhere, however, have I found a reliable source for this assertion. The naval archives, the national archives, and the FDR Library at Hyde Park reveal no record that Roosevelt's approval was requested, or, in fact, that any communication on this subject ever took place between Washington and Nimitz.

President Roosevelt had left Washington by train the day before, on 13 April 1943, for a sixteen-day tour of southwestern states. During that time, the only related messages to him from Washington was one on Sunday, 18 April, telling of Japanese planes downed in the

---

**Ed. note:* Indeed, British intelligence officials in charge of Ultra, who did not learn of the plan until after its completion, were incensed for this very reason. Cf. Brown, *"C": The Secret Life of Sir Steward Graham Menzies,* 469.

Shortland area, and a follow-up message next day noting that Yamamoto may have been in one of the planes. You know the rest of that wartime drama. P-38s from Guadalcanal shot down the two Japanese bomber aircraft. One, carrying Chief of Staff Ugaki and four other staff officers, crashed in the sea; Ugaki and two others were saved. Yamamoto's plane crashed in the jungle, killing all on board.

All of this and more is today a matter of public record. My remaining remarks arise from an unpublished personal experience. In 1949, for Admiral Morison's history, I was interviewing Japanese naval officers. These included Capt. Yasuji Watanabe of Yamamoto's Combined Fleet staff, and—as mentioned—the man who had laid out Yamamoto's last itinerary.

In two days of discussion he had answered my every question. Now I was gathering my notes, finishing a last cup of tea, and expressing my appreciation. Watanabe said, hesitatingly, "Lieutenant Pineau, you have asked me many questions. May I ask one of you?" It seemed only fair, since I had quizzed him about myriad topics ranging from Pearl Harbor to Midway, and I readily consented. His query was totally direct: "How did you know to shoot down my chief?"

I can tell you now that I knew the answer to his question. At that time, however, I was under a wartime oath never to reveal to anyone anything connected with my comint duty. Not until 1978, in fact, was I permitted to publicly discuss comint information that had by then been declassified.

Incidentally, this matter had already been a burden in my work for Admiral Morison. Although President Roosevelt had chosen him to be naval historian, Morison had never been cleared for comint. Accordingly, he wrote of our successes at Coral Sea, Midway, the Yamamoto shootdown, and of spectacular submarine achievements as being merely "fortuitous." I had to sit silently by, unable to explain to him that these victories had been possible only because of communications intelligence. Morison's fifteen-volume history was completed in 1961. Its readers should bear in mind that this was seventeen years before World War II comint was declassified for publication. Throughout my ten years as his assistant, my oath forbade unauthorized mention of comint to anyone.

"Captain Watanabe," I replied, "our Morison research is now on events in the year 1942. When we work on 1943 I will know more about the death of your chief, and then may be able to answer your question. Since you ask, do you have a theory about it?" His solemn nod showed that he had given much thought to the matter. Watanabe went on to explain that in releasing the 13 April itinerary message, he had directed that it be sent only by naval communications, because he believed the army code to be insecure. After Yamamoto's death, an inquiry revealed that—contrary to Watanabe's instructions—the message had gone out over both systems. Watanabe concluded, therefore, that the army broadcast had been intercepted. At that time, I could not tell him he was wrong, that we had broken his precious naval code.

From a cabinet he brought out a pocket notebook that contained his working draft of the fateful Yamamoto itinerary and showed it to me tenderly. From the precise calligraphy I saw that Red Lasswell's translation had been 100 percent correct. And now, seeing it in Japanese, I also noticed what appeared to be a slight error on Watanabe's part, and I had the temerity to mention it. Astonished, Watanabe sprang to my side and asked what it was. I pointed out that he had allowed forty minutes for the boat ride from Ballale to Shortland, but forty-five minutes for the return trip. Watanabe gave a sigh of relief, and managed a smile. It was not an error, but rather his careful five-minute allowance for the set of tide and current on the return trip. Touché!

Watanabe told other details about this, the greatest tragedy of his life. News of the crash reached Rabaul at noon on Sunday, 18 April, but a seasonal squall delayed his arrival at Buin until early Monday morning, 19 April 1943. Search parties found the Yamamoto aircraft wreckage that afternoon. All of its seven-man crew and four passengers were dead. Watanabe brought the bodies to Buin by minesweeper. During the trip he examined Yamamoto's body. One bullet had pierced the lower left jaw, emerging at the right temple; another had entered the left shoulder blade, traveling upward. Watanabe probed with his finger but could not reach the bullet.

Next day, on 20 April 1943, Watanabe supervised his chief's cremation, placing the ashes in a stout wooden box lined with leaves of the papaya—Yamamoto's favorite fruit. On Thursday, 22 April, Watanabe brought the box back to Rabaul. The next day he carried the ashes to Truk and on board the flagship *Musashi*. There, they were placed in the commander-in-chief's cabin for the last voyage home.

On 21 May 1943, more than a month after the attack that killed Admiral Yamamoto and six of his staff officers, Japanese leaders finally informed the public of his death.

The shootdown of Yamamoto was probably the most spectacular single wartime event ever to result from the breaking of one message in communications intelligence.

Was It Right to Gun for Yamamoto?
Paul B. Woodruff

I feel awkward raising a question of ethics when we are here mainly to celebrate the courage and skill of the pilots engaged on both sides in the air battle that brought down Admiral Yamamoto's airplane in 1943. There is no ethical question about the *conduct* of the mission; what I have to say has no bearing on what the pilots actually did.

Ethical evaluation of an action usually depends in part on the intention that lies behind the action. In this case the relevant intention is not that of the American pilots (who quite rightly intended to do their duty); the relevant intention is that of their commanders, who sought to kill Yamamoto. It is this primary intention—the intention to kill Yamamoto—about which I will be speaking.* Was it right to launch an attack that was intended to kill this particular man?

---

*The intention to do one's duty—to carry out orders—does not relieve a soldier from ethical responsibility in every case. The Yamamoto case is unusual because the

1. *I want first to anticipate the objection that ethical considerations do not apply in warfare.* At this point many may want to say that I am on the wrong track. There is nothing unusual about killing in wartime. After all, war routinely involves acts of violence against persons and property—acts that would be considered unethical in peacetime. Nevertheless, we do not condemn normal acts of war on ethical grounds. We accept, as ethically permissible, acts of violence in wartime that we would otherwise condemn. The reasons for this are controversial, and I will not go into them here. The point I want to make initially is this: not all acts of violence in wartime are ethically permissible. Sad to say, there are such things as war crimes, ethically speaking. We must not be misled because some cases of war crimes are hard to distinguish from permissible acts of war. History abounds with clear cases of unethical acts of war: the senseless torture of prisoners, for example, or the mass killing of innocents, or even the attempted massacre of an entire race. I do not want to invite comparison with these atrocities; I mention them only to make my point that however hellish warfare may be, there are still ethical and unethical ways to go about it.

True, modern technology has pushed back the limits of war by expanding enormously the range of targets that can be destroyed on the order of a single commander. This, however, does not affect issues in ethics. If it is easier now to kill innocent civilians than it used to be, it is no less wrong to do so. Total war—war governed by no ethical considerations whatever—is still an atrocity.

So I come back to my original question: was it right for U.S. forces to set about killing Admiral Yamamoto?

2. *The Yamamoto mission was unusual in being directed at a person.* Conventional military targets are forces, or weapons, or installations. The mission we are discussing, however, was directed spe-

---

mission falls within the usual ethical boundaries: normal weaponry used against a military target. An ethical issue arises here solely because of suspicions we have about the intentions behind the decision to kill Yamamoto. The pilots who carried out the mission did not make the decision, and so their intentions are not relevant.

cifically at Adm. Isoroku Yamamoto and no one else. As we have heard, he was the builder of Japanese naval air power and the designer of the attack on Pearl Harbor. He was also a brilliant chief of staff of the Imperial Japanese Navy, which depended heavily on his devoted and intelligent leadership.

I have said that part of evaluating an action ethically is examining the intention behind it. Intentions are not blind. They aim at specific things understood in certain ways. To say that the intention behind the mission was to kill Yamamoto is far too simple. As ethicists, we should want to know more: was this intended as an act of punishment? . . . of revenge? . . . or as part of a plan to reduce the effectiveness of the Japanese Imperial Navy? This is closely linked to another question: under what description was Yamamoto considered as the target for the operation of 18 April 1943? As the admiral responsible for Japanese success in the war? As the criminal who committed the sneak attack at Pearl Harbor? Or as an enemy officer who was expected to continue inflicting great losses on U.S. forces? Yamamoto was all those things and more.

3. *The motive of punishment may have played a part.* This is unusual in the context of active warfare. Although we have many reasons for being angry at enemy troops, we rarely think of them personally as guilty of crimes for which they deserve to be punished. Simply carrying a rifle in an enemy army—and shooting it at our troops in battle—is not a crime. If it were, we would treat prisoners of war as criminals. But we do not do this. When we do think of an enemy as a war criminal, we hope to bring him to public trial and punishment after the war is over, as an example to the world.

It is a fact peculiar to Yamamoto (and a few others) that as a military man he was considered to be a criminal by many on the Allied side during the war itself. Moreover, he was someone we could not wait to punish. (Halsey held a different view. When his colleagues applauded the news of Yamamoto's death, he is reported to have said, "What's good about it? I'd hoped to lead that scoundrel up Pennsylvania Avenue in chains, with the rest of you kicking him where it would do the most good.")

Top: Former adversaries confer. Kenji Yanagiya and Rex Barber in Fredericksburg, Texas, 17 April 1988. (Photo courtesy of the Nimitz Museum.) *Bottom*: Mission panel, Yamamoto Retrospective Symposium, Fredericksburg, Texas, 16 April 1988. Left to right: Nimitz Museum director Bruce Smith, Louis Kittel, Julius Jacobson, Delton Goerke, Douglas Canning, Roger Ames, Cargill Hall, John Mitchell, Rex Barber, Besby Holmes, Makoto Shinagawa (translator), and Kenji Yanagiya. (Photo courtesy of the Nimitz Museum.)

Top: Yamamoto mission aviators, Fredericksburg, Texas, 17 April 1988.
Left to right: Roger Ames, Rex Barber, Douglas Canning, Kenji Yanagiya,
Delton Goerke, Julius Jacobson, Besby Holmes, John Mitchell, and Louis
Kittel. (Photo courtesy of the Nimitz Museum.) *Bottom*: Admiral Isoroku
Yamamoto and his staff on board the battleship *Yamato* in the inland sea,
ca. 1942. Yamamoto is seated, first row, fifth from left. Rear Admiral
Matome Ugaki, chief of staff, is seated next to Yamamoto, fourth from left.
Commander Yasuji Watanabe is standing, fourth from the right. (Photo
courtesy of Roger Pineau.)

Top: Captain Yasuji Watanabe, staff gunnery officer on Admiral Yamamoto's combined fleet staff from 1940 to 1943, June 1949. (Photo courtesy of Roger Pineau.) *Bottom*: Admiral Isoroku Yamamoto at Rabaul, saluting pilots taking off during Operation "I," early April 1943. This is the last known picture of the admiral. (Photo courtesy of Roger Pineau.)

A photo mosaic of Fighter Two on Guadalcanal, ca. January 1943. (Photo courtesy of Rollins Snelling.)

Top: Members of the 70th Fighter Squadron, Army Air Forces, on Fiji Island, ca. August 1942. (Photo courtesy of Douglas Canning.) *Bottom*: P-40s of the 68th Fighter Squadron, Army Air Forces, over Guadalcanal, ca. late 1942. (Photo courtesy of Rollins Snelling.)

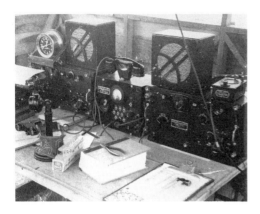

Inside the control tower at Fighter Two, Guadalcanal, ca. early 1943. (Photo courtesy of Rollins Snelling.)

A P-38 on a mission from Guadalcanal, 339th Fighter Squadron, ca. early 1943. (Photo courtesy of Douglas Canning.)

Left to right: Douglas Canning and John Mitchell on Fiji Island, fall 1942. (Photo courtesy of Douglas Canning.)

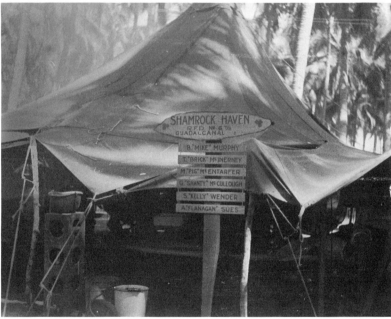

Top: A P-39 on Fiji, prior to move to Guadalcanal, fall 1942. (Photo courtesy of Douglas Canning.) *Bottom*: Headquarters of an unknown company, 25th "Tropic Lightning" Division, U.S. Army, on Guadalcanal. The 25th was commanded by Maj. Gen. J. Lawton "Lightning Joe" Collins. After the marines departed in December 1942, this particular unit, which contained its share of Irishmen, served on the front lines for forty days and nights. The 25th Division played a major role in driving the Japanese from the island. Ca. January 1943. (Photo courtesy of Rollins Snelling.)

Now that forty-five years have passed, I think we all recognize that whatever else he was, Yamamoto was not a scoundrel. Arguably, he shared responsibility for a criminal act, owing to his prominent role in the attack on Pearl Harbor. I am inclined to doubt that this attack was a war crime in the proper sense. But that should not concern us here. Our question is this: if the Allies had considered him a criminal, would it be permissible for them to punish him in mid-war, without trial? The question answers itself. *No act of war is justified on the grounds that it punishes a guilty individual.* Those killed in war are rarely thought guilty of any crime; and those who are thought guilty are, when possible, held for trial. So if the intention were to punish Yamamoto, it would not pass the usual ethical tests.

4. *The case of revenge is more complicated.* The desire for revenge against the enemy plays a part in the motivations of troops at all levels, from commanders to privates in the field; and anyone who has been in action soon has some cause for vengeance against the enemy. Yamamoto, the most prominent and dangerous of the Japanese leaders, was naturally a lightning rod for American resentment against Japan. The American people had suffered much in this unsought war, and in so many ways, that it would have been superhuman of them not to want vengeance. The many Americans who wanted revenge on Yamamoto were not superhuman. So what? We cannot blame them for that.

Still, the case is worrying, mainly because anger at what a nation had done was directed against one individual person. The revenge motive that operates in familiar military situations is impersonal. It does not matter who, in particular, occupies the enemy foxhole. He is the enemy, and the enemy killed your buddies . . . and so you act. But the case of Yamamoto seems to have been intensely personal. And that raises both practical and ethical questions. The thirst for personal revenge does not make for good soldiering on the whole, and it can lead, as we all know it did in Vietnam, to atrocities against helpless enemy prisoners and even against innocent civilians.

There are precedents for personal revenge, of course, in military history and in myth alike. The most famous is the oldest: sulky Achilles was brought back into the war of Greeks against Trojans when his buddy, Patroclus, was killed by Hector. The story of Achilles' terrible revenge is the centerpiece of Homer's *Iliad,* which begins with the word "wrath": "Of the wrath of Achilles, who was son of Peleus, sing to me goddess . . . " But we soon learn that Achilles' proclivity for anger was not entirely a good thing. The anger of that first line was Achilles' anger at his general over a skewed division of the spoils of battle. True, it is anger that brings Achilles storming back onto the battlefield, intending to kill the enemy's top spearman and drag his body by the heels through the dust. "Here is the man," says Achilles when he first spies Hector, "who beyond all others has troubled my anger, who slaughtered my beloved companion" (425 — 26, Lattimore). Achilles has become "a man with no sweetness in his heart" (467), and when he loses Hector in the mist, he launches into a merciless assault on every Trojan he can catch. When at last Hector is cornered by Achilles and sees that his time is up, he begs Achilles to return his body to Troy for proper burial. But Achilles is too angry to have any respect for the gentle and heroic Hector: "No more entreating of me, you dog . . . / I wish only that my spirit and fury would drive me / to hack your meat away and eat it raw for the things / that you have done to me" (xxii.345-46).

Now it is interesting that Achilles does not do that. When his fury is spent, and Hector's elderly father comes by night to beg for the body, the two men sit down and grieve together over their losses, the young man and the old. And then Achilles, reminded of his own father, relents and restores Hector's body to Troy.

I tell this old story here because I think it helps to clarify the issues, as myths often do. Achilles' great intention is personal vengeance, moved by anger. That makes him an awesome soldier, but not a particularly good one, since his anger moves as readily against his commander as it does against his enemies. No commanding officer would want an Achilles as his subordinate. Personal revenge is not a reliable motivation in warfare (or anywhere else, for that matter). But that is not yet precisely an ethical consideration, merely a practical one.

Is it wrong to kill enemies in war out of a desire for revenge? In itself, there is nothing wrong with Achilles killing Hector. He would have been right to do so even if he was not personally angry at Hector, for Hector was the most prominent and dangerous officer in the enemy's forces. There is something ethically wrong, however, when Achilles storms into battle with his mind totally clouded by his lust for revenge. The results are terrible for the Trojans, who sustain great losses. More serious in its ethical significance is the fact that Achilles' perception of his enemy is warped. Hector, whom we have just seen as a loyal son, a kind husband, and a gentle father—Hector, who never wanted war but fights it bravely only for the sake of his father and his country—this Hector becomes in Achilles' eyes a beast who deserves to have his flesh eaten raw and bleeding from his bones. This attitude extends to all of the Trojans in Achilles' mind, and that no doubt explains why Achilles in his anger slaughters prisoners of war when there is no military need for doing so. The ethical problem about revenge in war is mainly this, that it leads to an attitude of blind anger toward the enemy, an attitude that can lead to atrocities.

So far I have not spoken directly about Yamamoto in the context of revenge, but I hope you have already noticed the analogy: like Hector, he was basically a good man and a reluctant but noble warrior, a man moved by exemplary loyalty to his country; also, like Hector, Yamamoto became the focus of a personal, vitriolic anger, but this time of a whole nation, not just an Achilles.

I think I have said enough. The intention to gain revenge brings with it a distortion of the facts; and that distortion may, in the long run, and in all its ramifications, have terrible consequences. The happier side of this story is that anger passes in time, and we are able to see Yamamoto more generously—even our Pacific veterans may sit down together with his countrymen to grieve over our respective losses. So much for revenge.

5. *Could the Yamamoto mission have been a legitimate act of war?* The evidence I have seen suggests that the primary intention of the United States decisionmakers was not punishment or revenge,

but the elimination of an exceptional leader who threatened American interests in the war.

While punishment and revenge look backward to what has been done in the past, legitimate military intentions look forward, toward what can be prevented, or toward what can be gained. Ethical intentions in war look mainly forward, toward bringing the war to an end. I do not mean to say that ending the war is all that matters, ethically speaking; I do mean to say that backward-looking aims, like punishment and revenge, are strictly irrelevant to proper military decisions and can lead in unethical directions.

Those who decided to "get Yamamoto" were probably looking more forward than backward—more to the devastating effect on Japan of the loss of their great admiral than to what that admiral had done in the past. United States decisionmakers evidently believed that the Japanese had no one equivalent to replace Yamamoto.

6. *The mission was not an assassination.* Assassination raises special ethical problems because it takes place outside the theaters of war. In an assassination, nonuniformed personnel behind the lines gain access by stealth to an enemy leader (who may also be nonuniformed) and kill him. I have nothing to say about this except that it is very unlike the Yamamoto mission. Yamamoto was in uniform in a military plane, and he was attacked openly in a theater of war by military aircraft. This is what happens when snipers aim at officers, or when soldiers throw grenades toward radio antennas knowing that officers are marked by radios nearby. Officers in action, if they are identifiable, have always been especially vulnerable. Everyone knows that the loss of top officers can paralyze an army.

What raises suspicions in this case is that Yamamoto was not identified in a conventional way, but through the decoding of a secret message intercepted by radio. But the use of such devices to detect enemy movements and dispositions has never seriously been in question.

7. Conclusion. *The action against Yamamoto was ethically permissible precisely to the extent that it was not intended as revenge*

or punishment, but as a forward-looking action, designed to weaken the effectiveness of the Japanese navy.*

The Killing of Yamamoto Viewed as Ethically Wrong

Manuel M. Davenport

To begin, I want to summarize, as carefully and accurately as I can, Professor Woodruff's arguments because I believe he raises the correct and necessary conceptual, factual, and ethical questions. He points out that the killing of Yamamoto was not, by definition, an assassination. He then argues that on the basis of available evidence it was not intended primarily as an act of punishment or revenge; rather, it was intended primarily as the elimination of an exceptional military leader whose continued existence could prolong the war.

In considering the ethical questions, Professor Woodruff argues that the killing of Yamamoto could not be justified ethically as an act of punishment or revenge, but could be justified ethically if intended to eliminate a military threat. Because he believes the intention was, primarily, to eliminate a military threat, he concludes that the killing of Yamamoto was ethically permissible.

I have tried to reconstruct Professor Woodruff's argument with care because I find myself in a most curious position. I agree with everything he says except his conclusion. In other words, I think that although the killing of Yamamoto was primarily intended as the elimination of an exceptional military threat, this was insufficient to make it an ethically permissible action. It is quite plausible to argue, I will contend, that it was ethically wrong.

---

*Whether killing Yamamoto did have this result is not relevant to the ethical issue. Whether the action could reasonably be expected to have this result, however, is relevant to the ethical (as well as to the military) propriety of the decision to target Yamamoto. Generally, acts of violence in war are not permissible if it is unreasonable to expect that they will bring about the intended results. Whether or not the Yamamoto mission falls under this principle is controversial, and beyond the scope of this discussion.

Such an argument is plausible for two different kinds of reasons. In the first place, in the conduct of war we must question not only the morality of our goals but also the morality of our means. In regard to the killing of Yamamoto, we must ask not only was it right to eliminate this exceptional military threat, but also was this the right way to do it? In the second place, in the conduct of war as well as in the conduct of life in general, simply intending to bring about a good result is not enough to make an action right. In the killing of Yamamoto we must ask whether this action did contribute to our long-range military objectives more so than not killing him would have.

Let me emphasize that I raise these particular issues not because I believe that war should be governed by some romantic code of chivalry but, to the contrary, because I believe that if we engage in war, we should follow those rules of war that result in winning the war. But to "win the war" it is not sufficient merely to end hostilities. We must end hostilities in such a way that the values for which we fought are maintained and continued rather than destroyed.

This is why we must ask, first, whether the means by which we killed Yamamoto were ethically right. Clearly, killing him in the way we did led to an immediate military advantage, but by establishing a precedent in terms of which members of the supreme military command of a nation can expect to be targets at any time and in any place, did we restrict the future capacity of our own military commanders to exercise leadership? Did we establish a rule of war that later resulted in our senior officers circling high above the jungles of Southeast Asia while second lieutenants on the ground made the critical military and ethical decisions? Not only is it possible that the way in which we killed Yamamoto created a bad precedent by limiting our own present and future military effectiveness, it is also possible that it increased the will to resist on the part of Japanese military leaders who respected him.

I am more concerned, however, with the possibility that our long-range military objectives, including winning the peace, would have been better served by not killing Yamamoto at all. During the war with Japan, we carefully avoided putting the emperor's life in danger because we believed that to win the peace with Japan we needed his cooperation and leadership. It is just as plausible to believe that Yamamoto's cooperation and leadership would have contributed to preserving the values for which we fought. Yamamoto never wanted the war with the United States in the first place; he urged throughout the war that Japan seek a negotiated peace. He fought not out of hatred for the United States, a nation he knew and admired, but out of love of home and loyalty to emperor.

When I think of Adm. Isoroku Yamamoto, I think of another reluctant but brilliant warrior who fought a war he never sought against those he knew and admired; I think of Gen. Robert E. Lee. And I ask myself, suppose Lee had been killed during the war by a special strike aimed specifically at him while visiting his troops behind his lines; what would have been the consequences? Would the Southern will to resist have been increased? Would normal relations with the Southern states have been the more difficult to establish?

Of course it may be objected that, given the bombing of Hiroshima and Nagasaki, whether the killing of Yamamoto immediately increased the difficulties of winning the war or establishing the peace is irrelevant. In the long run, it may be argued, given our eventual acquisition of atomic power, the Japanese had no choice but to surrender and accept peace on our terms. But, I would counter, if the killing of Yamamoto in terms of our long-range military and political objectives was of no consequence, then it has no ethical justification at all.

To summarize, I have argued that our nation and all other nations should agree in the conduct of war to adopt rules that promote our long-range interests. It follows that we should not adopt rules of war that prevent us from winning, but it does not follow that we cannot show respect for our enemies as fellow human beings. Quite often, even in war, a failure to show such respect for our enemies creates precedents that restrict our own future ability to wage war effectively. In my opinion, the manner in which we killed Yamamoto reinforced, if it did not create, such a precedent.

Though we should not adopt rules of war that preclude winning, it does not follow that we should kill each and every enemy combatant whenever we have the opportunity. Quite often it is the case that certain individual enemies should be spared because their survival after the war would contribute more to establishing normal relations than their extinction during the war would contribute to ending hostilities. In my opinion, if Adm. Isoroku Yamamoto had survived the war, his continued efforts in life would have served our interests better than did his death during the war.

Questions and Answers

Academic Panel

Dr. Allard: The floor is open to questions.

Mr. Phillips: I'm Bill Phillips from San Antonio. In light of this mission review, Dr. Beaumont, I've heard about such things as cruise missiles today that can be used for assassinations, and also of the recent mission against Libya with the possible attempt to kill Colonel Quaddafi. Do you believe it is becoming part of our military policy to plan to take out high-ranking officers, and, if it's not, should it be?

Dr. Beaumont: We can review very quickly the 1975 Church hearings, the special Senate hearings held on the question of assassination as national policy. Congress subsequently passed legislation, which became law, making it illegal to use assassination as a tool of American foreign policy. Whether that would extend to the conduct of an undeclared war is uncertain. Addressing your question, however, I think the answer is yes; it is a general trend in the twentieth century that has become more common and, as others have pointed out, it is a function of the increasing technology of identification and surveillance, the increasing accuracy of weapons, and the increasing number of special units that can carry out these missions on land, sea, and in the air.

Mr. Kauslick: My name is Al Kauslick. I've worked for Bougainville Copper for several years. I'd like to address my question to Captain

Pineau. At what point in time was the Japanese code broken, and could you give us a description of the method or the mechanics used to break the code?

Captain Pineau: The history of American successes with Japanese codes goes back to the early 1920s. In fact, our first cryptoanalytic unit in the Navy Department started in 1924, and during the 1920s it was a very basic effort at code breaking. It was all pencil and paper, no computers, no IBM cards, and it was a long, slow process. It was also a process that could be speeded up if you could steal the enemy's code book. And so, in the 1920s we went up and broke into the Japanese consulate in New York City and photographed the code book that a naval officer had there. Now he was acting as a consular agent, but actually he was a naval officer, so we felt it was all right to go in. Since they were not playing cricket, it was all right for us not to play cricket. And that gave us a very clear opening into their codes; in fact, we were actually reading their codes for much of that period as rapidly as their own addressees were reading them.

Then the Japanese code system changed; the Japanese became more sophisticated and our efforts slowed down. We were not reading details in them again until the 1930s. We had successes then, helped out once again by breaking into the consul general's office in New York City and photographing their code books. We weren't alone in this, for the Japanese were doing it to our consulates in Japan. So, to the extent that it was done by both sides, I guess it was accepted as cricket by both sides. But this never traveled in a smooth ascending line, it was up and down.

During World War II, if that was the thrust of your inquiry, the Japanese tended to change codes every six months. Every time they either changed codes or changed additives—two major parts of the coding and deciphering business—we could count on a very slow period, usually lasting between six and twelve weeks, before we broke back into the system. But strangely enough, we'd usually get back into the system at crucial moments. During the war we weren't able to photograph code books surreptitiously, although some of the code books did fall into our hands, and that helped. But when the Japanese suspected that we had broken a code they might change it even more frequently than the usual six months, so it was still an up-and-down thing. Luckily for us, we were reading them enough at the most important times.

Allard: Captain Pineau, I believe he also asked about the techniques; do you have any comments on the techniques in World War II?

Pineau: The IBM mechanization of the sorting process on punch cards was a godsend to our people because it relieved them of the pencil and paper drudgery. Any time you can get enough messages in a given system and put them into an automatic sorting and comparing routine, you're way ahead. Now, today, I'm sure it's done by computers, and it has been speeded up a great deal. So by the time you can eliminate the nulls and the voids and the insignificant things, the significant things pop out and the codes become increasingly easier to break. But they have also become increasingly difficult, increasingly more sophisticated and more complicated. Our successes with them in World War II were quite complete. We intercepted Japanese navy messages at a rate of about 120 messages per day in our three stations. Those messages are today available in the National Archives, some 165,000 of them.

On the other hand, the Japanese had almost no successes; they never did break a major code of ours. They did succeed with aircraft carrier communications, the talk between ships, and between ships and shore. My friends in the coding business in Japan told me that they always knew when an American aircraft carrier was going in or out of harbor because the American practice was, as the carrier approached harbor, to fly all the airplanes to fields ashore, where they would be serviced while the ship was being refitted and overhauled. Then, when all the servicing was completed, the aircraft carrier would sail out to sea, and the planes would fly out and land on her flight deck at sea. That involved a lot of chatter between the pilots and the landing officers on the carrier decks. The Japanese understood that quite well, but that's the only real success they had.

Mr. David: Jack David from San Antonio. I would like to ask Captain

Pineau if he would agree with the assessment that one of the historical lessons of the Yamamoto interception, in the modern context, is the adequate collection and analysis of intelligence. I offer the Battle of Midway and the Yamamoto mission as examples of American intelligence successes, and the Battle of the Bulge, the Chinese intervention in Korea, and more recently the 1968 Tet Offensive in Vietnam, as examples of American intelligence failures, where a lot of brave men died as a result. Would you agree with that? My second question is, did it ever occur to any of the Japanese officers at any time during the war, the Japanese admirals and high-ranking officers that you interviewed, that we had broken their code? Did they ever receive any indication that we were able to decipher their messages?

Pineau: On the first question, I can in fairness respond only to the World War II part. After World War II my interest remained focused on that war, I'm afraid, but there is no question that Midway and the Yamamoto shootdown and our later submarine successes against the Japanese shipping were magnificent examples of the efficacy of intelligence, intelligently acquired and properly analyzed and disseminated. You must always remember there are three essentials of intelligence: the gathering, analyzing, and disseminating of information. You can gather and analyze until hell freezes over, but if you don't get it to the people who need it to make the proper military decisions, it's not intelligence. It requires all three of those points in order to be intelligence. On the second question, . . . would you repeat it, sir?

David: The second question was, in your interviews with the staff officers, did it ever occur to any of them during the war that we were able to break their codes?

Pineau: Some of them were very astute and sensitive to it. Captain Yasuji Watanabe was one of those. He was one of the most brilliant men I've ever known and he had a great mind, historically and analytically. Most Japanese officers whom I interrogated were not as bold as Watanabe; it was really rather bold of him to ask the code break question of me, but he felt that we were friendly enough that he could put this straightforward question to me. Others were reluctant to ask such questions. I became friendly with two of the commanders-in-chief of the Combined Fleet, the successors to Yamamoto—not immediate successors, his immediate successor, Admiral Koga, was killed a year later in an airplane crash in the Philippines. But two other commanders-in-chief [Soemu Toyoda and Jisaburo Ozawa] survived the war. It was always interesting to talk with them. They didn't raise the question about codebreaking, but we did discuss strategy. I asked them if they understood our Third Fleet and Fifth Fleet arrangement during the war. That both involved the same ships, but it was Third Fleet when Halsey commanded, and the Fifth Fleet under Spruance. Toyoda and Ozawa suspected something like that, but had not understood exactly how it worked. One thing they did agree on, though, was that it was too bad Halsey wasn't in charge at the battle of the Marianas and Spruance in charge at the battle for Leyte Gulf. If that had happened, they felt there would have been a complete reversal of the two situations.

Mr. Pruitt: I am Joe Pruitt from Kansas City, Missouri, and I'd like to reinforce what Captain Pineau has said. John Brannon, who defended Admiral Nagano, met with him constantly during some three trips, each trip lasting three-and-one-half months. In his letters, Brannon addressed that question to Admiral Nagano: "Did you know that we had broken the code?" He just could not believe it up to the time of his death, but finally admitted he had a suspicion that it might have been broken, but never admitted to his colleagues that he thought the code had been broken. If I'm not mistaken, Nagano was commander-in-chief of the navy. I could send you a copy of that letter if you wish.

Pineau: I'd be very interested.

Mr. Mouselman: My name is Tom Mouselman and I'm from Fredericksburg. I'd like to say that I think God has cursed us with philosophers because they make us think. I would ask Professor Davenport, would it have been more moral and right for Halsey to have taken his carrier group and sunk Yamamoto's ship and killed Yamamoto in this fashion than to send out airplanes purposefully to shoot him down? The second question concerns Professor Davenport's statement that Yamamoto might have been beneficial in establishing peace after the war was over. Do you believe that General MacArthur would have treated Yamamoto any differently in Japan than General Eisenhower treated General Jodl in Germany? It always seems as if the war criminals are on the side that loses.

Dr. Woodruff: If I may, I'd like to answer just the first part of that question—whether it would make a moral difference if Halsey had sunk Yamamoto's ship rather than shot down his plane. From my point of view, it would make no ethical difference, since I have no ethical objection to what was actually done. I prefer what was done, because fewer people were killed in the process.

Dr. Davenport: I don't think it would have made that much difference. My point about the way in which it was done was simply to raise this question: do we, by the way we conduct war and address any number of problems that come up in war, adopt a mode of operation that creates a precedent that would restrict future modes of operation? That question is always present and needs to be raised. I have thought a great deal about the second part of your question. I was thinking about this last night; would MacArthur have made the best possible use of Yamamoto?

I really can't answer that question, for it is a "what if" question. I don't know what would have happened. Again, the issue I wanted to raise is this: we've got to win wars, and I'm in favor of winning wars. I was in the army during the Korean police action—as I guess it is called—and I'm in favor of winning. But I think we've got to ask the question: How will this affect our future relations with those that we have conquered? If it was going to make winning the peace much more difficult, that has to be considered, too, and that's the question I think should have been considered at the time the mission was planned; what would the act do to us in the future? Roger, would you care to comment on whether we would have treated Yamamoto as a war criminal if he had survived the war?

Beaumont: That's a good spot to be put in! I suspect that at least an investigation would have been conducted; whether that would have led to an indictment or involvement in the Far East war crimes trial or not, I don't know.

Pineau: A glimmer of light may be shed if we consider for a moment Gen. Douglas MacArthur's treatment of one so-called Japanese war criminal. In the case of General Yamashita,* he showed no mercy. He named a military commission of five generals to try Yamashita. The trial began on Monday, 29 October 1945, and ended thirty-five days later on a Wednesday afternoon. Before adjourning, the president of the commission, Maj. Gen. Russell B. Reynolds, declared, "The commission will announce its findings at 2 o'clock in the afternoon, Friday next." As Capt. A. Frank Reel, one of Yamashita's four defense attorneys, has noted, "That was less than forty-six hours away. In that time they could not review the more than four thousand pages of record and the more than four hundred and twenty-three exhibits. They could not even properly study and digest the closing arguments."† How could the commission know how long it would take to discuss and vote on the issues and then write its decision unless these details had already been taken care of? As a final MacArthurian dramatic touch, that "Friday next" was more than just another Friday—it would be the seventh of December, the fourth anniversary of the Pearl Harbor attack.

I had the good fortune to interview General MacArthur with Admiral Morison. We spent two-and-a-half hours with him in his impressive office at the top of the Dai Ichi building. At one point Morison said to him, "How do you feel about the war crime trials, General?" MacArthur took a suck on his corncob pipe, looked out the window at Mt. Fuji, which you could still see then from Tokyo, and replied, "I'm glad you asked that question, Professor Morison. They were a fine bunch of men." (Dramatic pause.) "I have had a long and varied

---

Ed. note: General Tomoyuki Yamashita, the "Tiger of Malaya," commanded the Fourteenth Army Group, Imperial Japanese Army, in the Philippines for the last year of the war.

†Reel, *The Case of General Yamashita,* 166-67.

career. In the course of that career I have had to perform many difficult tasks. But the most difficult task I ever had to perform was to pass judgment on a man who had opposed me on the field of battle." (Another pause.) "It almost made me sick to my stomach" (pause), "and I have a very strong stomach."

People talk about MacArthur's being a ham actor; there is no question in my mind that he ranks with the best of them. He had my heart right up in my throat, and I felt extremely sorry for him at that moment. That evening, however, I got Frank Reel's book and read it through a sleepless night. It changed my mind and feelings about MacArthur. I have never forgiven him for his treatment of General Yamashita, for playing fast and loose with my emotions, and for lying to me and Admiral Morison.

Captain McGregor: I'm Captain Don McGregor, a representative of the 347th Fighter Group. My question is directed to Dr. Davenport and Dr. Woodruff on the question of ethics. I think we all realize that in the next conflict, God forbid, that command control structures will be targeted. For example, if you had a column of tanks or a group of fighters coming into a target, someone will decide who is part of that command control structure, who is the commander within that group, and they're going to be targeted. My question is, where do we draw the line as to what level of command we make this pinpoint surgical removal? Do we stop at the field commander, the army commander, or the theater commander, such as Yamamoto? Where do we draw the line, even though we don't have the names of those smaller people?

Davenport: I was assuming that the decision made in World War II would affect the future conduct of war. I'm not sure if decisions that will be made in the next war would affect the conduct of future wars at all. But assuming there might be wars after the next war, then we could raise the question in the same context: if command control centers are targeted, the question I will raise is, does that limit the effectiveness of the commanders to exercise leadership, and I think quite clearly it does. Now the fact that they are going to be targeted isolates commanders from the individuals that they're trying to lead. That's the kind of precedent that interferes with our capacity to exercise leadership. This is going to continue, this is going to escalate to the point, I suppose, where all commanding will be accomplished by remote electronic devices of some sort, and I think that's not as effective.

Woodruff: The question was at what rank and at what level should the targeting of enemy commanders be stopped, if any? Obviously, in future wars enemy command posts will be targeted as they always have since the Stone Age, but we will be able to do it much more accurately and at much higher levels of command. I can't see an ethical objection to targeting commanders at any level in wartime. If this is really a case of war, and the commanders we're talking about are enemy commanders, the question of whether killing them actually promotes our war aims is a practical military consideration that can be dealt with independently from the ethical point.

I would like to add an important footnote to this. The practice of targeting leaders in wartime is a very old practice, but our enhanced technical ability has led us to take this more and more for granted in wartime. It would be terrifying to me, however, if this practice were taken out of the arena of war and used as a method of carrying out foreign policy; destabilizing foreign nations with which we are not at war by this means seems to me quite atrocious.

Ms. Viles: I'm Patty Viles from Dallas, and I have a question for Dr. Davenport. Do you believe future relations with the enemy to be a higher good than preserving the lives of our countrymen in wartime?

Davenport: I think it depends on how many lives are preserved. You see, ending hostilities quickly does not always preserve as many lives as establishing a long-lasting international relationship. I think, perhaps, we learned some lessons in this regard between World War I and World War II. The manner in which peace was established after World War I left a great deal of bitterness and resentment. The seeds of the next war were planted in the manner in which peace was established in Europe. So, the manner in which we establish peace can prevent the killing of people in the future. You can't always say if you end a war quickly that is going to guarantee that we'll lose fewer lives; it also depends on the postwar relationships we establish with the enemy. Can we make and keep the peace as a lasting peace? That's the important thing.

Mr. Jones: My name is Jack Jones, and I also was a participant in World War II. I flew P-39s and P-38s against the Japanese in New Guinea, and in my squadron alone we lost about half shot down in about the first 38 days. I never thought as a fighter pilot I'd be coming to the rescue of some philosophers, but I'm always for the underdog I guess. I grew up in that generation. Dr. Davenport, before you answer my question, let me say this. I just spent some time here with a fellow I fought, Saburo Sakai. At the time of my first mission, as a matter of fact, he was a veteran of six years of fighting, but we both came out alive. The question is whether ethics is an individual matter. We youngsters used to argue in that squadron over whether or not we would assassinate an enemy pilot after he'd bailed out. Fortunately, Saburo and his crowd didn't use parachutes so we didn't have to confront that problem. I just asked him again today to confirm it. But in World War II we argued among ourselves about this, and half of the outfit I served with said, "Never shoot a guy in a parachute." The German Air Force never shot a fellow in a parachute unless he was a commando.

Allard: Sir, excuse me, what is your question?

Jones: I'm sorry, I'm taking too long. Do you speak of applying your ethics on an individual basis, or is it applied to the government of a nation?

Davenport: Let me say first, I appreciate any help I can get. To answer, I would say, both. I think ethical decisions have to be made on the individual level, but you can't give full responsibility to people in the lower ranks for foreign policy decisions of a government. The ethics of those decisions has to be made generally by higher level commanders and by the nation's leaders. What I was talking about here, more specifically, was the decision to order the Yamamoto mission; not about the ethics of the manner in which it was conducted, because I have no quarrel with that at all. I think it was carried out in the most skillful possible manner.

Concluding Comments

Allard: We have just run out of time. I would like to congratulate each of the panelists for their remarks, which seemed to me to show imagination, honesty, and sound scholarship. I also admire their ability to stay within the required time so that there was ample opportunity for discussion from the floor. In addition, I extend our thanks to the people at the Admiral Nimitz State Historical Park here in Fredericksburg, who organized this retrospective with the assistance of Professor Davenport and other members of the panel. I commend the audience for the excellent questions, and the panelists for an excellent discussion.

Chapter 3

The Mission Panel

R. Cargill Hall

I am honored to chair this second and concluding session of the Yamamoto Retrospective sponsored by the Nimitz Foundation. Our session this afternoon is significant on two counts. First, the participants will discuss the planning and conduct of what is arguably one of the most important aerial missions of World War II. Second, this is the first time since the war that all of the survivors have assembled in one place; moreover, it is likely the last time they will be so assembled. The American aviators navigated a course of some four hundred miles, over water, at altitudes of about fifty feet, and they intercepted the Japanese flight proceeding from Rabaul southeast toward Bougainville at a remarkably precise instant; they were extremely close to the planned intersect when the encounter occurred, and that in itself must be considered a truly remarkable feat. A "million-to-one shot" it has been called. Indeed, if you talk to some of the P-38 aviators here today they will confide that they flew many a mission in the Pacific to intercept and fly top-cover for American heavy bombers, only to fail to find them. They could hear over their radios the bomber crews talking with one another and complaining that the P-38 aviators were rather callous chaps who perhaps would have difficulty finding their backsides with both hands.* But in this case, they succeeded very well indeed.

We are also honored to have with us today the surviving Zero pilot, Kenji Yanagiya, and speaking for him, his translator, Makoto Shinagawa. I might add that Mr. Yanagiya has in the last day or so given numerous interviews, answered numerous questions, and is suffering from jet lag in the bargain. He is quite fatigued and we hope to give him every indulgence here this afternoon. I will offer a few observations of my own at the end of the session. Colonel John Mitchell, the flight leader, will introduce the American participants and lead the discussion. I turn the proceedings over to Colonel Mitchell.

The Flight to Bougainville
Colonel John W. Mitchell

Thank you, Mr. Hall. It is great to be here, ladies and gentlemen, and to have taken part in this memorable mission. The mission is still not over, I think, for we still have some controversy, but we want to go through the mission as we planned and flew it. My job as the squadron commander was to lead this mission and I was assigned by the navy on the evening before it took place. I think at this point I should introduce the people that were on the flight. I have them listed here in no particular order, but at least you will have a chance to meet them. The first one on the list is not here because he's not living, and that was Tom Lanphier. Tom died just a few months ago, I think on Thanksgiving Day if I'm not mistaken, and we are very sorry that he could not be here with us. Rex Barber, Besby Holmes, and Ray Hine are next on the list. Ray was the one man that we lost on this mission. The next one is Lou Kittel, then Albert Long, who has since died. William Smith has also passed on. Eldon Stratton was later killed in action. Julius (Jack) Jacobson—Jack was my wingman most of the time I was in the air, and was on this particular mission.

Ed. note: P-38 radios could receive at some distance, but could transmit to communicate back and forth with the bombers only at very close range—not more than about three miles.

Then, next to Jack, Doug Canning, Delton Goerke, and Roger Ames. Everett Anglin is also no longer with us. Lawrence Graebner is not here, and Gordon Whittaker was killed. Not up here on the stage, but having every right to be, is Jim McLanahan. I'll tell you what happened to Jim a little bit later.

To get on with the mission, I was called over to Navy Operations, which was on another field about a mile away from where we had our fighters. The navy had a dugout there, that's where their operations took place, and they called me over late on the afternoon of 17 April 1943, and the mission was flown on the 18th. I was told they had a special mission for me, and when I walked into this dugout, this hut, I was handed a message by somebody in the room that briefly stated that they had intercepted a message that Adm. Isoroku Yamamoto was going to be visiting the Japanese bases on the southern tip of Bougainville Island. The message said that Yamamoto would be coming down to visit his forward bases, and that we were to make every effort to get Yamamoto; in other words it was an all-out effort, we were to get him at all costs. The information available was that there would be one bomber, a Betty-type bomber, which was their standard bomber, and that it would be escorted by six Zeros. This was important because later in the flight it helped us to determine whether we had intercepted the right people.

In this meeting, a lot of people who weren't going on the mission had a lot to say, but as usual in a crowd like this there's always a bunch of big mouths, and so quite a hassle developed. For instance, some navy personnel suggested that we try to get Yamamoto in a boat that he was going to take between islands, after landing. He was to land at Ballale and go across to Bougainville by submarine tender. Some said, "Why don't you sink the submarine tender and we'll get him that way?" I said no, I didn't want to do that because, as an air force pilot, I didn't know one boat from another and, moreover, even if we sank the boat, he could very easily jump into the water and survive. That wasn't what we were up there for. So it was finally settled after much discussion, by Rear Adm. Marc A. Mitscher, who was the head of the air operations at Guadalcanal—

you may recall that the navy was in overall command out there— and after a lot of arguments, he said, "Mitchell's got to do the job, let's do it his way." So thank God that we had an admiral that could see my point of view, because I'm sure the mission wouldn't have been a success if we had done it any other way.

This was just the beginning of my job as the commander, and the first order was to plan the mission. I had eighteen P-38s in commission at the time, and we had external tanks, but they were 165-gallon tanks. You could hang two on a P-38, but that still wasn't enough fuel to get up to where we had to go and accomplish our mission and get back to base again, so we had to have some larger tanks. There were some over on New Guinea, and they flew some in that night. Our ground crews, there are some of them here, worked all night to get those external tanks hung. We didn't have enough to put two 300-gallon tanks on each P-38, so we had one 165-gallon tank and one 300-gallon tank. These are technical things, but they enter very much into the picture because fuel was a major consideration on this mission. The reason that the navy selected the Army Air Forces to do the job was because they didn't have the fighters with the range, even with external tanks, so the P-38 was selected. The navy didn't come down and pick me out because my name is John Mitchell, they picked me out because I had the equipment that would get up there. Even with these large external tanks we still faced a critical situation with the range, and I had to figure that all in. With that one external 300 tank and the 165 tank, we could go up there and make our mission, and we could loiter, that is, stay in the area where we expected the target to be for fifteen minutes, still fight our fight and then come home. It's always important to have enough fuel to come home. So you've got to think about all those things.

After we settled the argument in the dugout, the next thing that I had to do was select a crew. This turned out to be a hard job, for soon the word got out about what we were going to do. A fistfight almost broke out on a couple of occasions, and Lou Kittel was on my back all the time trying to get a bunch of his men in there, for he was in another squadron with experienced P-38 pilots. He had some good crews and so we couldn't afford to leave them out, so he selected some of his people and I selected the others. Somebody asked me just a while ago, how do you select people like that? You select them because you think they're the best pilots you have for a mission like this, and after you have flown with those people for a number of missions, you get to know them, and you know who you can depend on, and this was one mission where we had to be able to depend on every man that went on it. So I picked the guys that I thought would be the ones that could perform this mission and fortunately it turned out that way. In picking the aircraft and making the assignment of the flight that evening, I assigned four aircraft to go in and attack; we call them the "killer flight." They were to go in and make the attack on the bomber; one bomber is all we thought we were going to have. There's no way that I wanted eighteen airplanes up there milling around trying to shoot down one bomber, and we knew they had six Zeros up, but that didn't really concern us that much either.

We were especially concerned with one other situation right here, on Bougainville, very close to where Yamamoto was going to land [points to large map]. Within spitting distance, they had seventy-five Zeros sitting out on the runway to be used for any purpose. Not knowing the Japanese thinking, how they thought about things like this, I had to fall back on something that had happened to us not too long before. Secretary of the Navy Frank Knox had come out to visit the troops on Guadalcanal, and when he approached we took all the fighters that we had available at Henderson and flew out to the extreme range of the fighters, picked up his aircraft, and escorted him back into Guadalcanal. Same thing going out, when he got ready to leave, we escorted him out as far as we could go with all the fighters we had. So, I had nothing other than that precedent to fall back on. I reasoned that the Japanese would come up with possibly as many as fifty of the seventy-five fighters that they had sitting on the runway down there, to bring the chief in, and it would be an honor more than anything else because I know that they had no idea whatsoever, not any idea, that we were going to be in the area at that particular time.

In making our plans that night before, much of which was accomplished by lanterns and flashlights, I briefed all the pilots, after making the selections, and I don't think anybody got killed [while making selections], just a few bloody noses I think by a few who wanted to go on the flight. Anyhow, we could only take eighteen and that gave us two spares. I wanted to try to get up there with sixteen aircraft if I possibly could, so it left us with two spares and thank goodness we thought about that the night before and made plans for it. We were going to take off down here, this was our field on Guadalcanal. We were going to fly this route running out and away like this, go way up like this, and then turn in on the last leg here and make our interception at this point. As you can see, this was the famous slot that many of you have heard of. It's between these two chains of islands. The reason we went around like this, made this circuitous flight over water, was because the Japanese had coast watchers on these islands and some radar. The radar wasn't all that good, but they had some so we wanted to stay away, we didn't want to alert them to the fact that we were on our way up there. Had they seen us they would have passed the word on up and told Yamamoto to turn around and go back, I'm sure. So this was the reason for flying in this manner, and it turns out that this is about 415 miles coming around this way, and about 315 miles had we been able to go there direct. For this one reason we had to have those extra fuel tanks.

For the flight next morning, great weather, hot as it always was out there, but nevertheless it wasn't raining and we had good weather. We were told that we would have a quartering wind at between five to ten knots off our port bow, this is navy language, but anyhow I had a pretty good idea of what they were talking about so I cranked it into my schedule. Remember now, this was going to have to work, it was going to have to be right on the button because the admiral was not going to throw out an anchor when he flew in, and as I told you we only had about fifteen minutes to fool around on the scene, so we had to be on time in order to catch him. In other words, we weren't commissioned just to waste the gasoline.

We started our takeoff with everybody taxiing and the section that was the killer section consisting of Tom Lanphier, Rex Barber, and Besby Holmes, who later filled in, and Ray Hine, who filled in. Joe Moore and Jim McLanahan were our designated shooters, and Jim was about the third guy starting off and he got halfway down the runway and blew a tire, so there went one of my shooters. Then we got into the air and were just circling—I allowed just fifteen minutes to get our squadron together—we were ready to set course, and Joe Moore came up close and gave me the sign that he couldn't draw any fuel from his external tanks, so we had to get him out of there. We were of course on complete radio silence—this was briefed the night before that no one was to touch that button on the way up there from takeoff until after the mission was completed. So without any words at all being spoken on the radio, we got Holmes into the right position, we got Hine in the right position, and we were on our way.

We started out on this first leg, and each one of these legs is timed, as you can see. Now, on the way up there we not only flew away from those islands that I just pointed out, but we got down 50 feet off the deck and we stayed at 50 feet off the deck all the way up. It got hot in all the airplanes down on the deck, and we spread out so we could have a fairly comfortable flight without having to just watch your leader all the time; it was kind of a dull flight, really. People ask, "What were you thinking about on the way up there?" I was thinking, "Am I going to be on time? God, it's hot in here," and things like that, and actually nothing happened on the way up. One of the guys got a little too low and his prop threw some sea water up on his windscreen, and of course he had to clean the windscreen off when he got back. At least I think that's the only thing he had to clean up. But word got around to me that he wasn't able to go back to sleep again for a couple of days. With the sun rising, and it was up pretty well, for we had taken off at 7:30 that morning, it was hot, hot as hell in those cockpits. On a couple of occasions maybe, I dozed off myself, but I got a light tap on the shoulder a couple of times and He said, "John, hold the course," and I did. I finally turned the squadron in on the last leg.

I kept looking at my watch and compass. The navy, incidentally, had given me an excellent compass the night before that I had installed in my airplane and you have to swing the compass. What that means is that you have to orient the compass to the environment that it's in, so you have to adjust it, which was done that night before by the crews. Then the next morning as I was rolling down the runway, giving power to the engines also effects your compass so I was concerned about that. But as I was rolling, of course I knew the heading of the runway, I checked my compass and it was right on, so I knew I'd be all right. Without any checkpoints from the time we left, we found ourselves turning in on the last leg some two and a half hours later. I flew these legs just exactly the way you see them plotted on this map. This wasn't the map I had, which was a small one that covered the whole area that you see here. Where we wanted to meet was just south of Empress Augusta Bay on Bougainville, which you can see very clearly on this map. On the map I had, it looked like a pin-head. We turned in here and I began getting nervous, and I was getting itchy because I hadn't seen checkpoint 1 from the time I left. One wave out there in the ocean looks just like another wave, so you don't get any help from that; all I had was my compass and my watch and my airspeed indicator.

So I held my course, timed myself very closely, and I was beginning to really worry that we weren't going to meet because something was wrong. I was about four minutes out and I tried to close the squadron in because I wanted them where I could see them. We'd spread out quite a bit, so everyone closed in when I rocked my wings and we had a fairly tight formation going in—and I still hadn't made landfall. Now this concerned me very much. I'm about four minutes out and I should have been able to see some pretty high hills, I should have been able to pick up the land. We're heading east and the sun was in my eyes; we're still down on the deck and it was a little hazy, but not bad. Between the sun and the haze, I guess was one reason I couldn't pick up the land.

About that time radio silence was broken. Who broke it? "Old Eagle Eyes" Doug Canning, that's who. What did he call on the radio? "Bogeys, 11 o'clock high." For you people unfamiliar with that language, you use the clock, and 12 o'clock is straight ahead, and 11 o'clock is just off to the left, and 1 o'clock just off to the right. So, we had made a perfect intersection, though we didn't know if it was the right aircraft or not. Eleven o'clock meant, of course, they were just off of our port bow. There were two bombers instead of one; we had been told the night before there would be one. I looked for the six Zeros in escort, I looked behind and there were three; I looked further behind and there were three more, and Mr. Yanagiya was in one of those six Zeros. They had not seen us at that point so I immediately turned, I knew when I saw the six Zeros that we had our target. I turned parallel with the bombers' course, and pushed everything to the firewall, meaning full throttle, and called the squadron and said, "Skin them off," which meant drop the external tanks, and that's what we did. We wanted to get up as quickly as we could, at least on the same level as the bombers, which were at about 4,500 feet and so, having dropped our external tanks, the P-38s reacted very well and had us up there in just about a minute or so, a couple of minutes perhaps, and we were up level with them.

I called Tom Lanphier who was leading the killer section as it had been planned the night before, and said, "He's all yours, Tom." I got back a "Roger" from Tom; Tom said "Roger, okay," and his flight turned and headed right into the bombers while we kept on climbing. Now, the night before we knew the Japanese had seventy-five Zeros on Bougainville, as I told you a while ago. I didn't want to have sixteen aircraft in there trying to shoot down one bomber, and I wanted to be where the action was. I thought, well, I'm going to go on up to a higher altitude and we're going to be up there and have a turkey shoot. That's where I pulled a boo-boo as far as I'm concerned, not as far as getting Yamamoto was concerned, but it cut me out of the picture. I got zilch that day, but we got there and completed the mission. Your chances of doing this were probably one in a million. Remember the old *Mission Impossible* series on television? This was in effect a "mission impossible," but it happened, and I think it was the same guy that was tapping me on the shoulder all the way up there. Now I'm going to turn this over to Rex Barber, because Rex is the one that did the shooting that day and, with the others, he has more interesting things to tell you about than just getting the flight to Bougainville.

The Engagement
Colonel Rex T. Barber

When Doug Canning let out his famous yell, "Bogeys, 11 o'clock high," we saw them and that really moved us all up. And there they were, six Zeros and two bombers as Mitch said, though we only had planned on one bomber. Well, we climbed, and then Mitch said, "Go get 'em, Tom," and Tom and his flight broke off and headed toward the bombers. Besby Holmes called and stated he could not get his external tanks to drop, so he and his wingman circled back over the water while he attempted to release his tanks. The bombers were probably about five or six miles inland from where we started. So Tom picked a course to intercept them at the shortest distance, and he picked a very good course. We went right in directly toward them. The six Zeros were up above and behind the bombers, and luckily we had not yet been sighted. But as we approached the bombers, we were probably a mile away, the Zero flight on the right side of Admiral Yamamoto's bombers suddenly broke down and dumped their belly tanks. We also saw the bombers had already started a slight letdown toward their destination, steepening their dive substantially, and so they were coming downhill pretty fast and we were staying level with them. We could see these three Zeros coming down and knew that just about the time that we rolled in on the bombers that they [the Zeros] would be right on our tail. So

Tom broke sharply left and up into the Zeros as they were coming down.

I continued straight in, rolled up, and leveled off behind the bombers. When I banked I momentarily lost sight of the bombers under my wing, and when I leveled off behind them there was only one bomber ahead of me. I didn't know where the other one went, whether he had circled around or where he had gone. I never did know until the book, *The Reluctant Admiral,* was published and translated into English. The pilot of the second bomber, whose name was Hayashi, stated that the first he knew they were under attack was when tracers went over his canopy and into Yamamoto's airplane, and he looked up and saw a P-38 right over him. He then broke down and out to the coast. I continued after Yamamoto's airplane and fired into his right engine, and moved through the fuselage into his left engine. The right engine was smoking badly at that time, and I started firing back into the fuselage again. As I centered my fire on the fuselage, he seemed to stop in midair, as far as I was concerned, and came up more or less on one wing, and I shot over him, just missing his upturned wing. I looked back and he had leveled off, but he was smoking very badly and going down. By this time he was less than 300 feet from the top of the trees.

At the same moment I saw a Zero flight behind me. I don't know which flight it was, but one of the flights. I think maybe it was the one on the left side had caught me, and they were shooting at me rather heavily. I broke for the coast and hit the deck as low as I could, right down on the treetops, and tried to avoid them. As I was going out and watching the Zeros, seeing where they were and which one was going to shoot at me next, two P-38s made a head-on pass at me; they were coming at very high speed and down, and they shot over me and into the Zeros that were behind me. The Zeros broke and scattered, and I concentrated on looking for the Zeros, and they were gone.

By that time I had regained enough speed so that I was not concerned about them catching me again. And then I saw a bomber over the water, right along the edge of the island, and he was so low that his props were kicking up a wake behind them. You could see a streak where the wind from the props was blowing on the water. Then I saw up above and over the water two P-38s, and I was sure that it was Holmes and Hine. They saw the bomber also and went into a steep dive toward it. I flew an interception course toward the bomber while they were coming down behind the bomber. As I say, I was real low and as they approached the bomber, the leader, which was Besby Holmes, started to shoot at the bomber. His bullets hit the water behind the bomber, went into his right engine and out ahead of the bomber. Hine was shooting also and his bullets were hitting either the water or the outer wing. He was in pretty close to Besby Holmes, and when they pulled up, I was just about to drop in behind the bomber, and when I did I gave him a long burst into the fuselage and he blew up.

Black smoke billowed up when the bomber exploded and hit the water; a piece flew up and hit my left wing and cut through my inner cooler, which supplied my turbo supercharger with exhaust gases. Another piece flew up and hit my gondola, the cockpit I was sitting in, and cut a gash in the bottom of it. Other pieces flashed over my head as I pulled up. At that point I looked up ahead and there was a P-38 with a Zero under him, and he rolled around on that Zero and exploded it. There was another Zero coming in, but he was not looking at me, evidently he was looking at this disaster that had just happened to his friend, and I managed a short burst into his fuselage and he also caught fire and crashed. The amazing part, going back to the bomber, is that Admiral Ugaki and two other people lived through that crash. In fact, in the book *The Reluctant Admiral,* Ugaki said that the pilot attempted to crashland the airplane in the water. I suspect that he crashed it and I shot him about the same time because of the explosion. If he had crashed solely into the water, those people would have been inside that airplane and I doubt if they could have survived. But I think the explosion blew the fuselage sufficiently apart so they were thrown clear, and into the water. Three of them lived; this is amazing, but they did.

I proceeded on back to Guadalcanal and the Fighter Two airstrip, then the operations tent, and that's the story of the mission as far as I know it. I have kept my story in the envelope that I flew and what I saw. What other people saw and reported, I have attempted to correlate with what I saw. Sometimes I can't and sometimes I can. Now we're going to have another gentleman speak who was on this flight, and that's Besby Frank Holmes.

The Engagement: Another View
Lieutenant Colonel Besby F. Holmes

Most of my thunder in the beginning of my speech has been stolen, so I'll try to skip over the great bulk of it. After we took off and formed up, as Mitchell mentioned, Mitchell signaled me to join Lanphier. Lanphier was looking at the other flights trying to recover his wingmen, and we were awfully low to the water and it was a dangerous situation. Ray Hine and I bracketed Lanphier, and I signaled him to settle down. So he did and pretty soon Rex joined us, and now we had an actual four-ship attack flight together. Of course the rest of the story you all know. We cruised at low altitude in a circuitous route avoiding radar. Anyway, Mitchell's twelve aircraft climbed skyward after we broke the Bougainville coast, after Doug Canning identified the Bogeys. The signal to drop tanks was given and unfortunately mine didn't drop, they stuck on. I jiggled the release, I checked the circuit breakers, nothing happened. I couldn't drop them. I said, "Wait a minute, Tom, I'll tear my tanks off, just give me a second." Well, Tom didn't answer me. I don't know if he didn't hear me or he was so intent on getting to the enemy aircraft and his mind was so concentrated he couldn't hear me, but he didn't answer.

From here on my story basically disagrees with Rex's, and that's what makes horseracing. Knowing I would have to shake my tanks before I could enter the fight, I poked my nose down very steeply, held it there until the airspeed needle showed 350 MPH indicated. I pulled back; I hoped I pulled 9 gs, though we had no g meters so I couldn't tell. As I was pulling back very hard, I booted a rudder and I don't think any stores external to a fighter plane at that speed with a side load could stay on. The tanks left, as I knew they would. Just as I stripped the tanks I heard Barber, his voice; there were so few of us we knew our voices and we didn't even have to identify our call signs. I heard what I thought was Barber's voice, "The tail fell off the Betty, he's going straight in," and I saw the bomber crash. It looked to me like he went straight in, from the size of the fire resulting from the crash.

I looked down and around to see what else I could see and then I heard Lanphier calling. It sounded to me like he had three Zeros on his back and he said, "I can't go anywhere but straight ahead." Just then, as I was looking down, I saw another Betty. I saw a P-38 chasing that Betty, and I saw three Zeros on his tail, so I thought it was Lanphier. It turned out to be Rex Barber, but at that point I didn't know and I didn't care. Ray Hine and I did a barrel roll, a vertical barrel roll. "Barrel roll" is a technical term. You've been to the funhouses where they roll the barrel around, and if you get the right speed, you can go in the opposite direction, you can run around and stand up and not fall. Okay, a barrel roll is that same thing; you take the barrel and roll it up, then over, and pull down and keep the g forces positive. In this case, we went straight down doing that because those three Zeros were, my Lord, I thought, 200 yards from Rex, maybe less. We had to get there quick, and I had to be in firing position. I couldn't go straight down, which wouldn't have accomplished anything.

During the barrel roll we came in behind Rex, and I told Ray to take the Zero on Barber's right and I'd try for the two on his left. I slid over to get behind the two and when I got behind the first Zero, I saw the Betty still fleeing in front of Barber and I said to myself, "Oh boy, we've got to get him, but first we've got to get these Zeros off Barber." I fired a long burst at the first Zero into his tail and he exploded in a sheet of flame right in front of me. I instinctively ducked, though it wouldn't have done me any good, but I did it. I quickly got my eye back on the gunsight and picked up the second fighter, and as I hit him I saw a flash of flame and he rolled over,

Top: Army pilots' living quarters, tents on the hill at Fighter Two, Guadalcanal, late 1942. Note navy Wildcats, center; army P-39 at right. An army artillery battery on the opposite side of the field fired over the tents into Japanese positions beyond, doubtless making for fitful sleep. (Photo courtesy of Rollins Snelling.) *Bottom*: Japanese ice plant near Henderson Field, Guadalcanal, late 1942. It was rebuilt and operated by Allied forces. (Photo courtesy of Rollins Snelling.)

Top: Lieutenant George Von Weller, USN, a PBY pilot, standing next to
Capt. Thomas Lanphier's P-38, early 1943. (Photo courtesy of Rollins
Snelling.) *Bottom*: A temporary military cemetery near Henderson Field on
Guadalcanal, late 1942. (Photo courtesy of Rollins Snelling.)

Captain William Hull, 68th Fighter Squadron, in foreground, atop an abandoned Japanese tank near Fighter Two, late 1942. (Photo courtesy of Rollins Snelling.)

A beached Japanese transport sunk by the "Cactus Air Force," just north of Fighter Two. Late 1942. (Photo courtesy of Rollins Snelling.)

Enlisted members of the 68th Fighter Squadron next to a P-40 at Fighter Two, late 1942. (Photo courtesy of Rollins Snelling.)

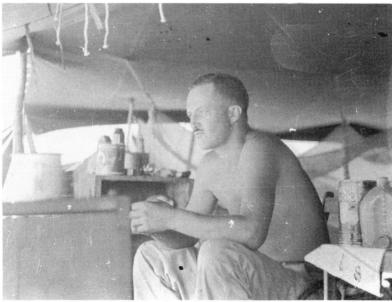

Top: Souvenir hunters inspect a Japanese antiaircraft gun just north of Fighter Two, late 1942. (Photo courtesy of Rollins Snelling.) *Bottom*: Lieutenant Colonel Henry Viccellio, USAAF, commander, XIII Fighter Command detachment on Guadalcanal, in his tent at Fighter Two, ca. February 1943. (Photo courtesy of Rollins Snelling.)

Official portrait, Adm. Isoroku Yamamoto, commander-in-chief, Japanese Imperial Navy. (Photo courtesy of the Nimitz Museum.)

First Lieutenant Rex T. Barber, standing second from right, next to wing of his P-38; tip sheared on the superstructure of a Japanese destroyer on the 29 March 1943 mission against a Japanese naval base on Shortland Island. (Photo courtesy of the Nimitz Museum.)

Top: Yamamoto mission pilots at Fighter Two, 19 April 1943. Standing left to right: Roger Ames, Lawrence Graebner, Tom Lanphier, Delton Goerke, Julius Jacobson, Eldon Stratton, Albert Long, and Everett Anglin. Kneeling, left to right: William Smith, Douglas Canning, Besby Holmes, Rex Barber, John Mitchell, Louis Kittel, and Gordon Whittaker. Not pictured, Raymond K. Hine, MIA. Stratton and Whittaker were subsequently killed in action. (Photo courtesy of the Nimitz Museum.) *Bottom*: The three designated shooters who survived the Yamamoto mission, at Fighter Two on 19 April 1943. Left to right: Thomas G. Lanphier, Besby Frank Holmes, and Rex T. Barber. (Photo courtesy of the Nimitz Museum.)

Wreckage of Admiral Yamamoto's Betty bomber on Bougainville Island, with small Shinto shrine in foreground, late 1940s or early 1950s. Note that the serial number 323 has not yet been vandalized. Missing segments of the vertical stabilizer may have been the tail pieces that Barber reported flew off the bomber. (Photo courtesy of the Nimitz Museum.)

Above: Admiral Isoroku Yamamoto on board ship, early 1940s. (Photo courtesy of the Nimitz Museum.) *Left:* Admiral Isoroku Yamamoto considering fleet movements, on board ship, early 1940s. (Photo courtesy of the Nimitz Museum.)

Top: In the control tower at Fighter Two, ca. early 1943. (Photo courtesy of the Nimitz Museum.) *Bottom*: Pilots relax in the operations tent at Fighter Two after a mission, with a "game of chance," ca. early 1943. (Photo courtesy of the Nimitz Museum.)

Top: Port engine of Yamamoto's Betty bomber, lying near the wreckage on Bougainville Island, 1972. *Bottom Right*: Aft section of the bomber that did not burn, 1972. *Bottom Left*: Tail empennage and rear gun turret protruding from the forest, 1972. (Photos courtesy of Charles Darby.)

Top: Starboard wing outer panel, held aloft, at the crash site on Bougainville Island, mid-1980s. *Bottom*: Port wing outer panel, located about 40 yards from the crash site. Note damage to leading edge of wing caused by impact with trees (mid-1980s). (Photos courtesy of Terry Gwynn-Jones.)

67th FIGHTER-BOMBER SQ. ⓒ

Emblem of the 67th
Fighter Squadron.
(Photo courtesy of the
USAF Historical
Research Center.)

Emblem of the 68th
Fighter Squadron.
(Photo courtesy of the
USAF Historical
Research Center.)

Emblem of the 70th
Fighter Squadron.
(Photo courtesy of the
USAF Historical
Research Center.)

Emblem of the 339th
Fighter Squadron.
(Photo courtesy of the
USAF Historical
Research Center.)

did a wing over, and I think we were at about 300 feet, I wouldn't swear to it, but he could not have survived even if he weren't on fire. Our indicated airspeed at that time was 425 MPH, and that's very high. We were fast overhauling Barber, and out of the corner of my eye I saw the third Zero, which appeared to be taking hits from Ray Hine's guns. Just about that time we passed Barber; I guess he was doing about 250, 260, something like that.

The Betty was flying straight ahead, a sitting duck as far as I was concerned. I pulled up even with it and did a classical high-side gunnery pass. Again, it was something we did in training consistently. We'd shoot at a banner flying along under tow, we'd get even or slightly ahead, turn in, and as the banner proceeded we would come in on a 45-degree angle or less. My first shots were just behind the Betty; I fired a short burst just to check elevation and deflection. The second burst I pulled further forward and hit him in the tail. I held the .50-caliber machine guns down and then I engaged the 20-mm when I was on him. I pulled through the Betty, all the way through the cabin up to the cockpit, and then I let the gunsight rest on the right wing and the right engine and I just held that firing burst there. The longest burst I've ever fired. It was having its effect on the bomber. I think they were shooting at me, but when I got in close nobody was shooting back.

We were now no more than ten miles from Kahili, and I could see a cloud of dust rising from the airfield as the Japanese aircraft were scrambling. That will get your attention, ladies and gentleman. Right then, I knew we had about run out of time and the Betty had to be polished off quickly if I expected to get back to Guadalcanal. Finally, extremely close, I lined my gunsight on the bomber's right engine and touched the triggers. The bullets tore into the engine and wing root. I could see little tongues of flame leap out, but the Betty wouldn't go down. I continued squeezing the trigger and sent long bursts again into the engine, and a huge puff of smoke, probably orange flame, burst out. I came to my senses just in time and I found myself about to ram the Betty's tail; in my haste and eagerness, I had forgotten how fast I was going compared to the Betty. For an instant, I thought I could pull over him and I saw I couldn't; the tail was too high, so I went under him. I don't think he was 50 feet off the water. For a split second the negative gs lifted me off my seat pack; I saw the shadow of the Betty pass over my canopy and I hauled back as quickly as I could—we had a wheel and yoke in the P-38, if you didn't know it. I hauled back on that thing and to keep from crashing as I pulled up to make another highside pass, I saw the Betty crash, hit the water with great force, break into pieces, perhaps the last quarter to the last third of the tail section came up and rotated backward and smashed right into the middle of a burning funeral pyre, and that's about the time Rex Barber went through it, and that's how he got all the shrapnel in the leading edge of his wing.

I called Rex and Ray to follow me and clear out of the area. I received no answer, for my radio was malfunctioning. Fortunately, both pilots were close enough and we all three headed out to sea in an attempt to disengage, and I sighed with relief. We had completed our mission; both Bettys were shot down. I believed I had knocked off two Zeros and Ray had probably gotten another one. But my relief was extremely shortlived. Out of the corner of my eye I saw an object streaking down at about a 45-degree angle on Barber's tail. I had no way of notifying Barber, my radio was out, and I quickly pulled my P-38 up and it started a little. I tripped my maneuver flaps, which was illegal, for when I looked at the airspeed I was still doing 350, I think the tech order said 260 indicated was the maximum speed to trip a maneuver flap. At that stage of the game I didn't care about that as long as the wings stayed on me. Unless I got there fast, Barber was a dead duck.

Pulling straight up, I rolled my P-38 into an Immelmann. Now this one I will have to demonstrate. An "Immelmann" is the first half of the loop where you pull up, get on your back and hold the wings level and then roll upright. That's an Immelmann. I pulled this Immelmann to get into position to first snap a burst at the Zero. The enemy pilot saw me, broke off his attack on Rex, and went straight up. I went after him, shoving the throttles all the way to the stop to get every ounce of power I could. I was practically on his tail at this time, firing as we climbed. Suddenly, my Lightning faltered, my right engine quit. The airspeed started dropping off so fast, thoughts flashed through my mind; boy, if I didn't get this Japanese pilot then and there, I was through. He'd split-S, come up under me, and knock me off. A P-38 against a Zero at low altitude on one engine is no match. I continued firing knowing this would be my only chance. My 20-mm cannon had run out and I was firing only 50s; "Oh, my Lord," I thought, "how many 50s have I got?" I kept my gunsight glued on his tail by pushing hard on the left rudder and increasing the pressure until I hit the rudder stop. I eased off on the rudder and let the good engine pull me over into a hammerhead.

I will have to demonstrate again. A "hammerhead" is where an airplane stalls and comes over on a wing as though it were a hammer. That beautiful airplane made the most perfect hammerhead I've ever seen. As soon as my nose got down below the horizon, I leveled my wings and considered the situation. I was alone, Hine and Barber were nowhere around; I later found that they were engaged in another fight. I believe in this battle Ray was lost. He was such a fine pilot and such a fine gentleman; I've felt his loss keenly, personally, ever since. I've never been in a tighter spot; about the only gratification was that I was still alive. I had saved Barber's neck a second time on that day and I'd also added another Zero to my list of kills. I didn't claim that last Zero; Barber claimed it for me after I landed. So I, at that time, thought I'd had only two Zeros and one bomber.

I did not have enough fuel to get back to the base; I checked. The reason for my engine failing, I found my main wing tank that held ninety gallons was empty, and all I could think of was battle damage. I quickly switched to another tank, and that engine started smoothly. Then I didn't know what to do. I was far enough from Shortland that I could turn straight for Guadalcanal, but I did not have enough fuel to get there. I made a double-check around the airplane and found out why my radio was not working. We had what we call quick disconnect jacks, and the jack had disconnected. I connected it and I had a radio. I called John Mitchell, and I told him what my plight was all about. He directed the squadron to spread out and look for me, and Doug Canning, bless his heart, his good eyes found me. I didn't know until last night that Delton Goerke also found me, but that's fine, two guys were watching me. The relief was so enormous, you can't imagine. I didn't have enough fuel to get home, and if I went down I wanted someone to know where I was so they could look for me. I immediately threw out the tech order, at least mentally, for, as I remember, the book said under no circumstance run those Allison engines under 2,150 RPM, but they ran fine at 1,600, really. Of course, they'd load up a little bit and I'd have to add a little power and clean out the sparkplugs, but at 1,600 RPMs and twenty-three to twenty-four inches of manifold pressure I was cruising at about 170; am I right, Doug, is that about right? We decided to try for the Russells, the Russell Islands, a little group about seventy-five miles short of Guadalcanal, I think, I'm not sure, closer to me, anyway.

A marine construction battalion had landed on the Russells just three or four days before, and they had started to build a runway. Unfortunately, they had run into an impasse; it was a great boulder in their way and they didn't have any dynamite to blast it. So they had 1,700 feet of dirt runway actually cleaned and leveled, and when we got close, I said, "Hey, Doug, I got it wired. Leave me and drag that strip." Doug put the power on his airplane and left me like I was standing still. He buzzed that runway with all that heavy equipment, steamrollers, road graders, sheep foot rollers, and he buzzed and pulled up. In the old days we used to put our landing gear up and our flaps up and come around, and he made another low pass and the steamrollers and the graders just left the strip and I landed. I was about fourteen seconds behind Doug.

The marine commandant wanted to know if he could help, and I said, "Yes, have you got any water?" That was the first thing I wanted, water; my Lord, that was a hot flight. The marine commandant said, "Yea, we've got lots of that." My next question was, "Do you have any 100-120 octane fuel?" and he replied, "No." I said, "Have you got a radio?" and he said, "Yes, I have a radio." I said, "Can you raise Tulagi?" and he said, "Certainly." I said, "Can you get PT Squadron 109 to send a boat here?" He said, "Well, I'll try," and I said, "Be sure and ask one to come with five-gallon jerry cans all over it, I need 120 gallons." What probably most of you don't know is that the PT boats that were in the South Pacific had four Allison engines, the same engines we used, and they used the same fuel that we did, and I knew they carried jerry cans all over those PT boats. Well, in about two hours, sure enough, along came a PT boat with all the jerry cans I needed. I had requested twenty-four of them and we actually used twenty-three, plus one gallon out of the twenty-fourth tank. I had four gallons of fuel left. I had also made a check of my ammo. I shouldn't have, I would have been better off if I hadn't, for I had four rounds of .50-caliber left and no 20-mm.

The return to Guadalcanal was surprisingly easy. I took off on the short runway with no problem. I think I hit maneuver flaps at about 100 miles per hour indicated airspeed. The airplane just came off the strip. I don't think I even pulled back on the yoke it was so light, with so little fuel and no ammo. The return to Guadalcanal caught me a little by surprise. There was absolutely no debriefing by anyone; I was never debriefed. I don't know what happened to the first group that returned, whether they were debriefed or not; I have heard claims that they had a little informal debriefing, but I don't know. It seems that Lanphier and Barber had both claimed a Betty plus several Zeros, and Ray Hine and my part was not mentioned. Lanphier didn't see it, Barber didn't know who initially chased the four Zeros off his tail and shot down the Betty in front of him until I landed.

Naturally, I was mad as hell. The victories had been distributed before I could report what Ray and I had done. And as a result, a few heated words were exchanged. The upshot of this discussion, in my memory, was that Rex did in fact confirm that we had taken a total of four Zeros off his tail and that I had also shot down the bomber that crashed into the water. Barber insisted that he had shot down one bomber, the one on the initial pass that crashed in the jungle. Each of them by their own accounts received credit for one bomber, but neither could confirm the other's claim, and we did not have gun camera film. Rex did confirm the bomber and some of the fighters I claimed, but I was only given official credit for one bomber and two fighters for a total of five for the record book. At this time it was a toss-up as to who knocked down the Betty carrying Yamamoto. Which one was he in? We didn't know at that point.

The passage of years hasn't clarified the subject to any great extent. Japanese accounts of the affair only add to the confusion, with one exception. There were only two Bettys, not the three that were first given official credit, given to Rex, myself, and Lanphier. I cannot honestly say who shot down Admiral Yamamoto's aircraft. There were credits established for three, all I can attest to is I shot down one of the bombers in the flight, the one that crashed into the sea. Three Zeros I claimed and Barber had at that time confirmed two. So I still don't know. I saw the other bomber crash into the jungle at what appeared to be the base of a hill; apparently it went straight in from the pattern and the resulting explosion. I have always thought that Barber shot the first Betty down. Originally, there were only six Zeros involved, three allegedly chasing Lanphier, and three on Barber's tail when Ray Hine and I entered the fight.

I believe that additional Zeros from Kahili could have bounced us after the last bomber crashed, while we were trying to withdraw. In the book *Zero,* by Masatake Okumiya with Martin Caidin, there's a chapter devoted to the Yamamoto mission. Of special interest are the excerpts from the diary of Vice Adm. Matome Ugaki, Yamamoto's chief of staff, that spell out in detail what this scene looked like to the Japanese. From Ugaki's diary comes information that there were two Bettys in the flight and that Ugaki was in one of the Bettys and Yamamoto in the other. One Betty crashed in the sea, and one on land. Ugaki, Rear Admiral Kitamura, and the pilot were the sole survivors of the Betty that crashed in the sea. Admiral Ugaki's diary recounts the finding of Yamamoto's body in the debris of the Betty that crashed, and the admiral was said to have been clutching his sword. After sifting the facts and accepting Ugaki's version of it, it appears that I did not shoot down the Betty carrying Admiral Yamamoto. Official reports are not clear in a lot of respects, but I must assume that I shot down the Betty carrying Ugaki and Rear Admiral Kitamura.

In conclusion, I wish there had been a formal debriefing. It would have cleared up many things years ago and perhaps made our lives a lot easier. I didn't have a clue for years, though I did receive hearsay evidence in 1967 or 1968 on why there was no debriefing.* I have formal certificates from 347th Fighter Group Headquarters, dated 23 July 1943, certifying that I was credited with one Zero and a Betty bomber on 18 April 1943. My recollection differs from Rex's in many respects; I have related for you what I thought I saw, and he has told you what he thought he saw.

The Engagement: Another View

Kenji Yanagiya (Makoto Shinagawa, translator)

The Zero pilots were notified to guard and protect Admiral Yamamoto's Betty, flying from Rabaul to Buin Airport.† They were informed of this special mission in the afternoon, one day prior to the actual Yamamoto mission, and their mission was only to guard the Betty that carried Admiral Yamamoto and his staff. They were to wait for two bombers flying in from Nishi Airfield, which is just a short distance from Rabaul Airport. The weather at that time, the visibility, was good; the altitude of the two Bettys was 2,500 meters, and the six Zeros flew right behind the rear of the two bombers at 3,000 meters. They were only about ten minutes from the Buin airfield when they encountered the P-38s. They never suspected the P-38s would approach from a lower altitude, and they were scanning the horizon and above because they had fairly high mountains on their left-hand side. They were surprised to be attacked unexpectedly from the rear from a lower altitude. Naturally, spotting the P-38s above the jungle was very late, almost nearing the actual commencement of the attack

---

Ed. note: The debriefing is covered in an interview with Maj. Gen. John P. Condon, USMC (Ret.), beginning on p. 120.

†*Ed. note:* Mr. Yanagiya recalls that the flight destination was the airfield at Buin, rather than the one at nearby Ballale. See the interview of Mr. Yanagiya, p. 105.

when they saw the P-38s. When the flight leader rocked his wings and then went immediately into a full throttle dive, Yanagiya realized that they were being attacked.

The immediate thought that went through his mind was to not to try and shoot the P-38s, but rather to repel them from the attack mode. So all of the six Zeros made a straight dive from their higher altitude to intercept [position themselves] in between the bomber and the oncoming P-38s. They kept firing, rather than at the P-38s, they kept shooting in front of the path of the P-38s trying to repel the P-38s coming toward the Betty. (This is off the record, but he told me during translation of the prior speaker's speeches that he would rather not to be in the middle of this controversy over who could claim credit.) Of course, after the initial attack by the first wave of P-38s they were all busy trying to recover their altitude and get ready for the second wave of P-38s. By the time he recovered his position, he saw smoke coming out of Admiral Yamamoto's Betty, and he saw the Betty of Admiral Yamamoto going straight down toward the Buin Airport, while his staff plane made a right turn toward the ocean trying to escape from the attack.

After he realized what had happened, he flew over the Buin Airport at an altitude of about 50 meters and with his machine guns gave a short burst. That was the emergency code or signal to notify that something had happened to the Betty flight. He then thought that he should give chase to the P-38s, which must be on their return flight. He gave chase toward Shortland Island, and shortly after passing over Shortland Island, while flying at an altitude of 4,000 meters, he spotted one P-38 flying at an altitude of 3,000 meters as if nothing had happened. He [the P-38 pilot] was at cruising speed as if it was just a casual return flight from any other mission. Without giving any warning, he shot at the P-38 from the rear and from above, but the P-38 was not an easy plane to set on fire, so to speak. It did not burst into flames, but he saw vapor coming out of one of the engines and that it was gradually losing altitude. He didn't see that plane make a landing, but he had always thought and wondered about the fate of this P-38. He had always thought that it made an emergency landing somewhere, or ditched in the water.

After the encounter he returned to Buin Airport, and he was the last one to return. This is where the controversy comes in. Only one out of the six Zeros made an emergency landing around the Shortland Islands. The other five, including him, landed safely at the Buin airport. So [none were lost, and] all six were accounted for. Of course, he was the last one to land, and the debriefing was made by the leader of the six Zeros; he was never asked to give any report. After two hours they were all given orders to return to Rabaul Airport.

The Engagement: Another View*

Colonel Thomas G. Lanphier

[SLIDE—Solomon Islands] Here is the route that John [Mitchell] prepared for us. We took off here, on Guadalcanal. We were to fly 375 miles over here to Bougainville. He [Admiral Yamamoto] was to come 230 miles to this island, Ballale. We were to arrive presumably 5,000 feet above him with my flight, and 15,000 feet above him with Mitchell's twelve planes, which would fly up and be prepared to take on the one hundred Zeros we assumed would be up there from Kahili covering the admiral's arrival. Now, we had done this for [Navy Secretary Frank] Knox about three weeks before, on Guadalcanal, and thought they'd do the same, but they didn't.

[SLIDE] This is the view that Yamamoto had of Bougainville coming from Rabaul; this is Empress Augusta Bay, and this is the line he was to fly to Ballale. We were coming from this point, on the deck, and we were just crossing the beach here at a thousand feet, when Doug Canning in Mitchell's outfit very quietly said, "Bogeys, 11 o'clock high," and there he was right up here. We were, of course, in a highly perilous position 4,000 feet below him and in front of him, rather than 5,000 feet above him. Earlier, when we saw that cablegram back on Guadalcanal, "At all costs, seek and destroy," Mitchell and I knew

---

*Excerpted from the General Electric Aviation Lecture, National Air and Space Museum, 11 April 1985.

perfectly well what that meant. We were going up there with eighteen P-38s, eventually sixteen, against one hundred Zeros. Each of us assumed that probably no one else but he alone would come home. That is the way you view aerial combat in these circumstances.

I turned in and started to fly parallel and to climb, and firewalled it until I could get out in front. And for a couple of minutes they didn't see us down there. Mitchell went on his way up to his altitude, and at this point I also lost my number three and four men. They couldn't get wing tanks off, and they went on down the coast, so it was just Barber and myself against the six Zeros. We finally got up to them, were parallel to them, when they saw us. I knew they [the Zeros] had seen us when they dropped their belly tanks and dove at us, the six of them. The first three [on the ocean side] came between me and the bombers.

The lead bomber dived down and away, the wing bomber came over at us, toward the sea. I pulled up into the lead fighter of the first three, because I couldn't get at the bomber with them in between. I fired, and he caught fire and went under me. I went between the other two and flipped over on my back and looked down and there was this bomber back down on the treetops heading again toward Kahili and Ballale. So I dove down from the altitude wherever I was—five or six thousand feet—to get ahead of him and cut across him. I got to going so fast—I ran at him for about two minutes, maybe ten miles—at some 300-plus miles per hour by this time. Then I turned into him and leveled out. I dropped my flaps to slow down and I was skidding to slow down, so at a point where I figured I'd better start checking my guns, I checked my guns—although they'd been working up above—I just squeezed the triggers on the P-38. I forgot to push the cannon button. I cleared the guns at him, and when I did, the right engine started to burn. I was at about 70 degrees to the bomber, which is an impossible angle to hit anything, but I kept on my curve of pursuit and his right wing began to burn also. Just as I went behind him, with his cannon shooting out the rear end, the wing came off and he bellywhopped into the jungle and I went on past. I came off down through here, through a cloud of dust, and the Zeros taking off were making the dust. I got out safely. Barber, meanwhile, followed the wing bomber out to sea and shot it down in the water some twenty-five miles from this point out here.

[SLIDE] Here is the wreckage, the fuselage and the tail, with the number 323 on it. There have been rumors that the tail was not on the bomber when it went in, that someone else had shot it off, and also that its wing had not been shot off.

[SLIDE] Here is the wing about forty yards behind. *Air Force* magazine this month [April 1985] has an article by an Australian RAF type who took pictures in 1977—and we've skipped a movie, to save time—that a friend of mine named Al Kauslick made, who went in and surveyed the crash site. It is twelve miles west of Kahili and about two miles north of a little village called Aku, that is a few miles south of the original line of flight. This wing, of course, is as I say about forty yards behind. Kauslick counted thirty-seven bullet holes in the fuselage, some in the wing, and some in the tail section.

[SLIDE] This is a memorial to Yamamoto in the jungle, which is still there today. People—twenty, thirty, forty people a year—still go there paying twenty bucks each to the natives to take them in and pick things off the wreckage.

Comments From Those Who Flew Top-Cover

R. Cargill Hall: I would like at this time to give the remaining members of the mission, those who flew top-cover and weren't directly involved in the fighting, an opportunity to offer their observations. Perhaps the easiest way to proceed is to start with Colonel Kittel and work straight down the line.

Col. Louis R. Kittel: All I can say is that after forty-five years, when you are asked to remember things, it's a little bit hazy, but when you do remember things there has to be some good reason for it.

When we speak of radio silence, that seems like a simple enough instruction. But when you realize that normally there's chatter when aircraft flights are trying to get organized, and for us to take off on a mission where we were briefed thoroughly for radio silence, it gave you a special feeling that this was a special mission. Next, when we got cruising along just above the water, and I could see the prop wash from the flight ahead of me, Mitchell had eight ahead of me, you realized that you are using a high-altitude interceptor for flying on the deck. Again, you know you're on a special mission. As we were flying over the water I remember patches of driftwood, people probably wouldn't pay much attention to it, but usually there's good fishing wherever you've got a ripple. When we approached the island [Bougainville], most of our concentration remained on the aircraft in front of us and holding our altitude. I never cross-checked; when it came time to rely on Mitchell running the program, he was there, you just followed. I did glance at my watch just about the same time that Doug said, "11 o'clock high." Now, this gave me my third thrill because I saw the Japanese were flying a three-ship formation of fighters—this was something that the Americans had abandoned back during my training at Selfridge.*

After we climbed, I saw nothing in the area of combat. I was aware that it was going on from a couple of very brief radio comments. When I looked down prior to passing over Kahili, I saw three distinct fires. I had no idea whether it was ours or theirs, but there were three separate fires with the last one being fairly close to the runway. Not finding opposition up above, we proceeded on home when Mitchell or someone gave us the signal: "Get your butts out of here." While going home, you think about the crews. They get those airplanes going and were key to the successful mission.

Julius "Jack" Jacobson: I don't have too much to add. I was the leader's wingman and my primary job was to see that he didn't get attacked. After hearing Lanphier say he needed some help, Mitchell

---

Ed. note: The three-ship "V" formation leaves one fighter without a wingman for defensive manuevers such as the "scissors." The British abandoned this formation in the late 1930s, and the Americans followed suit in 1941; thereafter, combat flights consisted of pairs or multiple pairs. The Japanese likewise adopted paired formations later in World War II.

and I started to dive down to ward off any Zeros. As we headed down, Mitchell got a short burst at a Zero that he thought had been on Hine's tail. I also got a short burst at the same Zero, but we were both going too fast and overran him. I didn't see anything of the actual combat involving Yamamoto's bomber. All I want to add is that I was understandably very proud to be on the mission. I believe I was lucky in three ways: First that I was picked for the mission, second, that I made it back, and, finally, that I am able to be here to participate today. Thank you.

Delton C. Goerke: I too am very proud to have been selected for the mission. I am proud to have been associated with this group of men and looking out at us now reminds me of what my grandson told his dad last night. He said, "Well, they just look like a bunch of grandpas." I guess we're no longer that lean, mean, fighting machine he expected to see. I remember being very hot and under a lot of tension. I can remember Doug Canning pointing out whales and I guess sharks that he saw in the ocean along the way. I can remember catching up—I too had trouble dropping fuel tanks and fell behind—with Doug and also Besby Holmes on the way back, and a big sigh of relief when we finally landed. I think that tells of my own experience on this particular mission.

Col. Douglas S. Canning: Believe it or not, this is the first opportunity we have had to get together and talk about the mission; we never knew the other guy's story in many ways, so today's my chance at last. I would like to say one thing though, about myself. I think I'm one of the few people that had combat duty in World War II, Korea, and Vietnam—and I'm still alive, thank God. One other thing I'd like to say about this tour: if I could have my life and start all over again, I'd like to be a fighter pilot in the United States Air Force, with John Mitchell as my C.O., and my wife Betty with me all the time.

I'm a tourist at heart, that's one reason I love the air force. I like to look at things, and they've been stealing my stuff here. But Goerke, the sharks! I had nothing to do on the flight up; we were spread out and so I started counting sharks. I counted forty-eight sharks on the way up there. I saw a pod of whales and a huge manta ray about ten feet across, and I thought it was very interesting; then, finally, I saw Yamamoto's flight. Mitchell didn't mention it, but when Tom and Rex went in, and we went up, our purpose was to go up and intercept what we thought would be seventy-five Zeros. Thank goodness they weren't there. Then we started down and, as we started down I noticed, I was on John's right, I looked down and I saw a Zero circling around behind us. I am fairly positive there must have been a lot more than six Zeros in that area because I saw this one out over the ocean. As I went down I had him bore-sighted; I was diving on him, right behind him ready to fire, when evidently I entered an inversion layer where the air gets colder as you go through it. My canopy fogged up and I couldn't see anything. I got out my handkerchief and wiped the canopy so I could finally see, and when I looked around there was not one soul there but me. I could see Kahili and all this dust being stirred up by seventy-five airplanes, or whatever, taking off, and I thought to myself, "This is no place for Doug Canning to be." So I went back up to 2,500 feet and headed home.

I've got to tell you about the widowmaker, for it made widows. These guys, these Navy Seabees, wouldn't get off the runway and bless their souls they're a wonderful group of people. So you come around and you dive right at the end of the runway, pull up real steep, and put the landing gear down and then your flaps will push you around and you can come on in. When I did that second pass and came on in they spread like flies. I'm telling you they went away and Besby Holmes came in right behind me. I then went on to Guadalcanal. I was the last one on the ground, and, again, I was never debriefed. I think it is one of the biggest shames of all times that it happened that way. I would also like to say one more time that the greatest fighter pilot that ever lived on this earth is John Mitchell.

Roger J. Ames: As far as I was concerned the thing that impressed me, after we spotted the Japanese flight and we started for altitude, was the performance of the P-38. We dropped those belly tanks and put everything to the firewall—I'd never really put that plane through its paces—and that thing just jumped up there; we just flew up there and it made an impression on me. Of course it's nothing like the jets we have now, but I thought it was great at the time. There I was flying at 18,000 feet in formation and I didn't see a thing. You just see the other airplanes; you don't want to run into your own partner. So, I didn't see a thing. But one thing I want to bring out. You know we had been briefed, John talked about this; don't let this get off of the island, don't say anything. We weren't supposed to let the Japanese know in any way, shape, or form that we might had broken their code. But Lanphier got on the open radio, I don't know why the rest of them didn't hear this, but on the way back [nearing Guadalcanal] he said, "That SOB won't dictate peace terms in the White House." That's all he said. But that would be enough for somebody listening to it, they could maybe put that together because Yamamoto had made the comment that he would like to ride down Pennsylvania Avenue and dictate peace terms in the White House.*

Anyway, eventually I got home; I had logged five hours thirty minutes on that flight. Then, about a month and half later, Joe Young and I rotated back to the States and arrived in San Francisco. We went into a little orange juice bar, someplace where you get juice and breakfast. And some little old gal came and sat down, and started up a conversation. Cute little thing, and she said, "I hear Yamamoto got shot down." Well, Joe and I just played dumb. We said we didn't know anything about that. There we were, yellow as Chinamen, because we had been on that atabrine for a year and a half, and we were just yellow, so she knew that we were from overseas. This is one of the things that I could not understand, how all this information got out, off of that island. It was not supposed to leave Guadalcanal at all and how in the world, a month and a half later on, some little

---

Ed. note: That comment, drawn from a Yamamoto letter to a Japanese leader that counselled against war with the United States, was distorted by Tokyo Radio for propaganda purposes. But that propaganda, widely reported in the American press, and his role in the attack on Pearl Harbor, made Yamamoto a lightning rod for wartime hatred. (The letter is reprinted in Chapter One.)

old gal in San Francisco could tell me what had happened, I don't understand it, I really don't.*

This happens all the time. I gave a talk recently to the Dadaelion Club at Barksdale Air Force Base. Somebody happened to find out I had been on the Yamamoto mission, so they asked me to give a little talk about it. So I did, and right at that time we had just completed that raid on Libya. So I compared our flight with the Libyan flight and again, we flew a low and circuitous route to avoid radar. We didn't want anybody to know about it, and our F-111s didn't either, you see. Likewise, some of them didn't make it, some of them had to turn back. We had two that had to turn back. But in both cases, we completed the mission. They flew six and a half hours just one way on the Libyan mission. I think they had two pilots aboard, so that helped. But after that mission I was watching television and William Casey, the head of the Central Intelligence Agency, said he wanted to prosecute some of the news agencies, including the *Washington Post,* for publishing details on how we received the intelligence information that led up to the Libyan raid. I don't know why we have to blab all the time, I really don't. But anyway, these are some of the little things I wanted to get off my chest and I'm glad I was picked for the mission.

Questions and Answers

Mr. Hall: The floor is open to questions.

Mr. Chandler: I am George Chandler from Pratt, Kansas. Two points I would like to clear up; perhaps John Mitchell can clear them up. First, do you know of anyone who physically typed or wrote the report of the debriefing? We have heard several of the pilots say they didn't get debriefed at all, yet a mission report was written; who wrote the report?

Col. Mitchell: It's been reported to us that Tom Lanphier actually

---

Ed. note: Tokyo Radio publicly announced the death of Adm. Isoroku Yamamoto some four weeks later, on 21 May 1943. That news had already appeared in the American press, unbeknownst to some of the returning American pilots.

wrote the report after the mission. This came to light not too long after the mission when Rex Barber and Gen. D. C. Strother, who retired as a four-star general here some time back, and Tom Lanphier were in New Zealand playing golf, and Rex brought up the subject, asking, "In the light of virtually no debriefing—how did anyone have enough information to write a factual mission report for higher headquarters?" Tom Lanphier replied: "Don't worry about that—I went in that night and wrote the report for them." So we have witnesses to that effect at this time.*

Chandler: I'm trying to address this rumor and I'm particularly trying to get this on tape, Mr. Hall, for future historians, because when I search these records myself, I know how hard it is to get something that's not hearsay. Second, one of the reports I heard was that the company clerk was writing the report that night and Tom Lanphier came in and said he would write the report, and he did write the report. Do you know who that company clerk was and whether he is here today?

Mitchell: No, I do not know his name. I was told yesterday he was here, but he is not.

Mr. Edwards: My name is Jack Edwards, and I am a former naval aviator in World War II in the Pacific. Some time ago I saw a taped interview of Tom Lanphier and he was giving his version of the shootdown. He said he made his approach on just a flat-side run, and he cleared his guns, which was the practice in our outfit, too. He said he looked up, after clearing his guns, and he had hit the bomber. I know from my own experience and I'll bet yours, too, it's hard enough to hit them on purpose sometimes, much less by accident

---

Ed. note: Made aware of this charge in a letter from Barber, Lanphier wrote to General Strother asking for his recollection. Strother replied, "The only thing I recall about the golf game in Auckland, when Rex, you, and I were there in May 1943, besides poor golf, was the concern over the security aspects of the mission that had emerged." He added, "It seems a great shame that this outstanding mission should be clouded with questions at this late date. Everyone concerned did a terrific job that has been widely recognized, and I, for one, would hope that it could rest there, with each one proud of his contribution." (Letter, Gen. Dean C. Strother to Thomas G. Lanphier, Jr., 21 January 1985.)

like that. Do you have any comments, or have you ever heard that before?

Hall: Let me address that first and then perhaps Colonel Mitchell or Rex Barber will add something more. The USAF Historical Research Center verifies aerial victory credits for the air force, and I sometimes think this is an undesirable assignment and the navy is much wiser, for it doesn't maintain an official list. But victory credits on this mission were examined several years ago and, given the primary evidence, the Yamamoto bomber was judged to have been fired on by two pilots; first, by Rex Barber, and subsequently, to the best of our knowledge, the plane was also attacked by Tom Lanphier. The credit is thus shared, presently, as is the credit for the second bomber between Holmes and Barber. So that is the present status and it is consistent, as I say, with everything we know today. Perhaps Colonel Mitchell can add a few comments.

Mitchell: Yes, I have quite a few comments. I am aware of the account you have just given. Tom Lanphier wrote a story way back, it was published right after the war was over, I think in September 1945, and in shortened versions in *Reader's Digest* and other publications, in which he claimed sole credit. And the stories written by Tom or by people who used his basic story, this became accepted as the story of the land. This was spread far and wide. It was believed by everyone for years. If you haven't read the story you ought to get a copy of it and read it sometime. I have here just certain excerpts from it and I think this is as good an opportunity as any for me to bring this up.

There's just too many discrepancies in these stories to let them go unanswered. For all these years we have remained pretty quiet and I have remained silent. When this happened I couldn't have cared less who shot down Yamamoto. We got him and that was the whole thing. I was remiss at the debriefing, as the squadron commander, in that I never signed it. Nobody ever brought it to me to sign. Actually, I can't remember ever being debriefed. I won't say I wasn't. I must have discussed it with someone to some degree, but it was certainly not a debriefing as we would consider it today.*

There's lots of controversy here and some of it is justified, but as I have said, everybody has leaned on the story that was published way back there without anybody arguing about it or publishing anything. Rex never wrote any books about it, or articles about it, nor have I. I want to make a point here that there is no evidence, no confirmation by anyone, that Lanphier shot down a Zero fighter that day, that he shot down a bomber that day, and for the sake of clarity I think we ought to pick out a few of these paragraphs that Lanphier had in his story.

I flew a lot of combat missions, had over four hundred hours of combat time during the war, and shot down sixteen airplanes. I know what it takes to get a confirmation. You have to have someone confirm that you shot it down. If someone said, "I shot down a plane over such and such a place," and somebody else saw a big fire burning at that time, you probably would be allowed a kill. We had no gun cameras, so you had to have confirmation by someone else besides yourself.

Even the position of the two Japanese bombers, when we get up to the actual combat, is important. Lanphier stated in his 1945 article that the lead bomber made a 360-degree turn, first going back in the direction from which it had come, after it broke to the left. Now the other bomber was on the lead bomber's left, and that would have meant that the lead bomber crossed right in front of his wingman.

It has been stated here, and in the book *The Reluctant Admiral,* that the wingman made a turn to the right, so Barber went after the lead bomber and stayed with it, and according to Mr. Yanagiya's statement on a videotape that I saw in the Nimitz Museum, he said he saw a P-38 continue on after the *lead* bomber and he saw the bomber get right down to the point of crashing. Whether he saw it actually hit the trees doesn't matter. There is what I call a confirmation.

Ed. note: The debriefing is discussed in the interview of Maj. Gen. John P. Condon, USMC (Ret.), beginning on p. 120.

Lanphier had stated that the lead bomber executed a violent wingover to his left while simultaneously, the number 2 bomber turned to his right. That means the lead bomber maneuvered right in front of his wingman, which could have caused a midair collision, and also he turned away from the attacking P-38s, thus inviting them to shoot his tail off. This doesn't make any sense.

Lanphier further stated that as they were approaching the bombers, practically in firing range, the Zeros started down, which is pretty well verified, and he turned upward then, back in the opposite direction that the bombers were headed, and made a head-on pass at the Zeros. He claimed a victory credit, though Mr. Yanagiya says none of their six Zeros were lost. As Lanphier got to the top of his turn, still flying in the opposite direction, the bombers were continuing in the direction they were supposed to go in the first place and I can imagine, although I wasn't in the cockpit with them, they had everything to the firewall, knowing they were under attack.

[Quoting Lanphier:] "I had lost sight of the bombers, rolled over on my back and looked down and there was the lead bomber down on the tree tops." At this time Lanphier says he was at 6,000 feet altitude. He says he positioned himself off the bomber's right wing. [Quoting Lanphier:] "The bomber was moving directly across my line of flight from my left," meaning, of course, he was off the bomber's right wing. [Quote again:] "I applied myself to my gunnery and taking no chances of missing him, began firing a long steady burst across the bomber's line of flight from approximately right angles. Long before I considered myself in range, the bomber's right engine and then his right wing began to burn." My comment on this is that while not an impossible shot, it is by far the most difficult and improbable shot a pilot can make.

Lanphier continued: "For just as I moved to within range of its cannon, the bomber's right wing came off and it plunged into the jungle and exploded." Fact: the aircraft was found and photographed, showing the right wing still attached or lying nearby the aircraft. This is important. We have color photos now in our possession that show it clearly. Lanphier says the wing came off before the bomber hit the ground. Now a wing coming off an aircraft in flight will cause that aircraft to immediately corkscrew. It's got to. It has lift on one side and none on the other. But when they found the bomber it was lying flat. There was none of the gyrations, so this makes it a very doubtful thing. In fact, it has been visited by an engineer, not an aircraft engineer, on two different occasions, who relates this to be a fact.

Lanphier further states in his original story that everyone in the top-cover, that would be the twelve of us up there, had seen the two bombers crash in the jungle and they were completely destroyed. That is an erroneous statement. There is not a man here that saw anything like that. Lou Kittel says he saw three fires; I only saw one. That's beside the point. The fact is no one verified that Lanphier did this.

There is some more, but these are the things that have bothered me for a long time, but I didn't ever rear up and say anything about them or write a book about them, or anything else. But I think, and so does Rex, that it should have been done. I should have sounded off about it a long time ago. I think you can gather from these remarks what my opinion about this is.

Edwards: Thank you very much. I appreciate that, I admire and respect every one of you even though you were in the Army Air Corps at the time. You're a good bunch, and I'd like to ask the gentleman from Japan a couple of short questions: Did the Zeros have radios, did you wear parachutes, and did you have self-sealing tanks?

Mr. Shinagawa [translating for Mr. Yanagiya]: As far as radios were concerned, they were standard equipment; however, none of the six Zeros carried them because of the weight. As for parachutes, they used the parachutes for seat cushions, so nobody wore a parachute.

Hall: We have time for one more question.

Edwards: Yes, about the self sealing tanks . . .

Hall: They were not on that particular model of Betty bomber. We are running a little late; one more question.

Mr. Kauslick: My name is Al Kauslick from Arizona. I have spent considerable time on Bougainville Island, and I'd like to address a question to Mr. Yanagiya from Japan. You stated that the six escorting Zeros made it back, but there were three air bases on or around Bougainville at that time, one at Kahili, one at Buin, and another on Ballale; is it possible that there were other Japanese aircraft operating in the area at that time that possibly got shot down on this mission?

Mr. Shinagawa [translating for Mr. Yanagiya]: The Japanese record states that yes, there were several fighter planes coming up from the other airfields; however, when they arrived at the encounter site none of the P-38s were present. There was a lapse of time before they arrived, so they didn't engage any Americans in dogfights, and they all returned safely to their airports. So, as far as the Japanese are concerned, none of the Zeros—the six in the cover flight or the Zeros that flew up from other airfields—were missing in action over Bougainville that day.*

Concluding Comments

Hall: You have now heard from the participants themselves, each one providing his own recollection of the Yamamoto mission. Quite obviously, recollections differ. Indeed, after forty-some odd years, one might expect as much and, as many of the participants have mentioned, the difficulties were the greater because of the secrecy involved in this particular mission. There were no special orders issued, the debriefing contained what I consider to be rather obvious errors in the number of aircraft involved: three bombers claimed destroyed when the pilots reported sighting two on the initial intercept. And there is another item of particular interest. Captain Pineau this morning discussed the importance of communications intelligence to the success of this mission, although, to be sure, the Magic and Ultra secrets of World War II were not revealed until many years after the war. Anthony Brown recently wrote the biography of the British

---

Ed. note: Japanese secondary source records confirm sixteen Zeros did take off from Kahili Airfield, but were airborne too late to engage the P-38s, which had already fled the area. No Zero fighter aircraft were lost in combat over Bougainville on 18 April 1943.

master spy for Winston Churchill, Stewart Graham Menzies, who was known as "C," which was published last year, in 1987. He touched on the Yamamoto mission and British dismay at the Americans' use of this intelligence data.* United States fighters working with Magic on 18 April 1943 intercepted and shot down the aircraft carrying Admiral Yamamoto as he was flying from Rabaul to Bougainville. As Brown describes it, since no cover story was disseminated to explain how American airman had been able to intercept a single aircraft in all the vastness of the Pacific, the Japanese could conclude that their codes had been compromised. Menzies thus believed that the Yamamoto mission was a compromise of the Anglo-American intelligence agreements. In Menzies' view, moreover, and I quote, "It demonstrated a predisposition in the command of the Southwest Pacific theater to use Magic for purely tactical or prestige purposes. It was not being used for great occasions only, as Churchill had said it should be. As 'C' argued at the Anglo-American meetings that followed, what was the use of Yamamoto's death to the Allies? By killing him, the Americans removed from the scene a man whose strategies and tactics were well known to them, and the likelihood was that he would be replaced by one whose conduct of battles was unknown. This could cause serious trouble. But more to the point of Magic security, the action accepted the risk that Magic might be compromised at the very moment when, on a grander scale, it was being used to transform Japan from a first-rate marine power to a third-rate naval power whose operating radius was rapidly being confined to home waters." Here he refers to the remarkable submarine activity that was going on during that period in the Pacific. Was that desirable state of affairs to be risked in the interests of vengeance? Again I quote: " 'C' thought the killing of Yamamoto was an act of self-indulgence, not a military operation, and he pointed out that on numerous occasions the British could have killed Rommel in much the same way as the Americans had killed Yamamoto, but had not done so because if they had, it would have cast suspicions

---

*Brown, *"C": The Secret Life of Sir Stewart Graham Menzies*.

‘

again on Enigma. There was, in consequence, a long pause in the negotiations to produce the Anglo-American agreements for a full exchange of Ultra and Magic. But when the pause was over, the Alliance was established." As you can see, it was a controversial mission at that time, at the highest levels. It remains a controversial mission today. But it was a successful mission, the objective was accomplished, and the American participants—each one of them—share in the credit. There is more than enough credit to go around.

Chapter 4

Interviews with Mr. Kenji Yanagiya, Major General John P. Condon, USMC (Ret.), and Mr. Hiroshi Hayashi

This interview of Kenji Yanagiya was conducted by R. Cargill Hall on 15 April 1988 in Fredericksburg, Texas. Mr. Makoto Shinagawa acted as translator for Mr. Yanagiya.

Hall: This is an interview, 15 April 1988, with Kenji Yanagiya, and with his translator, Makoto Shinagawa. Actually, it might be best if you just read these questions in Japanese; subsequently, you will have to interrupt periodically to translate so that he doesn't go on at such a length that you cannot remember.

Shinagawa: So I won't have to repeat the question in English. Good. Is this going into one single tape—I cannot do a simultaneous translation, right? All you hear is a voice doubling—in other words, you don't have a separate tape recorder to tape my voice onto another?

Hall: There's a single tape running with three mikes.

Shinagawa: Okay, good. Can we start?

Hall: Yes.

Shinagawa [asks Yanagiya the first question in Japanese]: Full name, rank, branch of military service at time of flight with Admiral Yamamoto in April 1943.

[Yanagiya replies.]

Shinagawa: I believe it can be translated as Warrant Officer of the Imperial Navy at the time of the Yamamoto Mission, Kenji Yanagiya. He belonged to the 204th Air Division.

Shinagawa [asks the second question]: What aerial combat experience did you possess at that time?

[Yanagiya replies.]

Shinagawa: He has the record with him, showing how many combat missions he had been involved with. At the time of the Yamamoto mission he had been an active combat flyer for eight months.

Hall: So he had not served in China?

Shinagawa: I believe he has the record with him that states everything. [Peruses record book.] In red ink it shows his combat record.

Hall: So he had been flying in combat since 1942?

Shinagawa: 1943, in June, he was injured—was wounded—until that time in June, 1943, he kept flying combat missions.

Hall: So he began flying in early '42, from what he says?

Shinagawa: In October 1942 he started to fly combat missions. He flew 50 missions, maybe 60. No, I take it back—over 100.

Hall: All right—now the third question.

Shinagawa [asks the third question]: How were you and your comrades selected for this mission (volunteered or detailed)?

[Yanagiya replies.]

Shinagawa: They were selected. Is that satisfactory?

Hall: Okay—they were selected and assigned to fly—it wasn't the case where they volunteered?

Shinagawa: No.

Hall: Go ahead with the fourth question.

Shinagawa [asks the fourth question]: What opinion did you and your comrades hold of Admiral Yamamoto?

[Yanagiya replies.]

Shinagawa: At the time, six men were selected to form two squadrons of three planes each. Piloting the number one plane was First Lieutenant Morisaki, and leader of the second squadron was also a lieutenant, but the rest, the other four, were enlisted graduates of the same year from the same school—same flight school, so they had a very strong buddy, comrade feeling toward one another. The feeling toward Admiral Yamamoto he did not elaborate, but his impression of that mission, of course, when he was selected and they were selected—hey, "tomorrow we are honored to protect him—it's quite an honorable position to participate in." That was his, and their, feeling. No personal feeling toward Admiral Yamamoto.

Hall: Okay, I would then proceed with the fifth question, or do you think we ought to skip that one?

Shinagawa: The Japanese side?

Hall: Yes, in other words, his own—well, he'd been in the theater but a short time, apparently since October, 1942, but in the period that he was there—what was his own assessment of his [the admiral's] contribution to the war effort?

Shinagawa [asks the fifth question]: What was your assessment of the admiral's importance to the war effort?

[Yanagiya replies.]

Shinagawa: Of course, his assessment at that time, Japan was an Imperial military power, was at the verge of, just about to fall apart, and then Admiral Yamamoto's decision to act, at the time [in 1943] it was one of the biggest planned attacks of reinforcement to retake many of the islands that they had lost, and he was in command of the fleet at that time. He didn't have to, but he decided to appear at the frontline, to command from the frontline.

Hall: I would gather that what you are saying is, with these war plans, of which he was an important part, that his role in the war effort was pretty crucial from his view?

Shinagawa: He [the admiral] did not want to sit back at the commanding position to command from a distance. He wanted to come to the frontline to command, so the admiral thought that it was imperative for him to come to the frontline to command his navy.

Hall: Now, the sixth question really revolves around the Betty bomber and the Zero, what types exactly were they, because there were different models. Were they locally based or special aircraft that flew in with unusual markings?

Shinagawa [asks the sixth question]: How many and what type of aircraft were selected for this mission? Were they locally based, or special aircraft featuring unusual markings or armament?

[Yanagiya replies.]

Shinagawa: The base was Rabaul.

Hall: Rabaul?

Shinagawa: Yes, Rabaul. The plane that Admiral Yamamoto was flying in was from Nishi Airport, which is located near Rabaul—a little bit higher altitude airport. A plain ordinary standard naval Betty—Isshikirikko, they call it—and six Zeros.

Hall: And the Zeros were new planes?

Shinagawa: 32 Model of Zero he was flying in, but nothing out of the ordinary.

Hall: Standard?

[Yanagiya continues to reply.]

Shinagawa: The 22, Model 22 Zeros—the 22 was the most common. But the one he was flying in was a Model 32 especially converted for flight from an aircraft carrier, which had a shorter wingspan, chopped off at the tip.

Hall: And standard armament?

[Shinagawa asks this question. Yanagiya replies.]

Shinagawa: There was nothing out of the ordinary. It was a standard equipped 20-millimeter [cannon] and 7-millimeter [machine guns]—there's nothing unusual or special about these planes that guarded Admiral Yamamoto.

Hall: A question of my own—were they equipped with radios that could communicate with the bombers?

[Shinagawa asks this question. Yanagiya replies.]

Shinagawa: Yes, they came equipped as standard equipment, they had a radio communication system; however, it was just a very basic and fundamental radio that could easily be jammed and that created such static that you could not easily communicate with each other, plus the fact that it was easily detected by the Americans if they used the radio, so, because of the weight of it, many of the pilots decided to dismount it to lighten the aircraft.

Hall: These were pilots on the mission?

Shinagawa: Well, generally speaking they [the pilots] did dismount it, and he recalls maybe all six of them didn't have radios—elected to dismount it, and they did.

Hall: So communicating with the bombers they could not do?

[Shinagawa asks this question. Yanagiya replies.]

Shinagawa: No.

Hall: Seven is the next question.

Shinagawa [asks the seventh question]: Were the two bombers armed, that is carrying gunners and guns?

[Yanagiya replies.]

Shinagawa: Yes, the Betty bomber had the [standard] crew of nine, not counting passengers, and, yes, there was the tailgunner and the side gunners. They were quite standard. But the mission plan stated that it was not an attack mission, but a transport mission, and he [Yanagiya] was advised to guard this transport mission.

Hall: The bomber carried guns and gunners?

Shinagawa: Yes, it did.

Hall: It wasn't briefed as a combat mission or anything, because they were a transport mission?

Shinagawa: Right.

Hall: So it was carrying guns and it did have gunners?

Shinagawa: Yes, nothing out of the ordinary, but just a standard crew of nine—pilot, co-pilot, navigators, the photographer, the gunners—three of them.

Hall: All right. Then of course, [in addition] the people they were transporting?

Shinagawa: Right.

Hall: We should move to question 8.

Shinagawa [asks the eighth question]: What did your intelligence officers say in the preflight briefing about the nearest American units and aircraft, the likelihood of encountering them, and the flying skills of American pilots?

[Yanagiya replies.]

Shinagawa: Nothing.

Hall: Okay. On question 9, read that to yourself carefully. He has already discussed radio communications.

Shinagawa [asks the ninth question]: Thinking back to 18 April 1943, to the best of your recollection, tell me about the mission events prior to the encounter with the American P-38s, that is, your launch time and destination, weather on the way, navigation checkpoints, and manner of radio contact, etc.

[Yanagiya replies.]

Shinagawa: Of course it happened forty-some odd years ago, memory is fading, and it doesn't appear as if it really happened as he recalls. But he said that at 6 o'clock in the morning they left the airport and the weather was clear and nicer than the average—the visibility was very good. They could observe some thunderclouds in the distance. They were flying the coastline with the Bougainville mountains on the left-hand side, thinking that if Americans come to attack the planes they cannot come from the mountains—they would naturally come from the sea, so they were flying with the mountains on the left-hand side with the two bombers, with Admiral Yamamoto flying at 2,500 meters and us [fighter pilots] flying on the right rear of the bombers at an altitude of 3,000 meters, 500 meters higher than the bombers, knowing and thinking that if they were to be attacked, then we can protect them from the rear.

Hall: All right.

Shinagawa [asks the tenth question]: What was the situation just before the encounter: the altitude and disposition of Japanese aircraft, visibility in the area, the heading, distance, and flight time remaining to destination?

[Yanagiya replies.]

Shinagawa: Of course the disposition of the Japanese planes was forestated in question 9. From Rabaul to Buin, which was the airport, the distance flying time of two hours, he doesn't recall the distance.

Hall: Remaining?

Shinagawa: No. That is the total distance. They could see the [Buin] airfield at the time of the encounter, so he assumed that they must have been only ten minutes away from the airfield.

[Yanagiya interjects in conversation.]

Hall: They were going into Ballale, I believe—Buin was the second stop.

Shinagawa: No. Buin was the destination.

Hall: Would you double-check because our records say that they were flying to the island of Ballale and then to return [next] to Buin.

[Shinagawa confers with Yanagiya.]

Shinagawa: Buin was the destination. He confirmed it three times. That was his mission to see to it that Admiral Yamamoto gets to Buin.

Hall: Okay. Let us move to question 11. [Discussion ensues regarding track of the American pilots from Guadalcanal to Bougainville].

Shinagawa [asks the eleventh question]: To the best of your recollection, describe the engagement and your role in it, from the moment the P-38s were first sighted.

[Yanagiya replies.]

Shinagawa: Of course it becomes a very, very long story, he recalls everything, but what he recalls is that his sighting of P-38s was a little bit delayed from first spotting by the squadron leader. And three of them first saw P-38s flying 1,000 meters below, coming very near the bombers, so they started to go down to repel some of the P-38s, off away from the bomber. As he realized that Admiral Yamamoto's plane was being attacked, of course, they all dove to try to repel the P-38s. They managed to do that, he feels, the first time, but as he tried to climb up to recover, to prepare for the second wave, as he looked down, Yamamoto's plane was already smoking and going down to the jungle. The staff plane, the plane that was carrying Yamamoto's staff, was going toward the ocean, to the right, and Yamamoto's plane was going down into the jungle.

[Yanagiya continues comments.]

Shinagawa: Delaying of the spotting was probably contributed by the camouflage painting on the top side of the P-38s, and also they [the Japanese pilots] were all looking toward the horizon and above, because Americans usually, and he stated almost a little bit stronger than usual, they . . . Americans, never normally started to attack from the lower altitude, because you know, whoever has the higher altitude has the advantage.

Hall: So they were expecting if anyone came, the Americans would come from a higher altitude?

Shinagawa: Higher altitude—that's why they were at a higher altitude than the bomber, looking toward the horizon upward, not downward, and because of the jungle underneath it was very difficult for them to spot the P-38s which had come for its mark.

Hall: I would be interested then to know—the P-38s obviously were spotted at the very last moment—how much time elapsed—just a few seconds before they attacked the bombers—they [the Americans] were obviously over the jungle and not really over the water by the time they spotted them, yes?

[Shinagawa asks this question. Yanagiya replies.]

Shinagawa: Yes. Correct. They [the P-38s] were above the jungle and they were already in the formation to attack.

[Yanagiya continues reply.]

Shinagawa: Were they [P-38s], of course, looking up, surely you find planes or any flying object much quicker than when looking down, because you don't have any . . .

Hall: Can't distinguish as easily . . .

Shinagawa: Right. And when they saw the P-38s they were in the formation just about to attack.

Hall: So it was a very few seconds then?

[Shinagawa asks this question. Yanagiya replies.]

Shinagawa: Of course it was a very tense moment, so he cannot recall the time that correctly, accurately, but not a couple seconds—maybe within ten seconds.

Hall: How many P-38s were there in the attacking element?

Shinagawa: Total or in that mode?

Hall: In the mode of attacking, how many in that element?

[Shinagawa asks this question. Yanagiya replies.]

Shinagawa: All he could observe—first four [P-38s] and the second four about to attack, and of course, he himself had to do his duty, so he assumed that everybody [P-38s] was in attack mode, but he didn't see personally whether or not everybody attacked simultaneously.

Hall: Would you ask him question number 17 out of order?

Shinagawa [asks the seventeenth question]: Which flight of three Zeros were you in, and at what position in the flight?

[Yanagiya replies.]

Shinagawa: Third of the second flight. One, Two, Three, One, Two, Three, so he was right here.

Hall: Closest to the mountain?

Shinagawa: No. The mountains were over there—furthest away.

Hall: So he was closest to the ocean?

Shinagawa: Yes.

Hall: So it was an element of three in a "V" and he was the third, closest to the ocean?

Shinagawa: Closest to the ocean, farthest away from the mountains. Not only the mountains, but farthest away from the bomber.

Hall: All right. I guess we should pick up with number 12 and just work our way down.

Shinagawa [asks the twelfth question]: After the engagement, where did you land, and what was the reaction of those on the ground.

[Yanagiya replies.]

Shinagawa: After the encounter, he saw the Yamamoto plane going down toward the jungle and the staff plane going out over the ocean. He saw these, and then P-38s, confirming these planes going down, scattered to go back to the airfield from where they came—Guadalcanal. His immediate reaction was that Buin was his final destination, and they [the Americans] were going toward that destination, so he thought, "I'm going to give it a chase." He flew toward the destination of the return route of the American planes, and right over Shortland Island he saw a P-38 flying, and he was flying 1,000 meters above the P-38, and he recalls that the P-38 was flying at an altitude of 3,000 meters, so that was about 9,000 feet. He wanted to ask, is that the average standard cruising altitude of a P-38, do you know?

Hall: I couldn't tell you off the top of my head, but we have a host of people who can, and I'll get an answer for you.

[Shinagawa advises Yanagiya. Yanagiya replies.]

Shinagawa: He recalls the approximate altitude of 3,000 meters, 9,000 feet, and he spotted the P-38 cruising, of course he was about a thousand meters, 3,000 feet, higher above and he attacked, and P-38 did not burn—it was one of the planes that does not burst into flames that easily—but he could clearly see that the gasoline gushing out as he hit the plane, with white smoke [vapor]. He wanted to know the fate—what happened to that particular plane, whether or not it made it back, or . . .

Hall: That plane was piloted by a Lt. Hine, who went missing in action and did not return, and it was the solitary American loss of the mission. They lost one P-38 whose engine was observed smoking. Others saw the engine smoking.

Shinagawa: And that was it?

Hall: Yes. He was still trying to fly, apparently it wasn't burning, but it must have been severe, so his recollection coincides, there was one P-38 lost. It was lost with one engine smoking, and that is the recollection of the other people that were nearby.

[Shinagawa translates this reply. Yanagiya replies.]

Shinagawa: Of course, he has mixed emotions. He doesn't want to say, well, whether or not he did shoot down the plane, it's irrelevant—I myself [Yanagiya] got shot. I don't know whether he [Lt. Hine] was shot in person or shot in the engine, or any part of the plane—it's the same thing, it's almost a sure death, but he doesn't want to confirm the kill, but of course he returned back.

Hall: How many P-38s were claimed destroyed during the engagement?

Shinagawa: Let me finish what he said and then let me ask him.

Hall: Surely.

Shinagawa: He made a U-turn to go back to the Buin Airport and when he arrived he was the last one to come in. Of course he gave a chase—that's why he was the last one to come in—and when he landed, the second lieutenant who was in charge of the squadron, by the name of Morisaki, reported to the commanding officer of the airport, so he was not asked to give the report. And about two hours later, after landing, they were given the order to go back to Rabaul, so he was never asked, and he didn't ask for their opinion or their emotion of the incident.

Hall [question 16]: After the encounter, how many P-38s were claimed shot down?

[Shinagawa asks this question. Yanagiya replies.]

Shinagawa: All unconfirmed, but they reported three—but none confirmed by anyone else. These are the total that six Zero pilots reported.

Hall: All right. [question 14] How many in the flight of Zeros, how many of his comrades were shot down?

[Shinagawa asks this question. Yanagiya replies.]

Shinagawa: Out of six [Zeros], one landed on Shortland Island—an emergency landing. Five others all landed at Buin Airport, so none were lost.

Hall: In question number 13, if you would ask, did Japanese intelligence suspect codes had been broken?

Shinagawa [asks the thirteenth question]: In the debriefings, did Japanese intelligence suspect that codes had been broken?

[Yanagiya replies.]

Shinagawa: He was not directly involved in intelligence, so he just does not know; he did not know before Yamamoto's death, but because of the unusual circumstances of the encounter—prior to the Yamamoto mission he had never seen P-38s in a group of sixteen or eighteen attacking from the lower altitude—and not only that, but to even ignore Zeros flying up above to go for the bomber and nothing else, from the lower altitude with a group of sixteen or eighteen, he was [himself] certain that the code had been broken. They [the Americans] knew who was flying in the plane. It was deliberate. It was not an accident.

Hall: So the Japanese officers of the day were satisfied that that was what had happened?

Shinagawa: Well, that was his opinion, his conception, and usually in the frontline airfield, when one plane lands, the dust created by the first plane—you have to wait for awhile for the dust to settle to land another one. At the time he recalls that when he landed and when all of them landed at the Buin Airport, the airfield was in such a condition that it did not create a speck of dust flying into the air because it was watered, it was well kept, because they were informed that Admiral Yamamoto was coming to the very extreme frontline for the first time and the message had been relayed to not only the navy personnel, but to the army personnel throughout the region. So it was his understanding that the code had been broken. If that many messages were given, no matter what form it took, to oversee the runway watering, for example, everybody would have known.

Hall: Were any other Japanese fighters from Kahili or Buin able to get up in the air and engage or not?

[Shinagawa asks this question. Yanagiya replies.]

Shinagawa: Immediately after the encounter, the P-38s just scattered to go back, ran full speed almost, and he doesn't recall and he doesn't think there was an encounter by the Zeros.

Hall: In other words, the airplanes on the ground did not have an opportunity to get airborne and engage at all?

Shinagawa: He didn't think so. He thinks that it was too late for them to encounter P-38s, because there was a time lapse.

Hall: None of them [Zeros from Bougainville] were reported lost?

[Shinagawa asks this question. Yanagiya replies.]

Shinagawa: No.

Hall: All right.

[Yanagiya asks a question.]

Shinagawa: He would like to add this question to the prior question—the cruising altitude of P-38—did the Americans usually water the runway?

Hall: At Guadalcanal, or?

Shinagawa: At Henderson Airfield or whatever.

Hall: Henderson's on Guadalcanal.

Shinagawa: They used to do that?

Hall: I don't know.

Shinagawa: Would you also ask?

Hall: Yes. The Americans frequently used that steel matting—it was a matting they laid down to make the surface firmer, but I imagine there would still be plenty of dust—I'll have to ask.

[Yanagiya and Shinagawa confer.]

Shinagawa: He feels that those steel plates placed on the runway would prohibit almost . . . but of course the runway was quite long he feels, and there must have been some uncovered surface that created dust.

Hall: Probably. Again, you must say that there are many from Henderson Field here and he can ask them. Mr. Chandler, whom he met earlier, was not on the mission but was stationed at Henderson Field also. He [Yanagiya] met him for pictures here earlier. Let's return for a few more questions, then we'll call it an afternoon. Returning to the engagement itself, as Yanagiya is undoubtedly aware, there has always been some dispute over how many American pilots actually engaged the bombers and how many didn't. Did he observe that more than one P-38 fired on Admiral Yamamoto's bomber?

Shinagawa: Is your question asking him whether or not he has seen them?

Hall: Yes. Did he observe—frequently in the middle of a firefight like this you don't have the pleasure of taking in observations, but did he observe in the conflict whether more than one P-38 attacked the bomber, or from his earlier statements he implies that several broke through to attack the bomber, but it was not too precise.

[Shinagawa asks this question. Yanagiya replies.]

Shinagawa: He is certain that almost all fired, but first two or three were repelled by the other Zeros. But others followed. They were all firing at the bomber and they were just going in rows, so to speak. They were all firing.

Hall: When one passed, firing, then another would follow?

Shinagawa: Shoot, flip, go down—just like that.

Hall: Did he observe the attempts made to escape attack by the bombers—did they do any special maneuvers?

[Shinagawa asks this question. Yanagiya replies.]

Shinagawa: When Zeros found the P-38s they did a maneuver to let the bombers know that there was an attack going on from the rear, wing-banking?

Hall: Yes. Rocking your wings.

Shinagawa: When they saw the Zeros doing this, the bombers speeded to shoot straight into the [Buin] airfield, but of course, P-38s had much quicker speed so they were caught in between.

Hall: But they did not make 360-degree turns—they didn't make big circles to try to . . .

[Yanagiya breaks in to continue comments.]

Shinagawa: Of course as he first stated, Yamamoto's plane was going straight toward the airport and then the staff plane was going— went out toward the ocean.

Hall: It didn't complete a 360-degree turn?

Shinagawa: No.

Hall: Did Mr. Yanagiya see either of the two bombers on fire or crash?

[Shinagawa asks this question. Yanagiya replies.]

Shinagawa: The Admiral Yamamoto's plane was heavily smoking, plus he saw the flame—a little bit of flame. The staff plane he thought had landed on the water, having seen very small smoke and the fumes spilling out as white clouds. But at the impact in the jungle of Yamamoto's plane, all he saw was just big smoke coming out of the jungle—he didn't see any flame because it's a heavily wooded jungle.

Hall: Then, he did see the crash?

[Shinagawa asks this question. Yanagiya replies.]

Shinagawa: Yes. He was in the middle of the chase, chasing a P-38, so he didn't see the exact impact, but then after the crash, he was sending the waving action over the [Buin] airfield and a short burst with the machine gun to signal the encounter or mishap. That was the time when he saw the big smoke coming out of the jungle.

Hall: All right. Did he attack any of the P-38s immediately after the bomber was attacked or did he proceed down the coast?

[Yanagiya asks a question.]

Shinagawa: He [Yanagiya] had a question. Did any of the P-38 pilots stay there to see the actual crash of the bomber, or did they just evacuate that area? He feels that there wasn't any P-38 left long enough to see the actual bomber crashing into the jungle. Of course, he himself was busy chasing P-38s.

Hall: The P-38s divided into two groups. One group went up high to fly top-cover, thinking that there would be fighters coming from Buin and Kahili, but they did not come. Four were selected to attack the bomber.

[Shinagawa translates Hall's comments. A discourse follows in Japanese.]

Hall: You've answered most of the questions of interest to the Americans. Did he attack the P-38s only once?

Shinagawa: At what site, after the chase at the Shortland Island? Yes, he did attack at Shortland Island.

Hall: But also before that, right?

Shinagawa: At the site?

Hall: At the [original] site, did he have an opportunity to attack any of the initial P-38s, or was he too far out over the ocean?

[Shinagawa asks the question. Yanagiya replies.]

Shinagawa: Yes and no. As P-38s attacked and flipped up to escape after the burst, he joined the fight to fire in front of the P-38s that were shooting at the bomber, as repelling shots—he just kept squeezing the grip—or pushing the button—to try to repel these P-38s from attacking—that was the extent of it. He did not engage in a dogfight after the [initial] encounter.

Hall: All right. So, he did not really fire on a P-38 until later over Shortland Island?

[Shinagawa asks this question. Yanagiya replies.]

Shinagawa: Yes. Correct.

Hall: One last question and then I'm going to ask him to add any observations he would like. The American debriefing reported that the first two P-38s to reach the scene—one of them flew up into the Zeros and the other one flew down to attack the bomber. Does he remember that—the second one apparently flipped over.

[Shinagawa asks this question. Yanagiya replies.]

Shinagawa: As he stated before, he was on the farthest right-hand rear from the attack, so he repelled the second formation, so to speak, of the P-38s, so therefore he does not recall and he did not see, and probably he didn't have the opportunity, if in fact one of the P-38s did that, he didn't see. He couldn't see.

Hall: It seemed to him that the first ones—all of the first ones were going directly for the bomber?

[Shinagawa confers with Yanagiya.]

Shinagawa: Yes, all of them.

Hall: All of them were going for the bomber. All right. I have exhausted all of my questions. I would like him to add any comments— any personal observations of his own—in retrospect.

[Shinagawa relays this request. Yanagiya replies.]

Shinagawa: The special impression and the feeling about that recollection was that as the P-38s attacked, they wouldn't attack because the gun here from the [bomber's] rear—the immediate rear— maybe from the side of the fuselage; and then immediate embankment to go up to escape. Maybe the P-38 that claimed to have gone up to attack the Zeros went and did this [flip-over] motion, but the fact remains that none of the Zeros had any bullet holes in any of the six, so it is not likely that they fired at any of the Zeros. But his recollection was that it was almost like a Kamikaze suicide attack that these P-38 pilots did, and it was very unusual and embedded in his mind and his vision to attack just one blow, and then just scatter to escape after the immediate shots. It didn't look to him like that they did think about coming back to confirm the kill or anything. Without confirmation, they just took off.

Hall: Yes. I want to thank him very much.

This interview of Major General John P. Condon, USMC (Ret.) was conducted by R. Cargill Hall on 8 March 1989 at the Marine Corps Historical Center, Washington Navy Yard, Washington, D.C.

Hall: By way of introduction, perhaps you might begin, General, by giving your date of birth, the names of your parents and their occupation, and the schools you attended before the war.

Condon: I was born December 20, 1911. My father, John C.

Condon, was a banker up in northern Michigan. My mother was from Lockport, New York, originally. Her father, Dr. Emmett Hall Pomeroy, was the head surgeon of the Calumet and Hecla Copper Mining Company in Calumet, Michigan. I went to the local high schools up there in Houghton and Hancock, Michigan, two little towns that are adjacent to each other. I graduated in 1929 and went for a year to Severn School, at Severna Park, Maryland, a preparatory school for the Naval Academy and West Point, right near Annapolis. The following year, in 1930, I entered the Naval Academy and graduated in 1934. At that time you had to do a year at the Marine Corps Basic School, Navy Yard, Philadelphia, first, so the Marines could "teach you how to be a Marine," followed by a year of sea duty. Then you were eligible to go into other specialties, and my choice was aviation. I went to NAS Pensacola in 1936 and finished flight training in December 1937. I then reported to Brown Field, Marine Barracks, Quantico, Virginia, where I was assigned to Marine Fighting Squadron 1, in January 1938. I stayed right there at Quantico for the next four years, except for assignments of the squadron on maneuvers in the Caribbean, or for carrier duty, gunnery, bombing, etc., right up to Pearl Harbor. We were flying the last of the biplane fighters, the Grumman F3F-2.

Hall: Between Pearl Harbor and April 1943, could you describe the assignments you had then?

Condon: Well, right after Pearl Harbor, we were ordered to San Diego with the entire First Marine Aircraft Wing, of which my squadron was a part. By that time I had become the executive officer of Fighting Squadron 121, one of the new squadrons, and the first one to get the Wildcat fighters in the Marine Corps. We were "launched" to the West Coast—and we thought we were going from there right out to do battle with the Japanese. But instead, we plumped down on the West Coast on a field outside of San Diego, at Carney Mesa, "Camp Carney," as we called it, now NAS Miramar. Then, it was strictly "boondocks." Then they took our Wildcats away and sent them out to an aircraft carrier. So we were bogged down with 75 or 100 brand-new second lieutenants—and six gas-leaking Brewster Buffaloes. We were hard up for aircraft for about two months, but then we began to get F4F Wildcats in quantity. The squadron became a fighter group, Marine Air Group, MAG-12, with four fighter squadrons and we began some real training and preparation. I became the Group Operations officer when MAG-12 was commissioned and remained in that job until attached to Fighter Command, Air Solomons.

Hall: This was most of 1942?

Condon: Yes. That was all during 1942, and on the first of January 1943 we were ordered overseas to Noumea, and then went into Efate and were based there. About a day after our arrival, the group commander, Col. Edward Pugh, was dispatched to Guadalcanal. The next day I followed him to take over what they called at that point The Fighter Command, which consisted of one officer. So the two of us took over a dugout up on a little bluff at Fighter Two on Guadalcanal, and began to operate from our "hole in the bluff." We were in charge of all the daily operations of all the fighters at Guadalcanal, all services and nationalities.

Hall: This was in January 1943?

Condon: The end of January 1943.

Hall: Was this field a part of Henderson Field?

Condon: No, it was nearby, about two miles away.

Hall: Was Henderson the main field?

Condon: Henderson was the bomber field by that time. There weren't any fighters on Henderson Field. There was a Fighter One, out of commission for rehabilitation at that point, on the other side of Henderson Field. Fighter Two relieved the congestion at Henderson and Fighter One. Fighter Two became temporarily, until March, the sole fighter field, from the time I arrived.

Hall: So these fields were just designated as Fighter One and Fighter Two?

Condon: Fighter One and Fighter Two.

Hall: And the P-38s were . . .

Condon: At Fighter Two, where the P-40s and P-39s were also. There were also about forty to sixty F4Fs and Corsairs there as well. You might say it was somewhat crowded, and it was.

Hall: What was your rank and assignment at the time of the Yamamoto mission in April 1943?

Condon: I was a major when I first arrived on Guadalcanal, and was promoted to lieutenant colonel in May, as I remember it. My assignment at the time of the Yamamoto mission was still operations officer of The Fighter Command. By that time, in April, we were back at Fighter One, and we had been augmented considerably with administrative support, communications support, and operations personnel. We had a group there in The Fighter Command headquarters of maybe ten or fifteen people, and we stood watches around the clock. I practically lived there, and that was what I had been doing for a couple of months beforehand.

Hall: The number of aircraft, in terms of the army and navy aircraft available, I know it fluctuated, but I gather there were about twenty or so P-38s and a number of P-39s at Fighter Two. How many aircraft did the marines and navy have at Fighter One?

Condon: At Fighter One, we had several squadrons from MAG-12 and the navy, mostly F4Fs, but also with growing numbers of marine Corsairs. Numbers varied with the situation and with training ops back at Espiritu Santo, but Fighter One had an average fighter count of about one hundred to one hundred twenty by April 1943.

Hall: A squadron was composed of twelve aircraft?

Condon: No, in the marine case, a squadron was twenty aircraft, approximately. It basically started off at eighteen and then if you could get two or four more operating spares, why you usually wound up with about twenty-some odd planes in a squadron. We still had some F4Fs at Fighter One, the Wildcat, but the Corsairs were beginning to come up in the overall percentage of marine strength. For awhile, we had to struggle to get a total of 100 fighters in commission at both Fighter One and Fighter Two. We had to have about 120 total to be able to launch 100 for incoming raids, or to escort dive bombers to New Georgia, or heavies all the way up to Bougainville. The dive bombers went as far as Munda and the closer targets that were within their range. I'd say that at the time of the Yamamoto mission, it was very seldom we had over 120 fighters total. Of that number, the air corps had at Fighter Two, I'd say, about 40 to 50, comprised of P-40s, P-39s and P-38s.

Hall: Captain Roger Pineau has observed that deciphering of the Japanese message was completed at Pearl Harbor late on Wednesday, 14 April. Now that's about four days before the mission transpired. Can you shed any light on whether the Yamamoto mission was in fact approved in Washington, D.C., later in the week, or whether the orders came down from Admiral Nimitz at Pearl?

Condon: It certainly was our understanding that the attempt to intercept him was "at all costs," that was the way they phrased it. And it was clear to us that this [message] had emanated from Washington, and that President Roosevelt or Secretary Knox of the navy had approved it. But we cannot find written proof of that. No one seems to know where it is today. Admiral King's dispatches have been researched. They are not easy to come by, what there is of them, and none reveal the message from Secretary Knox that all surviving participants seem to remember.

Hall: But to those on the scene, when the order arrived, there was a clear understanding, The Fighter Command understood that this wasn't just a local order, but came down from . . .

Condon: Oh no. It obviously had concurrence at all levels of command. I'm positive of that. But I can't hand you a document right now.

Hall: Captain Pineau has stated that that is the case [documents are unavailable]. And there is one book written by a Frenchman that alludes to Knox asking that the message be destroyed, so . . .

Condon: Oh really!

Hall: Yes, it's called *Flames in the Sky.** I will have to send you a copy of those pages. He has no footnotes, so it's not possible to know. It was published in 1952 and it is conceivable he might have talked to the principals. He tells of a luncheon with Secretary Knox

---

*Closterman, *Flames in the Sky*, chap. 4.

and somebody else, where this mission was discussed, but again there are no footnotes.

Condon: I'd say he was pretty accurate. I searched through all the files here trying to find it about four, five or six years ago. But I remember just as about as clearly as I can recall anything, it [the message] was on a special kind of paper. It was different from our normal dispatches, our normal message traffic. At the end of the message it said something like: "Knox sends," or "Secretary Knox sends." No one can find that message now.

Hall: All right. Did those orders for the mission arrive at Guadalcanal one day before, on Saturday, 17 April, or at an earlier date?

Condon: To my recollection, and I'm pretty positive on this, we got word of it, meaning Colonel Pugh and myself, The Fighter Commander and me—I was his number two—we received it on the 16th of April.

Hall: Which would be Friday.

Condon: Yes, Friday, the 16th.

Hall: So the air corps pilots weren't called over until Saturday.

Condon: They weren't called over until the next day. Colonel Pugh and I were called into Rear Adm. Marc A. Mitscher's COMAIRSOLS* headquarters on the 16th, I can't remember if it was morning or afternoon. We sat down with Admiral Mitscher, and I can't recall for sure the names of the others. Brigadier General Field Harris, USMC, chief of staff, was there, and another was Stan Ring, a navy captain and Admiral Mitscher's operations officer. Another, I believe, was Comdr. William A. "Gus" Read, but I am not sure of all the names. There were not any air corps types there at all. We discussed the message, of course, and who was involved. We read the detail of the message to the minute, where Yamamoto would be and at what time, where he would board a boat to make the run to the seaplane base, when he would come back to fly over to Kahili for the return to Rabaul. It was very detailed, and we talked about how best to do the job. Well, in the course of the conversation and the discussion,

---

*Commander Air, Solomon Islands.

it became pretty clear that we had no aircraft that had the range to do that except the P-38s.

We were very confident that if anybody could do it, they could, as far as aggressively pursuing the assigned mission. I might say right here, when they first arrived with the P-38s, it was just about the time I got there. The 38s' first deployment forward to Guadalcanal was before I arrived, I think, in late 1942.* That initial deployment was not a success. I don't mean to cast any aspersions at all, but I think that some of the pilots who brought the P-38s up there the first time didn't have the confidence in the aircraft that the later pilots did. When I arrived, some of them would be drifting back to Guadalcanal a half an hour before the strike part of a mission returned or had even been heard from. I'm sure that the air corps pilots of that day heard about it, but other pilots, marine, navy, etc., referred to the P-38 as a "high altitude foxhole." The 38s were always given high cover, because they had the altitude performance. They often failed to see things that happened. They were up at 35,000 feet and didn't see any Zeros, didn't see any action. Not all the time, mind you. I don't mean to imply that, but some of the time.

Hall: So it wasn't until later, in February or March 1943, that they began to be employed more effectively, using them at lower altitudes?

Condon: Colonel Pugh was concerned in February and discussed it with Brig. Gen. Dean C. "Doc" Strother, who was the XIII Fighter Command Commanding General, and was at Guadalcanal often. He came over on the order of three or four times a month from Espiritu Santo or Noumea. He was on Guadalcanal a lot and we liked him and had good rapport with him in every way. So we registered a comment with Gen. Doc Strother about the P-38s on that initial deployment. He said he would see if he could do something about it, to make them more aggressive.

The next deployment of P-38s brought Lanphier and a detachment of the 70th Fighter Squadron. As I recall, the 339th Fighter Squadron,

---

Ed. note: The first P-38s, aircraft of the 339th Fighter Squadron, arrived on Guadalcanal on 12 November 1942.

with Mitchell and Kittel, came just before the Y-mission to relieve the 70th Squadron. Major Kittel got into the searchlights at night one time and you could hear a roar all over the island when he flamed a couple of Bettys up there. Two in one night. God, it was just like a standing ovation on that island, no less! Major Kittel, with his little beard that fitted under his oxygen mask. He was a real hero to all the people on Guadalcanal because they saw what he did right over their heads in the dark of night.* Anyway, when Lanphier came, it was another ballgame with that kind of aggressiveness at any altitude, down on the deck, or up at 35,000 feet. It was like turning night into day.

I emphasize that I understand that the transition to the P-38s was a chore. It was something new—twin engines, a wheel instead of a stick, it was just a little different—a lot of airplane. I saw some of that in San Diego where there was a P-38 outfit when we were at Camp Carney in 1942. The P-38s were at North Island, right there at Coronado. And that was wild. So it was either Jimmy Mattern or someone like him from Lockheed came down to calm these guys down. He feathered a prop, one prop, on takeoff. He just took off and did everything with one prop feathered as part of his act. And he came by low and slow, to show them that this wasn't a "killer" airplane. Some of that type of concern might have occurred in the transition to P-38s in the South Pacific. In any case, I attributed the initial situation to a hurried transition and the lack of time for confidence-building of the type that Mattern showed them on North Island could be done. That's the way I meant those comments, not in any other way. When Lanphier and Mitchell came later, it was a total turn-around—about the best airplanes and the best pilots we had.

Hall: Lou Kittel, John Mitchell, and Lanphier. How long had they been on Guadalcanal before the April 18th mission?

Ed. note: Louis R. Kittel pioneered night-fighting techniques using the P-38. He would loiter at high altitude awaiting Japanese aircraft at night, and then dive on them when they were caught in the search lights. The incident above occurred on 19 May 1943.

Condon: Lanphier was just finishing a very successful P-38 tour. He and his 70th Squadron detachment were held over for the Yamamoto mission. He was to end his time on the 17th and, along with Barber and the other 70th pilots, was leaving the next morning for a rear area for rest. The point about holding Lanphier and Barber over for the mission was a "bet-hedging" operation. John Mitchell, I'm sure, could have done whatever Lanphier and Barber did without any question, and no doubt about it. He was a marvelous pilot and he had been there as an outstanding pilot in P-39s, in the really tough days on Guadalcanal. That was his background and general reputation, I remember very clearly. But Lanphier and Barber had been in the southern Bougainville area a few days before. It was the "best bet" to hold them over.

Hall: The team had been there a month or so already?

Condon: Lanphier and Barber had been there for about six weeks. That was about the length of their stay.

Hall: And Kittel and Mitchell?

Condon: Kittel and Mitchell came the day before the mission.

Hall: They arrived on the 16th?

Condon: Right, on the 16th or the 17th even, to relieve the group that Lanphier had up there.

Hall: I see. They had eighteen aircraft in commission at that time?

Condon: That's right, and two of them went down as I remember.

Hall: One blew a tire on takeoff.

Condon: Yes, that's right. I'd just like to mention one other thing. When we were discussing the mission on Friday the 16th with Admiral Mitscher, the 38s came into the discussion, particularly because Lanphier had, about four, five, or six days before, led a predawn similar type of flight at low altitude, out of sight of land and so forth, into the Shortland Island seaplane base.* He shot up the float planes on the water, and at the time Barber was on his wing. They also encountered a good sized ship in the area of the seaplane base. It just happened to be an unfortunate ship. It was right there, near the

---

Ed. note: The mission occurred on 29 March 1943.

seaplanes. So they strafed the hell out of this ship and sunk it. It was later found from a photographic reconnaissance plane that just happened to come by and took pictures, a B-24 photoplane—the navy had some of those—that it was a destroyer. And that was rather an unusual occurrence. The crew was jumping over the side, the ship was afire, and it just went down right there.

Hall: It was a powerful airplane.

Condon: Yes, and it was a powerful performance! So Admiral Mitscher was well aware of one Capt. Thomas G. Lanphier and Lt. Rex T. Barber. Barber, I think, left part of his wing on the stack of that destroyer. Now that's the kind of aggressive performance we were getting out of the P-38s at the time of the Yamamoto mission.

Hall: On the 16th, on Friday, the decision was made that you would use P-38s and that you would bring these people in. How did the planning then fold into the events of the 17th, when John Mitchell and others came over.

Condon: The one thing on the 16th, it was P-38s that we needed, and additional long-range tanks, extra drop tanks, to make that long, low-altitude mission. That was part of the discussion. It was to be out of sight of land, down on the deck, which was a hell of a long way to go, at one hundred feet max over the water. That's about close to a two-hour flight without ever getting above a hundred feet. That was rather unusual. They should have had terrain-following gear or something, but we didn't have that then! On that mission, I guess it would have had to be "wave-following gear."

Hall: So you were saying the decision was made right there?

Condon: Right there by Admiral Mitscher, on the recommendation of Colonel Pugh, that Lanphier and his flight, particularly, be held over and should be the ones to be the hit element. The hit element was for the initial attack on the bombers with a higher cover element to protect them. There is some argument about that, who made that decision. I can tell you who made that decision: Admiral Mitscher.

Hall: Now, this was on the 16th still.

Condon: Yes, this was on the 16th. And on the 17th then, in his meeting, secrecy was stressed by Admiral Mitscher because of the need to protect communications intercept ops which gave us Yamamoto's schedule. After the 16th, all we could do for the next twenty-four hours, approximately, was just keep thinking about the other things that had to be incorporated in the mission plan to enhance its chances for success. There wasn't any way we could talk to the pilots who were going to do the job before we identified all the mission elements, until the 17th. Well, on the 17th they came over late in the afternoon, as best I can recall, because time was moving on toward nightfall. We did send a message on the 16th to the Air Forces Command in the Southwest Pacific, General Kenney's Fifth Air Force, asking for those fuel tanks, to please have them over on Guadalcanal by the 17th. That was done on the 16th, and they got there on time. The crew that prepared those airplanes, checked them, and installed the tanks and a few other things that night of the 17th, turned in a truly superior performance which was an important part of the mission success. Only two of the eighteen planes went out of commission, one with a blown tire, the other one with no feed from the drop tanks. They both were off the mission, of course, and the two spares then joined Lanphier's flight as briefed.

Hall: On the 17th then, Mitchell arrived, Kittel arrived . . .

Condon: I'm not sure what day Mitchell and all his pilots came. It was either late the 16th or on the 17th. I'm not clear when Kittel arrived exactly. I know he came with Mitchell as a part of the 339th Fighter Squadron.

Hall: So they arrived to replace Barber and Lanphier and others, a day or so before?

Condon: It was about a day overlap. That's what they normally had.

Hall: Then they were called over to Fighter One?

Condon: No. They were called over to Admiral Mitscher's headquarters. Mitchell and Lanphier and Henry Viccellio came to the meeting, and that was all. I don't remember Lou Kittel being there.

Hall: Well no, I think Kittel argued about getting some of his men in on the mission later. But Henry Viccellio, what was his position?

Condon: He was the senior air corps officer from the XIII Fighter

Command, and head of the Air Corps Detachment. He was commanding officer of the 70th Fighter Squadron during most of 1942 and had trained Lanphier, Barber, etc., in P-39s.

Hall: So Viccellio was the senior air corps person in charge on the island?

Condon: Yes, of the air corps fighters attached to The Fighter Command. He was the former commander of the 70th Squadron that was just being relieved, at the time of the mission,* to go to the rear area. Vic, that's what we called him, was the head man of the air corps at Fighter Two. They always kept someone like that in charge. For instance, when I first got there it was Col. Kermit Tyler, who was at Pearl Harbor, a wonderful guy. When the radar operator at Pearl Harbor said, "Lieutenant, there's a big flight coming in here, I don't know what it is, but you better take a look at this." He did take a look at it, and he said: "Those are carrier planes coming back in." That was Pearl Harbor! He got pretty famous for that. But that was unjust, he was a P-40 pilot and a damn good one. A very reliable guy, and we liked him in every sense. The other one that I can remember is Aaron Tyre, "Pete" Tyre. He was there after Vic Viccellio left. Pete was later, unfortunately, killed in a P-80 accident during the Korean War.

Hall: Let us return to the meetings then on the afternoon of 17 April. Lanphier, Mitchell, and Viccellio came over and Admiral Mitscher advised them of the mission?

Condon: Yes. He, the admiral, asked us to hand them the Yamamoto schedule, and they looked at it and saw it and saw that you could tell where he was going to be by the minute. It was secret, mentioned no name, but they knew who it was. We all did. No question about that, we all did. I'm afraid the whole bloody island eventually knew who it was sooner or later, later mostly. Anyway, then the admiral said we wanted to try with the P-38s to make that intercept.

Ed. note: Major Viccellio served as commander of the 70th Fighter Squadron between December 1941 and October 1942. Promoted to lieutenant colonel in March 1943, he was at the time of the Yamamoto mission the executive officer and A-3 (Operations) of XIII Fighter Command on Guadalcanal.

Hall: You'd already established that they should fly at low altitude?

Condon: Those parameters of the mission were already set, including the need for radio silence, the need to avoid any possible detection from observers on islands, either visually or by radar. These requirements were now mentioned, and then, based on the intercept schedule, the discussion [on 17 April] went into where the highest probability of success would be achieved. When he was landing at Ballale, with all its AAA? When he was in the boat enroute to the seaplane base? The naval officers thought that they could hit that boat on the way to Shortland and that would be a good place to get him for sure.

Hall: Rather like that destroyer incident.

Condon: Right. Especially in view of that. And they also felt that the time it would take to go from Ballale over to the seaplane base on Shortland would allow for some flexibility. In other words, if you were two minutes late making the air intercept, you weren't going to see him, he would be gone. But with that boat going at the most ten or fifteen knots, you had a hell of a lot more leeway during a fifteen-minute trip in a boat. So, these things we all discussed. Finally, Admiral Mitscher said, as John Mitchell has observed in a couple of statements, "Wait a minute, I think we have discussed all these alternatives long enough, and we'll leave that to Major Mitchell. He's going to make the flight. He should make the choice." So John Mitchell said, "I like the air intercept because, although the probabilities might be fairly low at that distance, and so forth, if it's made, it's a sure thing. I mean, if we shoot that plane down, nobody is going to survive."

Hall: You can't jump into the water.

Condon: No, you can't. If that plane blows up and goes into the jungle, it's gone. So that was that and it was settled. Then, there were a few other things as I mentioned, the need for radio silence, etc.

Hall: So Mitchell then left with his charge, returned to the squadron, and apparently after, as he has said, some near fistfights, selected a crew.

Condon: [Laughs] Well, that I know nothing about.

Hall: He has related some of these things. And then he charted out the times and so forth over the course legs and . . .

Condon: Well, that's his version. I'm sure that forty-six-year-old memory circuitry changes just like everybody else's with respect to this mission. The way I remember it is, when we were finished with Admiral Mitscher, Colonel Pugh, myself, John Mitchell, Tom Lanphier, and Viccellio got together at Fighter Command headquarters. I think a couple of intelligence officers, I know a couple of ours from The Fighter Command were present. It wasn't Joe McGuigan, because I knew him well and I remember him. It was someone from the Air Corps Fighter Two detachment. Anyway, we went back to The Fighter Command headquarters dugout at Fighter One. We had a table there with a chart of the area, and we went over the parameters of the mission as laid down by the admiral: no closer than twenty miles to any land until Bougainville, and the need for precisely maintaining the courses, speeds, times, and legs that were prescribed, because otherwise there would be no intercept.

Hall: The timing would be crucial.

Condon: Absolutely. It was a marvel of performance on Mitchell's part.

Hall: As a matter of fact, the Japanese pilot in his interview mentioned that they were descending, and the airport was in sight.

Condon: There was one other thing before we left, I don't remember if that was in Admiral Mitscher's place or over at Fighter One. Mitchell said, "Well, we ought to back everything up so that the intercept, if it happens, will take place about right here." Now that was just south of Empress Augusta Bay. I don't know, twenty or thirty miles, maybe forty miles away from Kahili airdrome. That was the spot. And, that's where the 38s later looked up—and there they were!

Hall: After Admiral Mitscher allowed Mitchell to choose the option, everybody adjourned and went over from his hut to Fighter One and the three or four of you worked this out in detail?

Condon: No. Then we reviewed all the mission specifications laid down by the admiral. All the low altitudes, the why and the needs. Not the speeds over courses yet; we had not yet worked out the intercept. We didn't even know the spot that Mitchell felt was desirable forty miles northwest of Kahili. That spot determined what the courses and speeds would be. We knew the speed that the P-38 could comfortably maintain, but the other details had not been worked out at that point. Then, having reviewed all of that and gotten as much settled as we could with the guys that were going to do it, they went back to Fighter Two and set everything in motion.

By that time it was late in the afternoon on the 17th, and I sat down at that same table and plotted with parallel rules and so forth, the true courses and true air speeds that had to be maintained to work the intercept selected, all based on Yamamoto's schedule. I had to make it come up to Mitchell's intercept point, so that's where the Japanese would be when the P-38s got there. We had to make some assumptions, and an important one involved the Japanese penchant for precise performance, punctuality, etc., and that wasn't a bad assumption—especially for a VIP like the chief of the Imperial Japanese Navy. They were not going to be one second off the timed schedule. And furthermore, I felt that they would do the same with the airplanes. We thought the bomber, there was only going to be one, and six fighters escorting him, would be all shined up and waxed up and everything, and so I even added five knots to what we normally gave them as a cruising speed. Right here I would like to point out that we measured everything in nautical miles and the speeds in knots. That's the way the navy and marines operated then and do to this day.

Hall: So, when you say indicated airspeed of 350, you're talking knots, not miles per hour.

Condon: That's right. We're talking knots, but it usually says on any plot what it is. If it's distance, it usually has a little "nm." The air corps at that time used statute miles and miles per hour. For mission planning, we used true headings. Of course, you have then to apply the variation for that region to get the magnetic heading—and then you have to apply the deviation to get the compass heading. So, if you just plot something and say 162 degrees, without a "t," an "m" or a "c," I don't know how you know where the hell you are. And if it is as precise as Admiral Mitscher wanted this one opportunity in a lifetime to be, everything had to be in order so that it could be converted by the flight leader to whatever the hell he wanted—statute miles, miles per hour, or whatever.

Hall: So, you worked it out over the course with all these things cranked into it. But in knots, in nautical miles, and the rest.

Condon: It was true headings, and times on the legs, knowing the true airspeed of the P-38. Now, what the indicated airspeed was, and certainly what the ground speed was, I knew only within a percentage point or two.

Hall: So, you turned that data over to Mitchell?

Condon: Yes. But first we checked it umpteen times within our own Fighter Command headquarters. Colonel Pugh and a couple of other officers who worked there had worked it out the same way, and everything checked out. Then we put it in pilot kneepad format: For the first leg, such and such a course, true, and for such and such a time; second leg, turn to such and such a course, true, for such and such a time, etc. Then we sent it over to Fighter Two. We couldn't do that for eighteen or twenty-five pilots or whatever. We just gave it to them as: Here are the mission parameters as we would like to see it flown. And that's what was received over there at Fighter Two. We sent it over with a guy named Pete Lewis, a navy intelligence officer assigned to The Fighter Command.

Hall: You sent one master chart over?

Condon: The chart was just a little table of the legs and times on each leg. I don't think there was anything else on there, I couldn't imagine what it would be. But then they had to convert that data to compass headings to begin with, and add to, and be damn certain that, the airspeeds that they were flying gave the specified times on each leg. Then Mitchell had to make the judgment as to what the wind was doing to them. Because, you know, that intercept was damn near four hundred nautical miles away. Right down on the waves; if you hit a squall line it can up your wind by fifteen to twenty-five knots and change the direction by ninety degrees or more.

Hall: You had no milestones?

Condon: No. And if you lost two to three minutes, and you weren't there in those two to three minutes—right on the button—they're gone, gone by.

Hall: Some have referred to it as one shot in a million.

Condon: It was. That's all it was. It was just that the Luck of the Irish was with us, I'll tell you.

Hall: Okay. The mission transpired then on Sunday morning, 18 April 1943. Doubtless everyone watched the pilots take off and assemble. Would you describe the post-mission debriefing that occurred later that day in the afternoon and who participated in it?

Condon: As near as I can remember, they dribbled back. A couple of guys as I recall landed in the Russell Islands, refueled, and came on in later. But as near as I can remember Vic Viccellio, John Mitchell, Tom Lanphier, and Rex Barber were present, and maybe the one who was credited with Barber for the bomber that went in the water.

Hall: He was the guy that went into the Russells—Besby Holmes. So he was delayed, he was never debriefed.

Condon: No, I guess he wasn't there. But usually, the pattern of The Fighter Command debriefing, strictly for air corps missions, would involve a senior air corps leader and those who had extraordinary experiences to relate about the mission. It didn't include everyone on a mission.

Hall: So, Mitchell, Barber, and Lanphier were brought on over to Fighter One with Viccellio, and you were present?

Condon: I was present, Colonel Pugh was present, and a couple of our intelligence guys were also there.

Hall: Who is McGuigan?

Condon: Joe McGuigan. Lieutenant Joe McGuigan was a navy ACI [Air Combat Intelligence Officer] who was assigned to the air corps at Fighter Two. He was an outgoing, marvelous guy. I understand he is dead now. Everybody liked him very much. He was their navy liaison-type intelligence officer, assigned with the air corps intelligence officers.

Hall: It was he who ultimately signed the debriefing, he may have been the recorder or acted as a recorder. I think his name is on it, yes, here it is. [Peruses XIII Fighter Command debriefing report.]

Condon: And Morrison, probably, Morrison and McGuigan.

Hall: Who is Morrison?

Condon: Captain William Morrison was an air corps intelligence officer, as I remember.

Hall: He, Morrison, was present also?

Condon: He was present at The Fighter Command debriefing, I believe. But I don't remember McGuigan being there, but he might have been. There were maybe eight or ten people altogether.

Hall: To the best of your recollection, could you describe what the pilots said. Did Lanphier claim he had shot down Yamamoto?

Condon: I think what they claimed was, they thought they shot down three bombers—but there were only two as it turned out after the war. They knew that Yamamoto wasn't flying in one of the Zeros, so they were confident that they had performed the mission objective fully. In other words, they had killed Yamamoto. I don't think there was any question about that. I didn't hear anybody say "Hey, I shot down Yamamoto," or anything like that. One thing, Lanphier, and I'm sure it was Lanphier, because we knew him well from other missions, relayed through to "Recon," which was their home base, to tell us—this was when he was within radio range—to tell us that "that son-of-a-bitch would not be dictating any peace terms in the White House."

Hall: So he broke radio silence?

Condon: Oh, it wasn't radio silence. That was on the way home.

Hall: They weren't briefed to maintain radio silence on the way home?

Condon: Coming back didn't matter.

Hall: Okay.

Condon: They could use the radio normally. Also, a couple of them came in and did rolls over the field.

Hall: To your recollection, Lanphier, Mitchell, and Barber recounted essentially what they saw and did?

Condon: That's all, yes. And just about the way you read it in the report. Lanphier said he had that beam shot, and saw the thing go into the jungle, and the wing came off just before it struck.

Hall: And Barber thought that a tail had fallen off?

Condon: He thought a piece of the tail had fallen off the one he hit; there is some dispute about that, I gather.

Hall: Well, apparently it was pieces of the tail that flew off when the cannon fire went in there, but not the whole tail, apparently . . .

Condon: No, the whole rear-end didn't.

Hall: In the middle of a firefight, it is not always easy to . . .

Condon: He said, something I read later, that a sizable portion of the vertical fin came off . . .

Hall: Now this is Barber?

Condon: Yes, that a sizable piece had flown off. Now the vertical fin on the Betty is a very prominent feature of the aircraft. It sticks up. If a "sizable portion" of that went off, and you found later that the fin was essentially intact, that would be an inconsistency. And I noted that. Now whether he later said, "Well, I didn't mean a sizable piece, I just meant a little piece," I don't know. I don't want to say anything about Rex Barber, or offer any reflection of what he said, because I don't want to get into that. I wasn't on the mission. The wing, regardless of whether it was the right or left, that came off just before it hit the ground, according to Lanphier, was apparently moved afterward by the people who decided to keep the wreckage as a shrine to Yamamoto and as a tourist attraction.

Hall: Yes, I've heard that.

Condon: And they brought it up and put it by the airplane. But anyway, I also heard that one Japanese came there with an idea of taking a wing—I never did decide which wing he was talking about—and he had it down to the landing and was hoisting it aboard a ship to take it back to Japan when they caught him.

Hall: Well, indeed, people have been cutting up and carrying away pieces of that wreckage for years.

Condon: I don't think the Japs are any different—excuse me, I'm not supposed to use that term—that the Japanese aren't any different from us. In the war zone, if pieces of a Japanese aircraft fell anywhere near American troops, immediately they were over there sawing and tearing metal to make souvenir watchbands, and all that sort of thing.

Hall: At the conclusion of the debriefing then, looking back at this, was there any discussion of who would prepare the record report of the mission results? Did everybody just leave? What do you recall?

Condon: The debriefing?

Hall: Yes.

Condon: They reported just the things we know from their statements. What happened, what they saw and did on the mission. That was all. That was sent in and was put in the COMAIRSOL's summary: who shot down so many bombers, so many fighters. Well, it turned out to be two bombers instead of three.

Hall: But my point is, at the end of the debriefing, presumably the mission participants left. Who sat down and typed it up, was it Morrison?

Condon: Nobody in The Fighter Command. I don't remember anything like that. We didn't do it that way.

Hall: Well, we've got a report, you see, issued by XIII Fighter Command.

Condon: But that's a XIII Fighter Command detachment document. That came from Fighter Two as an air corps debriefing output. It must have been written right there at Fighter Two by Morrison and McGuigan, the two that signed it, I guess, and sent it to General Strother through XIII Fighter Command channels.

Hall: So, this wouldn't have necessarily been the same record that the navy prepared?

Condon: No. You see, what we got out of The Fighter Command debriefing of the principals on the mission, with Viccellio participating and so forth, we would then pick up the phone and call over to Admiral Mitscher's headquarters and say, "Here are the results: how many enemy shot down, how many losses, who was lost and who got hit." Then we would do a written summary of that in dispatch [TWX] form. But it wasn't a formal thing at all. Things were pretty informal, you understand.

Hall: So this [The XIII Fighter Command Mission Report] was prepared after the debriefing over at Fighter Two.

Condon: This was prepared by the air corps and, even though McGuigan happened to be a naval officer, he was as much an air corps officer as Viccellio was. He was very loyal to everything over at the Fighter Two Air Corps detachment.

Hall: But the contents of this XIII Fighter Command debriefing report coincide with your recollection of what was said at the debriefing?

Condon: This? [Examines the report].

Hall: Yes.

Condon: I don't see anything particularly different about this report from what was said orally after the mission when they came over to Fighter Command.

Hall: This was obviously typed up later.

Condon: Oh sure. They always were. They couldn't type them up at the moment. We didn't have court reporters!

Hall: Well, there has been some argument apparently, among participants, that perhaps this [debriefing report] was "cooked" after the fact.

Condon: That makes me ill, frankly. To think that about any of the men involved! It doesn't matter to me one damn bit what somebody thinks today about Tom Lanphier. Nobody thought that about him then, to my knowledge. It was evident on Guadalcanal that he was a full-time colleague and fellow fighter pilot, and a respected one. I must say that his former buddies ought to keep that in mind. They flew with Lanphier on many missions. Forty-six years later they're implying, almost, that something crooked was going on there. I don't like that at all, because I had every bit of respect for Tom Lanphier and so did everyone else I knew who also knew him—army, air corps, navy, and marine.

Hall: Was it obvious to you that neither Lanphier nor Barber had really seen what the other claimed to have accomplished?

Condon: Except for their statements, I couldn't make a comment on nor evaluate that right now. They were enthusiastic, and they were all agreed. Let me put it this way: The kind of controversy and difference of opinion and evaluation of the mission that exists today was not in any way evident at the mission debriefing. Not one dissent was expressed.

Hall: From Mitchell, from Barber?

Condon: From Mitchell, from Barber, from Lanphier, Viccellio. Nothing. And nobody made any claims about individuals. The only "claims" were those that are recorded—the bombers, and two or more fighters.

Hall: Would you care to offer any other observations of your own, what you believe actually transpired, for example?

Condon: As far as who did what to whom on that mission, I just don't have any observations to offer. I think it is pretty poor form for someone who was not even on the mission to be making any comments in that regard. Fighter pilots are fighter pilots regardless of what the hell service they come from. Things happen very fast, you know, and for someone who wasn't even there, you can't be sure you're following it exactly as it happened. And for someone who wasn't even born at that time to offer observations, I know damn well he doesn't know what was going on.

Hall: I want to thank you very much; I appreciate your time.

This interview of Hiroshi Hayashi was conducted by Jay. E. Hines on 22 June 1990 in Yakushima, Japan. Mr. Hisashi Takahashi acted as translator for Mr. Hayashi. All of Mr. Hayashi's answers and any questions addressed to him by Mr. Takahashi have been translated here by Noriko Iwai.

Takahashi: Shall we begin?

Hayashi: Yes.

Takahashi: Question 1: To begin, would you please give me your full name, rank, branch of military service, and unit of assignment on 18 April 1943?

Hayashi: My name is Hiroshi Hayashi. At that time I was a flight petty officer second class in the Japanese Navy, assigned to the 705th Air Squadron.

Takahashi: This questionnaire asks about your military career. Let us proceed with the questionnaire. The second question is: What combat experience did you possess at that time?

Hayashi: Do you mean after I joined the navy?

Takahashi [to Hines]: This second question concerns his military career. The meaning of this question is that Cargill Hall wants to know his military background, right? Right from the beginning?

Hines: Up until the Yamamoto mission.

Takahashi: He [Hayashi] is wondering if he should start from the first time he joined the navy maybe? [To Hayashi] Please explain from the beginning.

Hayashi: You mean when I joined the navy?

Takahashi: Yes, and your war experiences.

Hayashi: I joined at the Sasebo Naval Barracks as a volunteer on 1 June 1939.

Takahashi [to Hines]: His first assignment was to Sasebo, a large training school which was called Sasebo Kaihei Dan. [Hayashi continues.] He received three months of training at Sasebo in communications and signals. After training at Sasebo, he went to the navigation school in Yokosuka. After spending six months training there, he graduated in March 1940 and was assigned to a torpedo boat named *Tomozuru*. His mission was to inspect Chinese junks around Tsingtao. He spent about three months there, in China. He was then assigned to the cruiser *Nachi*. He was asked by his superior, a navigation officer who later died in the Pearl Harbor attack, "Why don't you try to take the test as a pilot?" He had never thought about becoming a pilot before, but at his superior's insistence, in 1940 he decided to try it. Being a pilot was more attractive than being a regular sailor.

Hayashi: I took the test to be a pilot, which was only for flying. I passed the exam and was sent to Tsuchiura.

Takahashi [to Hines]: He was sent to Tsuchiura to be trained as a pilot, for basic ground training.

Hines: To where?

Takahashi: Tsuchiura in Ibaragi. Tsuchiura had a flight school.

Hines: On Honshu?

Takahashi: Yes. [*Note:* Ibaragi Prefecture is just north of Tokyo on the east coast of Japan.]

Hayashi: After training at the school, I became a student pilot in the Kasumigaura Air Squadron.

Takahashi: He was in Class 18. [To Hayashi] Was that Showa 18 [1943, the eighteenth year of the Showa Era (1926-1989)]?

Hayashi: No. It was the eighteenth class.

Takahashi: Then where did you go?

[Hayashi replies.]

Takahashi: It took him six months to finish the pilot training school at Tsuchiura. He then went to an air base at Oita in Kyushu. There he trained to become a bomber pilot for the Type 96 attack plane. [Hayashi continues.] Then he went to Xinzhu on Taiwan, where he took multi-engine training. This was at the beginning of 1942. The war had already started. He was sent to Rabaul around May 1942. He spent two years in Rabaul, staying there until August 1944.

Hines: After the Yamamoto mission?

Takahashi [to Hayashi]: Did you stay in Rabaul after Admiral Yamamoto was shot down?

Hayashi: Yes, I stayed in Rabaul.

Takahashi: Then what did you do?

[Hayashi replies.]

Takahashi: He was heavily involved in fighting in the Solomon Islands, while stationed in Rabaul, and in attack missions against Guadalcanal and Port Moresby. He was also involved in reconnaissance flights.

Hayashi: Almost all my combat experience was in the Solomon Islands.

Takahashi: What happened after August 1944?

Hayashi: I went back to Japan in 1944. By then, our squadron was only one-third of its former size. Then I was sent to the Matsushima Air Squadron near Sendai.

Takahashi: His new mission was as an instructor at the flight school.

[Hayashi speaks.]

Takahashi: He taught college graduates there. [Hayashi continues.] This was around October 1944. He did not like the cold. He hated cold weather. He needed more than three blankets to keep warm. He asked his superior to be sent back to the battlefield because he couldn't bear the cold, but his superior scolded him for this. Then he was sent to Kanoya in Kagoshima, Kyushu. Kanoya was one of the bases for Kamikaze pilots. The Okinawa campaign was about to start. His plane crashed and his face was injured very badly. [To Hayashi] Did you fly Zeros?

Hayashi: No, I flew Betty bombers. My mission was to spot the location of the enemy and lead attack planes to the enemy forces. The Betty bombers were called "one-shot lighters" because they went up like a torch.

Takahashi: They were dangerous, weren't they?

[Hayashi responds.]

Takahashi: He also had a plane crash at that time, when Tokyo suffered its biggest air raid by B-29s on 9 March 1945.

Hines: Did he get injured in the air raid?

[Hayashi replies.]

Takahashi: No. He also didn't get injured at the time of the Yamamoto mission. He only got cut at that time. [To Hayashi] Then you weren't injured at all, were you?

Hayashi: No.

Takahashi: He was unharmed. [To Hayashi] To get back to Question 2: You didn't have any combat experience, then, did you?

Hayashi: Yes I did.

Takahashi: How about air battles?

Hayashi: The Battle of the Solomon Sea.

Takahashi: All in Betty bombers?

Hayashi: Yes.

Takahashi: Did you ever shoot down an enemy airplane?

Hayashi: No, that was not my duty.

Takahashi: He mainly dropped bombs and torpedoes. [To Hayashi] Did you ever take part in air combat?

Hayashi: Yes I did. Since my comrades were involved, I was involved, too.

Takahashi: His plane was involved in dogfighting, but since he was the pilot, he was not able to see everything that happened. He had gunners on board shooting at the enemy fighters. As the pilot, he just carried out the mission of bombing. [To Hayashi] Then question number 3: How were you and your comrades selected for the Yamamoto mission (volunteered or detailed)?

[Hayashi speaks.]

Takahashi: It was a direct order from above. For security reasons, the order was given after the lights were turned off after 9 o'clock at night.

[Hayashi speaks.]

Takahashi: The order was transmitted after the lights were turned off.

Hines: How was the order transmitted?

[Hayashi speaks.]

Takahashi: When he was asleep, he was awakened and given the order verbally. He received very detailed instructions for the mission next day, for the Yamamoto mission.

Hines: The question of volunteering never entered anyone's mind?

Takahashi: No. [To Hayashi] Question 4: Did both of the bombers that transported Admiral Yamamoto and his staff come from the airfield at Rabaul, or from another airfield?

[Hayashi replies.]

Takahashi: Usually the home base for the Betty bombers was the west airfield at Rabaul, but for this particular mission they flew them to and left from the east airfield, where the fighters stayed. On this mission, Yamamoto was to get on the airplane at the east airfield. So Mr. Hayashi moved from the west airfield to the east airfield to pick up Yamamoto. That's how this trip started.

Takahashi [to Hayashi]: Then question number 5: Were these bombers ordinary military aircraft, or of a special design?

Hayashi: They were "one-shot lighters," standard Betty bombers used for attack, nothing special.

Takahashi: Okay, then question 6: Were both bombers fully armed, that is, carrying guns and gunners?

[Hayashi speaks.]

Takahashi: That proved to be a problem. The airplane was fully armed; however, it did not carry extra ammunition. Before the mission, they were told to unload the extra ammunition. Usually they carried extra ammunition in a box for each gun. The Betty bomber had 13-millimeter guns—three of them—and one 20-millimeter gun. But because of the weight of the boxes, the squadron leader ordered only one belt for each machine gun. His bomber had a normal crew, including gunners. At the time of the battle, four people were engaged in shooting at the enemy. Also, Buin was the destination, and because they held air superiority there, they did not expect on this transport mission that they would be attacked by the enemy at all. [To Hayashi] How about question number 7: What did your preflight briefing say about the nearest American units and your likelihood of encountering them?

[Hayashi speaks.]

Takahashi: Nothing at all. There was no information given to him or to his colleagues about the position of the enemy or about the possibility of meeting the enemy during the flight.

Takahashi [to Hayashi]: Then question number 8: Thinking back to 18 April 1943, to the best of your recollection, tell me about the mission events prior to the encounter with the American P-38s, that is, your launch time and destination, weather along the way, navigation checkpoints, radio contacts between the bombers, etcetera?

[Hayashi speaks.]

Takahashi: His plane and Yamamoto's plane took off at either 6 or 7 o'clock in the morning, on the hour. The destination was Buin. The weather was clear. What he did was simply follow the first bomber which carried Yamamoto.

Hines: He was the wingman?

Takahashi: Right. So he didn't have to worry about the navigation. All he had to do was to follow the first bomber. Okay? [To Hayashi] How about communication with the first bomber?

[Hayashi speaks.]

Takahashi: What he did was just keep an eye on the first bomber. The communication was handled by the captain of the bomber. [To Hayashi] Were you co-pilot?

[Hayashi speaks.]

Takahashi: No, he was the command pilot. There was only one pilot in the airplane. There was a Mr. Taniguchi, flight petty officer second class—he was several years senior to him—who served as the navigator and the navigator was responsible for communications. In Japanese it is termed "kichoo." Just like a captain.

But he was not the pilot. Mr. Hayashi was the pilot. The captain was in charge of communications, so Mr. Hayashi has no knowledge whatsoever about what kind of communication was conducted between the navigators of the two bombers.

[Hayashi speaks.]

Takahashi: As a pilot, he flew as the wingman, carrying out formation flying.

[Hayashi speaks.]

Takahashi: Admiral Ugaki, who was Yamamoto's chief of staff, was his passenger sitting behind him, so he had to really act like a perfect soldier and a perfect pilot. [To Hayashi] Question number 9: The original flight plans intercepted by the Americans called for Admiral Yamamoto to land on the island of Ballale. Was this destination later changed, with the landing rescheduled at Buin on the island of Bougainville?

[Hayashi speaks.]

Takahashi: What he was told on the previous night was that his destination was Buin, not Ballale.

[Hayashi speaks.]

Takahashi: From the beginning, the destination was Buin. Okay? Any additional questions?

Hines: The question presumes that the first American radio interception of the destination identified Ballale. Obviously, that was changed before Hayashi-san was informed of the mission, so he has no knowledge of the change.

Takahashi: He has no knowledge. He doesn't know. He was told that the destination was Buin, not Ballale.

Hines: It was changed before he flew the mission?

Takahashi: He doesn't know. He doesn't know anything about it. He has no knowledge whatsoever about the change of the mission destination. His mission to the best of his mind was always to land at Buin. [To Hayashi] Question number 10: Did Japanese military forces on Bougainville in 1943 have two military airfields at the southern end of the island, Kahili on the coast, and Buin, about five or ten kilometers inland?

[Hayashi speaks.]

Takahashi: He had never landed at Buin, and that concerned him.

[Hayashi speaks.]

Takahashi: He knew the name of Buin, although he had never landed there. His military mission was usually attack bombing of Guadalcanal.

[Hayashi speaks.]

Takahashi: Buin was probably the southernmost air base of all the naval air bases. [To Hayashi] Question number 11: Were the six Zero fighters that flew cover on this mission equipped with radios that could communicate with your bomber, or had the fighter pilots removed them?

[Hayashi speaks.]

Takahashi: He has no knowledge about communications—whether or not the Zeros were able to communicate with the Betty bombers. [To Hayashi] Question number 12: What first made you aware of the American attack?

[Hayashi speaks.]

Takahashi: One of the Zero fighters flew forward just in front of the first Betty bomber and made movements.

[Hayashi speaks.]

Takahashi: But at that moment he didn't have any knowledge whatsoever about the approaching attack by the Americans.

Hines: But then he knew something was wrong?

Takahashi: He knew something unusual had happened.

[Hayashi speaks.]

Takahashi: When the Zero flew forward, that is how he noticed that something was going on.

Hines: Rather than use a radio if they had one—perhaps the Zeros did not have a radio—the way they chose to communicate with Yamamoto's airplane was through visual contact.

[Takahashi explains Hines' idea to Mr. Hayashi. Hayashi replies.]

Takahashi: He agrees with you on this hypothesis.

Hines: Otherwise, they would have used the radio. Security would have been irrelevant at that point.

Takahashi: That's right. You've made a good point. [To Hayashi] Question number 13: To the best of your recollection, describe the engagement and your role in it, from the moment the attack began until your bomber crashed.

[Hayashi speaks.]

Takahashi: The first Betty bomber dove down very sharply, about 60 degrees, at high speed. [Hayashi continues.] He followed the first bomber in order not to break formation, but overspeeded, and the radio antenna mast started to flutter.

Takahashi: In the front, was this antenna coming loose?

[Hayashi answers.]

Takahashi: Then the whole body of the bomber started to vibrate; he thought a bolt or fastener must have come loose.

[Hayashi speaks.]

Takahashi: At that time he still did not know that the enemy was approaching.

Hines: He was just being a good wingman, following Yamamoto's airplane.

Takahashi: He just followed. The navigator did not tell him that the enemy was going to attack them.

Hines: No radio transmissions?

Takahashi: No. The first bomber knew that it was being attacked, so it tried to escape.

[Hayashi speaks.]

Takahashi: He wanted to stop the flutter and vibration.

[Hayashi speaks.]

Takahashi: So he throttled back, slowed down, and his plane rapidly fell behind the first bomber.

Hines: To keep the airplane from breaking up?

Takahashi: Right.

[Hayashi speaks.]

Takahashi: Then he saw bullets passing over his head. This is a special bullet which makes a light.

Hines: Tracers.

Takahashi: Right. That's the word.

[Hayashi speaks.]

Takahashi: But these bullets—tracers—did not hit his plane, and were directed at the lead bomber. The P-38 flew over him. He was lucky.

[Hayashi speaks.]

Takahashi: Then the navigator—the captain—shouted: "Oh, the enemy is attacking us!"

[Hayashi speaks.]

Takahashi: Admiral Ugaki was sound asleep taking a nap. He had no knowledge whatsoever that he was under attack. Then he woke up.

[Hayashi speaks.]

Takahashi: Ugaki was seated just behind Hayashi; the captain—the navigator—was standing beside him [Ugaki].

Hines: The captain was the airplane commander; Hayashi-san was the pilot; and the admiral was the ranking officer on the plane?

Takahashi: That's right, the highest-ranking officer. Admiral Ugaki was the chief of staff of Yamamoto. Then Ugaki shouted, "What happened to Admiral Yamamoto's plane?"

[Hayashi speaks.]

Takahashi: The navigator pointed forward to the left, and Ugaki spotted Yamamoto's plane. [Hayashi continues.] The P-38s never attacked his plane—never challenged him. All of the P-38s were concentrating their attacks on Yamamoto's plane. [Speaks to Hayashi] Maybe they knew Yamamoto was in the first plane. Did you think that they knew that?

[Hayashi speaks.]

Takahashi: He was surprised; all the P-38s were attacking Yamamoto's plane. And I asked Mr. Hayashi whether or not he realized that the enemy knew that Yamamoto was on the first plane. It was not on his mind. He was trying his best to escape. He did not have such a realization.

Hines: Did he receive any orders from the admiral or the captain?

[Hayashi speaks.]

Takahashi: Ugaki issued an order telling Mr. Hayashi to follow the first Betty bomber, to follow Admiral Yamamoto's plane.

Hines: Even though it was being attacked?

[Takahashi speaks to Hayashi. Hayashi replies.]

Takahashi: Even though he tried to follow the first bomber, Yamamoto's plane, he noticed and was surprised that no P-38s were trying to attack his plane.

Hines: Was it possible that the P-38s did not see his plane?

[Takahashi asks Hayashi and Hayashi replies.]

Takahashi: He doesn't think so. He was following Yamamoto's plane all the way through. He was really flying very low—at the lowest altitude over the jungle.

Hines: The P-38s must have known Yamamoto was in the first plane.

[Hayashi speaks.]

Takahashi: Since he was flying at the lowest altitude, it is very unlikely that the P-38s did not notice his bomber.

[Hayashi speaks.]

Takahashi: He caught up with and followed Yamamoto's plane as closely as possible. [Hayashi continues.] And now he saw fire coming out from the two engines. He felt it was a long time that he followed, but it wouldn't have been too long. Then Yamamoto's plane dived into the jungle. He didn't have to commit suicide, right? It was Japanese territory, so he could have escaped. The reason why it dived that way in a very sharp angle was because he thinks the pilot was killed or the control cables sheared. Either the pilot was killed or injured or the mechanical instruments were shot away. After seeing Yamamoto's plane dive into the jungle . . . He could spot the Buin airfield from above. He knew that it wouldn't take many minutes to reach it—it was only a matter of a few minutes to get there. After seeing that Yamamoto's plane had crashed, he decided not to go inland because he might be attacked, but instead fly on to the ocean to escape.

Hines: This was Hayashi's decision?

[Hayashi speaks.]

Takahashi: That was his own judgment as command pilot. [To Hayashi] Did Ugaki say anything?

[Hayashi replies.]

Takahashi: Ugaki did not say anything. [To Hayashi] Then what happened next?

[Hayashi speaks.]

Takahashi: He brought his plane down flying very low just close to the waves of the ocean, just above the water. [Hayashi continues.] Then he felt a shock, a movement of the lever—his control stick.

Then he hit the water. If he had been flying higher, most likely his plane would have crashed and nobody would have survived. Simply because he chose to fly very low, at the lowest altitude, in a good angle, he could survive.

Hines: Then why did the plane crash? Did it lose power?

[Hayashi speaks.]

Takahashi: The reason why he felt a shocking movement in the control lever was the flap at the tail of the plane . . . what do you call that?

Hines: The elevator.

Takahashi: He knew instantly that that had been attacked. [To Hayashi] Finally, was your plane attacked by a P-38?

Hayashi: Yes.

Hines: It was damaged by gunfire from the P-38s. So it crashed from combat damage. Since he was close to the water, it was not a serious crash.

Takahashi: That's right. That's his point.

Hines: But he said earlier that he was not attacked by the P-38s.

[Takahashi speaks to Hayashi and Hayashi replies.]

Takahashi: Probably after the crash of Yamamoto's plane, the P-38s came to attack *his* plane, but he does not think he was attacked earlier. Any further questions about this? [To Hayashi] Then let's move to question number 14: How many P-38 aircraft first attacked the bombers—only one or more than one?

[Hayashi speaks.]

Takahashi: More than one. He is not sure about the number of P-38s.

Hines: How many approximately?

[Hayashi speaks.]

Takahashi: He counted as many as eight. [To Hines] How many were there?

Hines: Sixteen.

Hayashi: Really? Then I counted only half.

Takahashi: He remembers that he counted up to eight. [To Hayashi] Question 15: In attempting to escape after the first attack, did you perform any special maneuvers? [To Hines] Question number 15 is irrelevant to Hayashi.

Hines: It's already been answered.

Takahashi: Then let's move on to question 16: After you reached the Bougainville coast and proceeded southward along it towards Shortland Island, did you look inland and see Admiral Yamamoto's bomber above the jungle, still flying?

[Hayashi speaks.]

Takahashi: He just followed all the way, as he said before. Question number 16 is very much irrelevant. He has already explained how he tried to keep up with the first bomber—Yamamoto's bomber.

Hines: Part of the controversy hinges on Yamamoto's plane flying a long time and then being attacked by two different aviators.

Takahashi [to Hayashi]: How about Question 17: Did you see the admiral's bomber crash?

Hayashi: Yes I did. I saw it crash into the jungle.

Takahashi: Question number 18: Did you see any P-38s attack the admiral's bomber again, just before it crashed in the jungle?

Hayashi: Yes, I saw a couple of P-38s attack.

Takahashi: How many do you think?

[Hayashi replies.]

Takahashi: He remembers just before Yamamoto's plane crashed, that it was attacked by two P-38s. Two.

[Hayashi speaks.]

Takahashi: From behind?

[Hayashi speaks.]

Takahashi: He saw Yamamoto's plane attacked twice. [Speaks to Hayashi] Do you remember the difference between the first and second attack? For example, did the first come as a single aircraft?

[Hayashi speaks.]

Takahashi: The first attack was by one P-38. The second attack was when he saw Yamamoto's plane flying and another P-38 attacked his plane.

Hines: He saw two separate attacks on Yamamoto's aircraft from two different P-38s?

Takahashi: At different times.

Hines: Yes. And he saw Yamamoto's plane crash in the jungle?

Takahashi: Right. [To Hayashi] So, did you see that Yamamoto's plane was attacked twice with your own eyes?

Hayashi: Yes. It was just before his plane went down.

Takahashi: Okay. His argument goes this way: Yamamoto's plane was flying low and had lost speed. And he finally caught up with Yamamoto's bomber and followed it as closely as possible. At that time he saw the fire from the two engines. And then the final attack came. One attack was made by one P-38, and a few moments later a second attack was made by another P-38. [To Hayashi] Do you remember the direction of the P-38s?

[Hayashi speaks.]

Takahashi: The first attack was made from the right-hand side.

[Hayashi speaks.]

Takahashi: The second attack was from the left side.

[Hayashi speaks.]

Takahashi: In the meantime, Yamamoto's plane crashed. So his supposition was that these two fighters made the fatal blow to Yamamoto's plane.

Hines: Both of them?

[Takahashi asks Hayashi. Hayashi replies.]

Takahashi: He thinks that either one of them was responsible.

[Hayashi speaks.]

Takahashi: Oh. He thinks maybe the one which came from the left was responsible for the fatal blow. [To Hayashi] Do you have any reasons why you think that way?

[Hayashi speaks.]

Takahashi: It was only a matter of seconds after the second attack was made from the left side that the plane crashed. So he thinks that the one which made the attack from the left-hand side was responsible for . . .

Hines: He thinks that the one from the right-hand side missed?

[Takahashi asks Hayashi and Hayashi replies.]

Takahashi: He believes that the one from the right-hand side missed Yamamoto's plane. He believes that the one which came from the left either killed or wounded the pilot or destroyed the control system.

Hines: Approximately how much time was there between the first and the second attacks?

Takahashi: Good question.

[Hayashi speaks.]

Takahashi: One or two minutes interval. That's what he thinks. Any additional questions? [To Hayashi] Question 19: Please describe the final attack on your bomber. [To Hines] Hayashi has already answered this question. [To Hayashi] Let's move to question 20: During this attack, approximately how far above the water was your bomber flying? [To Hines] Hayashi already explained this to us as well as Question 21: "Did your bomber break apart or explode before it hit the water?" [To Hayashi] Question 22: Approximately how much time elapsed between the first American attack near Empress Augusta Bay and the crash of your bomber near Moila Point?

[Hayashi speaks.]

Takahashi: Three to five minutes.

Hines: That can be a long time in combat.

Takahashi: Question 23: Are there any observations of your own that you would care to offer?

[Hayashi speaks.]

Takahashi: After the war ended he heard a rumor that Yamamoto committed suicide. He could not believe such a stupid story. This argument said that Yamamoto wanted to commit suicide, so he let the Americans read the coded messages. He thought that was stupid.

Hines: After crashing in the ocean, was he the only survivor?

Takahashi: Admiral Ugaki survived. [Asks Hayashi] Only three survived from the crash: Mr. Hayashi, Admiral Ugaki, and the chief paymaster.

Hines: There were nine people on board?

Takahashi: We have a record somewhere, but he remembers there were seven men.

Hines: How were they rescued?

Takahashi: There's a good description of that in our official records. The army was responsible for rescue.

Hines: Was there any further attack on his plane by the P-38s after he crashed?

Takahashi: P-38s never attacked his plane after . . .

[Hayashi speaks.]

Takahashi: This is what happened: After the crash, he was out of his mind. His mind was a total blank. He was in shock. He felt that the P-38s were trying to hit them in the water because he heard the sound of bullets, but later he found out that these bullets did not come from the P-38s, but from the Japanese army. The Japanese army was there, and they shot at the plane thinking that his plane was the enemy, so Ugaki shouted at him, "Shout out and tell them that we are here." That's how they were rescued.

Hines: They were picked up by a boat?

Takahashi: Ugaki was carried away by army soldiers in a boat. Hayashi was able to swim to the shore.

[Hayashi speaks.]

Takahashi: The chief paymaster was adrift over a long distance, and when the boat went back to the crash site to find floating materials, they picked him up.

[End of Interview]

Appendixes:
Related Documents

Appendix A

XIII Fighter Command Debriefing

13th FIGHTER COMMAND DETACHMENT
APO #709

SUBJECT: Fighter Interception
TO: Commanding General, USAFISPA

1. **Date:** April 18, 1943.
   Time: Take-off 0725—Return 1140.
   Place: Kahili-Shortland Area.
2. **Weather:** Ceiling and Visibility Unlimited.
3. **Our Forces:** 16 P-38's.
   Enemy Forces: 3 Type 1 M/B "Betty" and 6 Type O SSF "Zeke".
4. **Our Losses:** 1 P-38.
   Enemy Losses: 3 Type 1 M/B "Betty" and 3 Type O SSF "Zeke".
5. **Target:** Special information was received, advising the command that an enemy bomber, with fighter escort, would proceed from Buka to the Kahili area on the morning of April 18th. Sixteen Lightnings were ordered to the point of interception to attack and destroy the bombers. Of these, four were designated to act as the attacking section, with the balance as their protective cover. Major Mitchell was named as the flight leader.
6. **Fighter Pilots:**
   a). Attacking Section: Capt. Thomas G. Lanphier, Jr.
                               1st. Lt. Rex T. Barber.
                               1st. Lt. Besby T. Holmes.
                               1st. Lt. Raymond K. Hine.
   b). Cover: Major John W. Mitchell.
                               1st Lt. Julius Jacobson.
                               1st Lt. Douglas S. Canning.

1st Lt. Delton C. Goerke.

Major Louis R. Kittel.

2nd Lt. Gordon Whittaker.

1st Lt. Roger J. Ames.

1st Lt. Lawrence A. Graebner.

1st Lt. Everett H. Anglin.

1st Lt. William K. Smith.

1st Lt. Eldon E. Stratton.

1st Lt. Albert R. Long.

7. **The Action:** From the takeoff at Cactus, the flight went 410 miles over the circuitous all-water route, flying all the way at an altitude of 10 to 30 feet above the water. The course had been figured and timed so that the interception most probably would take place upon the approach of the P-38's to the Southwestern coast of Bougainville at the designated time of 0935. As this point was reached *the Enemy was sighted.*

It was almost as if the affair had been pre-arranged with the mutual consent of friend and foe.

The picture was this: the Lightnings were at 30 feet, heading in toward the coast, and just about to begin to get their altitude for the presumed attack. The enemy was sighted, in a "V", about 3 miles distant proceeding down the Southern coastline toward Kihili [Kahili]. The two bombers were together, flying at 4500 feet, with two sections—3 Zeroes each—1500 feet above them and slightly to the rear. As the enemy force, apparently unaware of opposition, pursued his course, Mitchell led his covering group in their climb for altitude, ultimately reaching 15-18000 feet, from which point they stood their protecting vigil. Lanphier led his force parallel to the course of the enemy, flying in toward them a bit, and indicating 200 MPH, in his 35° climb. The P-38's actually climbed at 2200 feet per minute. When level with the bombers, and about 2 miles away, Lanphier and Barber dropped their belly tanks and swung in to the attack at 280 MPH indicated. Holmes had difficulty in releasing his tank, and Hine remained with him until he could do so.

When Lanphier and Barber were within one mile of contact, their attack was observed by the enemy. The bombers nosed down, one started a 360° turn dive, the other going out and away toward the shoreline; the Zeros dropped their belly tanks and three peeled down, in a string, to intercept Lanphier. When he saw that he could not reach the bomber he turned up and into the Zeros, exploding the first, and firing into the others as they passed. By this time he had reached 6000 feet, so he nosed over, and went down to the tree tops after his escaping objective. He came into it broadside—fired his bursts—a wing flew off and the plane went flaming to earth.

The Zeros were now pursuing him and had the benefit of altitude. His mission accomplished, he hedgehopped the tree tops and made desperate manuevers to escape. He kicked rudders, slipped and skidded, tracers were flying past his plane,—but he finally outran them. In all the action he had received two 7.7's in his horizontal stabilizer.

Barber had gone in with Lanphier on the initial attack. He went for one of the bombers but its maneuvers caused him to overshoot a little. He whipped back, however, and although pursued by Zeros, caught the bomber and destroyed it. When he fired, the tail section flew off, the bomber turned over on its back and plummetted to earth.

By this time, Holmes had been able to drop his tank and with Hine, who had stayed in formation with him, came in to ward off the Zeros who were pursuing Barber. A dogfight ensued, many shots were exchanged, but results were not observed. The flight was on its way out of the combat area (in the neighborhood of enemy bases at Kahili, Ballale and Shortland-Faisi) when Holmes noticed a stray bomber near Moila Point flying low over the water. He dove on it, his bursts getting it smoking in the left engine; Hine also shot at it and Barber polished it off with a burst in the fuselage. The bomber exploded "right in my face"; a piece of the plane flew off, cut through his left wing and knocked out his left inner cooler and other chunks left paint streaks on his wing—so close was his attack driven home.

Holmes, Hine and Barber then turned up for home, their mission—to destroy the bombers—a complete success. However, Zeros were coming in on Barber's tail and Holmes whipped up and around and shot one down in flames. Another attempt to draw away ended in another dogfight during which Barber exploded a further Zero. During these minutes, Hine's left engine started to smoke and he was last seen losing altitude south of Shortland Island. It is believed that Hine also accounted for a Zero as a total of three enemy fighters were seen to fall into the sea during this part of the combat.

Barber and Holmes were forced to use extreme evasive measures in order to successfully escape from the enemy hotbed and their course out, as was Lanphier's, was further complicated by the sight of a huge cloud of dust fanning out from a swarm of planes taking off from Kahili airfield. Holmes eventually ran out of gas and made a successful emergency landing at the Russell Islands, from which he later brought his plane safely home to base. The damage to the cooling system of Barber's left motor prevented him from pulling more than 30 inches of mercury at low levels and 25 inches at 4/5,000 feet but despite this limitation to his speed and rate of climb he also brought his plane safely home to base.

8. **Comment:** The success of this extraordinary mission—a 425 mile interception by land planes largely over water—was due in large measure to the leadership of Major Mitchell. On the eve of the flight, the mission was thoroughly explained to each pilot—there were no generalities. Each minute detail was discussed, with nothing taken for granted; take-off procedure, flight altitude, exactly when and how to drop belly tanks, radio silence, the tremendous importance of precise timing and position of covering elements, until Major Mitchell was sure that each of his pilots knew both his part and that of each other pilot from take-off to return.

The results bear witness to the thoroughness of this briefing. Radio silence was absolute until Canning's quiet "Eleven o'clock" announced contact with the enemy. The timing resulting from Major Mitchell's close control of the flight's speed and the unwavering formation maintained was so exact that the enemy was met on the minute, where a few minutes' delay would have meant complete failure. The covering flight covered the combat action—as it should have—and when help was called for by the attacking element, Major Mitchell immediately diverted the pre-arranged section and the balance remained on station. This discipline—intelligent discipline—was throughout the mission flawless, not one of the twelve covering planes yielded to the temptation to peel off and mix it with the enemy.

Once again the following fundamental principles of modern, organized air attack—the first instruction which new pilots receive from Col. Viccellio—have proven their soundness: "When you are on a mission, whether leading a flight or flying a wing, know exactly what your mission is, where you are going and how to get back—and be on time".

Distribution: Army Intelligence
    W-2, MAW, APO 709
    Fighter Intelligence, APO 709
    Strike Intelligence, APO 709
    CO, 13th Fighter Command, APO 708
    A-2, 13th Air Force, APO 708
    G-2, USAFISPA, APO 502
    NACI, COMSOPAC, APO 502
    S-2, 347th Fighter Group, APO 502
    S-2, 18th Fighter Group, APO 709

Appendix B

Excerpts from Narrative History, 339th Fighter Squadron

30 October 1942–31 December 1943

SUBJECT: Narrative History of the 339th Fighter Squadron Two Engine from Activation until 31 December 1943.
TO: Commanding General, Thirteenth Air Force, APO 719. (Thru Channels)

The history of any squadron in the time of war can be recorded in the accomplishment of the task assigned to it. The tougher the job the more glorious will be its history when that work has been well done. The annihilation of the Mikado's South Pacific air power and the recapture of the Solomon Islands was no easy assignment. It was the fortune of the 339th Fighter Squadron of the Thirteenth Air Force to play a part in the accomplishment of this task. Its record speaks for the contribution it has made.

Born in the heat of battle, nurtured and reared on repeated aerial clashes with the Japs it matured rapidly. From then on, having attained its full stature, this composite of alert, determined pilots and efficient hard work-crew, justified the name that was given to it, The Sun-Setters.

It was early September, 1942. The place was Guadalcanal. The Marines, just a few weeks before had taken Henderson Field. The 67th Pursuit Squadron, flying P-400's and stationed at Tontouta Air Base, New Caledonia, had sent some pilots and a ground crew of approximately 33 men to Guadalcanal for combat. The P-400 was the British version of the P-39 Airacobra. They had been built in the United States to British specifications, but instead of going to England they were sent to the South Pacific. The rest of the 67th remained at Tontouta training for combat, while the ground crews worked assiduously to keep the remaining planes in flying condition. More pilots, anxious for combat, were beginning to trickle in from the United States. Everyone had heard that this theater of war was to receive P-38 Lightnings, but as yet none had arrived. Then there was the question, who was to fly them? What outfit? Soon it was common talk that the 67th Pursuit Squadron was to be split up, to form a new squadron, and that new squadron was to fly the P-38's. Speculation and anticipation ran high. Then it happened. It was all contained in a Secret Letter, File A.G. 320.2 of the Headquarters, War Department, The Adjutant General's Office, dated 29 September, 1942. The 67th Pursuit Squadron was split in two, and from it came the 339th Fighter Squadron and the 347th Fighter Group Headquarters. Effective 1201, 3 October 1942, the 339th Fighter Squadron was activated and along with the 67th Pursuit Squadron was assigned to the 347th Fighter Group. When all was said and done and the first 339th Fighter Squadron morning report was completed, it showed 33 pilots and 102 enlisted men, of these 7 pilots and 16 enlisted men were in combat on Guadalcanal. Major Dale D. Brannon of Chardon, Ohio, became the first Commanding Officer. . . .

It was on the morning of 12 November 1942, that the first P-38's left Tontouta for Guadalcanal. What a beautiful sight it was for those who witnessed this first departure, to see 12 Lightnings take off, circle the field and then head for the land of combat. Stopping for lunch and gas at Esperitu [Espiritu] Santo Island, the P-38's continued to the 'Canal, landing on Henderson Field at 1530 that afternoon much to the awe and encouragement of all who witnessed the landing of the new arrivals. Hundreds of battle worn troops lined both sides of the runway, shouting and waving their arms as the Lightnings came in to land. The Japs undoubtedly heard of the arrival of the new interceptors also, as daylight raids ceased from then on. The next night Jap battleships heavily shelled the Henderson Field area again and one of the new P-38's was lost. On November 15th three more Lightnings were ferried up from New Caledonia. The pilots of the 339th Fighter Squadron were now flying P-38s, P-39's and P-400's. A few of the crews which had worked on the Lightnings at Tontouta were sent up to maintain them at the 'Canal. It was the intention from the start, however, to make the squadron strictly a twin engine squadron. This was to be realized in time as more P-38s arrived from the States and the pilots had checked out and trained in them at New Caledonia. . . .

The 339th Fighter Squadron has the distinction of being the first to fly the P-38 in combat in the Pacific Theater. For the first few weeks they flew mostly patrols. However, before the first week had passed, they had flown their first escort mission and had shot down their first Jap planes. . . .

On March 18th an order was published making the 339th a Twin Engine squadron. From this time on it was strictly a P-38 squadron, although from time to time a few of its pilots still flew P-39's on missions.

April, however, provided its share of aerial clashes with the pilots of the Rising Sun. There were more photo escort missions to New Georgia, barge sweeps to Vella Lavella and Cape Alexander on Choiseul Island, and escorting SBD's in addition to regular patrols. It was particularly notable for the enemy contacts on April 7th and 18th. Both instances were outstanding pieces of P-38 interception. The one on the 7th was a high tribute to teamwork, its effectiveness and practical necessity when fighting a numerically superior enemy. On this occasion 4 P-38's with Lanphier, Moore, Barber, and McLanahan were scrambled along with P-39's and P-40's to intercept a strong enemy fromation [formation] headed towards the 'Canal. This flight of P-38's intercepted 11 Zeros, and by working together and protecting one another they definitely shot down 7 of the 11. Captain T. Lamphier [Lanphier], who at the time was with the 70th Fighter Squadron but later became a Sun-Setter, got 3, while Lt. Rex Barber was credited with 2, with Lt. McLanahan and Lt. Moore getting one each.

On the morning of April 18th, at 0725, 16 P-38's took off from Guadalcanal to intercept a force of enemy planes over southern Bougainville. Special information had been received that an enemy bomber with fighter escort was to proceed from Buka to Kahili. A flight of 4 Lightnings with Captain Thomas G. Lanphier, Lt. Rex Barber, Lt. Besby Holmes, and Lt. Raymond Hine was to be the attacking section. Twelve other P-38's led by Major John W. Mitchell, with Julius Jacobson, Lt. Douglas S. Canning, Lt. Delton C. Goerke, Major Louis E. Kittel, Lt. Gordan Whittaker, Lt. Roger J. Ames, Lt. Lawrence A. Graebner, Lt. Everett H. Anglin, Lt. William E. Smith, Lt. Albert R. Long, and Lt. Eldon E. Stratton were to provide the cover.

Flying all the way at an altitude of 10 to 30 feet, the P-38's flew 410 miles over the water to make the interception. The course had been figured and timed so accurately that the enemy was sighted as though the encounter had been arranged with the mutual consent of both sides. As the P-38's approached the coast of Bougainville, flying 30 feet above the water, the enemy was sighted about 3 miles away heading down the coastline towards Kahili. There were 2 bombers flying at 4,500 feet with an escort of 3 Zeros apiece at 1,500 above them. Apparently unnoticed at first, Major Mitchell led his forces into a climb for altitude and after reaching 15,000 to 18,000 feet, they commenced their protective vigil. Never once did they break formation to participate in the battle raging beneath them, although the temptation was great. The attacking section of 4 P-38's climbed to the level of the bombers. They dropped their belly tanks and closed to within a mile of the contact before being observed. The bombers then nosed down and started evasive action. The Zeros dropped their belly tanks and dived to intercept the P-38's. Lanphier saw he could not reach the bombers before the Zeros reached him, so he turned up into them, firing at them as they passed. Soon he was at 6,000 feet so he nosed it over and dived down to the tree tops after an escaping bomber. He came into it broadside, fired his shots, a wing flew off, and the bomber burst into flames as it plummeted to earth. Barber had gone in with Lanphier on the initial attack. He went for one of the bombers, but its evasive action caused him to over shoot a little. So he whipped back and, although pursued by Zeros, caught the bomber and destroyed it. As he fired the tail section flew off and turning over on its back the bomber nosed into the ground.

By this time, Lt. Holmes, who had trouble getting rid of his belly tank, had dropped it, and he along with Lt. Hine, who had stayed with him, came in to fight off the Zeros pursuing Lt. Barber. A dog fight ensued, many shots were exchanged, but results were not observed. The flight was on its way out of the combat area, which had been mostly over the Kahili and Shortlands regions, when Lt. Holmes noticed a stray bomber near Moila Point flying low over the water. He dived on it with Lt. Hine right behind him. His bursts started the left engine smoking. Lt. Hine poured in his shots which added to its destruction, then Lt. Barber joined in and polished it off with a burst in the fuselage and the bomber exploded in front of him.

With the bombers destroyed, and their mission accomplished, Lts. Holmes, Hine, and Barber headed for home. However, the Zeros, who were greatly stirred up by that time, were coming in on Barber's tail. Lt. Holmes whipped up and around and shot one down in flames.

In another dog-fight, Barber got himself a Zero. It was during this melee that Lt. Hine's left engine began to smoke and he was last seen losing altitude south of the Shortland Islands. However, another Zero was seen crashing into the water during this part of the fight and it is believed that Lt. Hine got this one before he himself was hit.

Lt. Holmes ran out of gas on the way home and made an emergency landing at the Russells. Lt. Barber's coolant system had been shot up, greatly reducing his speed, but he brought it home and landed safely. The score for the day was: 3 bombers and 3 Zeros definitely destroyed. The squadron had lost Lt. Hine. Lts'. Barber and Holmes became squadron Aces this day, each getting a bomber and a Zero, bringing their totals to 5 apiece.

Preparing for this mission, Major Mitchell had worked it out down to the minutest details. In his briefing before take off, he made sure that each pilot understood not only his own part, but also that of the others. The success of this extraordinary mission bears witness to the thoroughness of the preparation.

After the squadron's success on the 18th, there was no further contact with the Japs in the air for the remainder of the month. On different occasions, the P-38's escorted photo planes to Rekata Bay on Santa Isabel and Munda Point on New Georgia, but the Jap interceptors did not appear. Occasionally the Lightnings were given a strafing mission and on April 21st, 15 P-38's flew to Cape Alexander, northwest tip of Choiseul Island and saturated the target with a rain of fire in an unopposed strafing run.

At the month's end, 8 sures and 1 probable had been added to the squadron total of destroyed Jap planes, which now stood 50 definitely destroyed, with 16 probables. In that time the squadron had lost 14 pilots. . . .

Kim Darragh,
2nd Lt., Air Corps, Historical Officer

Appendix C

Assistant Chief of Air Staff, Intelligence, Digest of 15 June 1943

Extract From Air Command Solomon Islands Intelligence Bulletin, April 18, 1943

Sixteen Lightnings contacted 2 bombers and 6 Zeros at about 0930 Love some 33 miles NW of Kahili at 5000 and 8000 feet respectively and destroyed both bombers and 1 Zero. Near Moila Point another bomber and Zero were contacted and destroyed. All 3 bombers were Type 1 Mitsubishis painted dark green with 20mm. in tail; 7.7's in the waist and top turret just off the middle of the wing. The Zeros were Mark 2 also painted dark green with silver belly tanks. All planes shot down were seen to burn or crash on the ground. Lt. Hine failed to return and was last seen going down just SW of Shortland Island, toward Heilson Strait. Other planes in the flight received hits, and one was damaged by pieces of a destroyed Jap plane.

Appendix D

Interviews with
John W. Mitchell
and Thomas G. Lanphier

Assistant Chief of Air Staff, Intelligence
15 June 1943

This is a digest of an interview with Major John W. Mitchell and Captain Thomas G. Lanphier, Jr., P-38 fighter pilots in the South Pacific.

Major Mitchell discusses the training and welfare of pilots in the Pacific area and in that connection takes up gunnery, escort missions, formation flying, training and acrobatics, instrument work and living conditions. He also makes suggestions with reference to the equipment of the P-38 plane.

Captain Lanphier relates experiences on some specific missions, and discusses tactics in the use of P-38's and some characteristics of this plane.

Major Mitchell: I would like to speak to you about pilot training, or, rather, pilot welfare in the Pacific area,—the squadron as a whole, the things that we have needed, the things we have done. Captain Lanphier will tell you of the tactical side. He has had varied experiences there—just as much, or more, than I have. So he will give you that side,—from strafing destroyers to shooting down Zeros.

The first thing I'll speak of is gunnery. We would like to have gunnery stressed more for pilots than it has been. The boys have been coming into the squadron with very little or no gunnery. I finished flying school in July, 1940, and have had two flying missions against the sleeve since I finished flying school. I have tried to get it everywhere I have gone. Before the war we were not able to get ammunition, and out in the Fijis we were able to get very little of it. It is certainly letting the boys down by not letting them get any more. The only way we can get the enemy is to get close behind him, jam on the machine guns, and let him have it. If we try to make long shots, we just don't hit him. I think gunnery should be stressed. That is the most important thing.

Pilots should have more escort missions. They should fly with heavy bombardment on some long missions where they will probably be intercepted by a different type of airplane. Let them get used to flying high cover. Sometimes it takes the hard way to learn it—but if you learn back here it will save pilots and airplanes out there.

The boys get out to the front and they don't know enough about formation flying. I used to talk to all the new boys who came into the squadron and found that most of their flying was done individually. They were sent out to do individual flying, and they were not getting the proper training in formation flying. Emphasis should be laid on sticking together when flying formation—at least in pairs. We used to fly four-ship formations, *but emphasis must be laid on the boys sticking together in pairs. They are certainly going to get in trouble if they don't. If they do stick together they are going to come out pretty well. One of them can pick the Jap off the other's tail.*

The boys should also be trained in acrobatics before they leave here. That is the only way in the world they can learn to handle the airplane. A goodly part of them come out there afraid of the airplanes which is due in part to the lack of proper indoctrination back in the States. We have to give them all this when they get out there. It would be better to keep them back in the States a little longer and teach them those things rather than have us teach them. It takes about three or four planes back here, at least, to make up for one plane out there.

The new boys need much more instrument work. They have had no instrument flying in fighter planes at all, and most of them had never done any night flying at all. On long missions from Henderson up to Kahili we would take-off at three or four in the afternoon, and get back at about eight or nine at night. Sometimes it would be raining and the boys would have to come back on instruments. We used to lose a few of them.

The new pilots should be given practice landing, in short fields, and told not to be afraid to go around for another try. The main thing is to give them practice in landing on short fields. *It is a bad thing to land on the first third of a runway, then have them encounter short fields out there. It is better to have them crack up over here.*

Some of the boys who came to us had never been on high altitude missions. When you fly P-38's you start taking oxygen at about 10,000 feet, and if you go up on a long daylight mission you are on oxygen for at least three hours. It is important that pilots have that experience.

Pilots should have more ground instruction in tactics, and know more about the Japanese planes. Many have evidently had no tactical training on the ground at all. An aggressive attitude should be instilled in the fighter pilot. He has to be looking for a fight, and has to carry it to the enemy, rather than wait for them to bring it to him. The boys who come out there are a little bit afraid of their airplanes, and are not sure of themselves. That could be corrected in part in the general training program.

We had been out there just about a year before the first pilots for relief and replacement started coming out. I understand that pilots were very few and far between then, but now there definitely should be some leave system. A definite system should be carried out providing relief for the pilots after six or twelve months. Twelve months is a little too long for a pilot to stay in an area where it is hot and there are mosquitoes, in places like Guadalcanal, and where they have to do quite a bit of fighting. *It is much too long. Six months is by no means too short a period of time.*

Our quarters at first were very poor out there. We lived in tents without floors. We had mosquito bars, but no mosquito-proofing for the tents and we had to sleep under mosquito bars every night. Sometimes we would chisel crates from planes and make floors for the tents but as a whole we didn't have any. The food was very bad.

There should be some way to have a refrigeration unit sent along with a squadron. We had none, and consequently, no way of preserving any kind of fresh meat. The only time we could get it was when a boat came in with extra meat and we could get some from them for one or two meals.

The fighter squadrons that were out there were away over the T/O strength. A fighter squadron calls for 27 pilots, and the squadron I had had over 90 pilots assigned and 30 or 40 more attached. That made promotion for the pilots in the lower grades very slow. In fact, there were no promotions. We were given no relief and had so many pilots that there was no promotion for the men in the lower grades. Now and then they sent men out from the States who had come out of flying school way behind the boys there, who would be at least one grade ahead—sometimes two—and had seen no action, *while our boys had been out fighting.*

There was no whiskey at all for combat pilots out there. There was whiskey on some of the islands, but we didn't seem to be able to get hold of it for some reason. I think a certain amount is all right. After a day when the boys have had a pretty tough job, when they are ready to go to sleep they can take two or three shots and get a much better rest.

General Grant (The Air Surgeon): Major, that has been corrected, or will be within the next month or two for combat missions. They should get it by that time. It will have an accumulated value. They can use it as they desire.

Major Mitchell: We were based in New Caledonia and went up to the Solomons for six weeks, and then were sent to Australia or New Zealand for a week's leave. Then we were sent back to New Caledonia to stay for about two or three weeks, and then into the Solomons again for another period of about six weeks. Six weeks is actually too long. The stay there should not be over four weeks at a time. However, we didn't have enough pilots to keep three shifts running that way. Of the 90 pilots that I had, many were in training, some were sick, some were on leave—and we needed that many pilots to run two shifts up there. In my opinion we should have one more P-38 squadron out there. The planes are going there, I understand, and we certainly need one more squadron to ease the load. I think the pilots are there.

The P-38's should have better heaters and better ventilating systems. The heaters are not sufficient to keep you warm when up at high altitudes especially when you stay at 25,000 feet for two or two and a half hours at a time. If you put on enough clothes for that altitude, and then get down to a lower altitude, you just about burn up.

While we have not had much trouble with the dropping of belly tanks and bombs from the P-38, there should be a manual release installed on the planes at the factory. We installed one on our own hook, which took time and equipment that we had to chisel around to get. If it could be installed back in the States it would save a lot. It would save a lot of lives, too, because the boys who can drop the belly tanks are better off. The planes will blow up as easily as the Jap planes, with the belly tanks on. They are not self-sealing. Also, if you are trying to drop bombs and you can't drop them at the proper time, you might as well not have them on there.

The instruments as a whole have been very poor. I know this is partially due to operations in the field, and also because the hot weather there causes a lot of the instruments to go out. There are no replacements, and many times we strip other planes to get them. Right now they are flying P-38's on missions without either tachometer working. You have to go on long missions where you need to save gasoline, and it is rather difficult to know how many r.p.m. you're pulling. Very often we had to strip airplanes with just one part missing—take more parts off of it to put on other airplanes to keep them going. We figured it was better to have one airplane out with several parts missing than to have two with one part missing on each of them. They also have too many lights. When something happens, six lights flash on and you start grabbing for everything in the cockpit. (Ed. Note: This is also in line with Colonel Cass Hough's recommendations). At night it makes it very difficult for it blinds you. The belly tank light especially, in my opinion, is not necessary. It stays on all the time and certainly blinds you at night.

We have been using P-38's for night flying out there with very, very good results, in conjunction with searchlights. They have proved more than satisfactory, and we usually get about two per night when we go up. They have been doing much better than the P-70's since the P-70 is not able to get to sufficient altitude. The P-38's, after the lights pick up the enemy bombers, can move in on them and knock them down. We must have night fighting devices on them.

Some of the gunsights that are still coming out are the old Christmas-tree sights,—the cross-sight. They are very unsatisfactory. *The boys are very well pleased with the circle sights which they have on a lot of airplanes, but some still have the Christmas-tree sights*. The cannon button on the P-38 is behind the wheel and should be moved out slightly. The machine-gun button is over in the front and a man with short fingers is unable to reach both of them at the same time. If they were moved over a little bit then he could press both at the same time. Some pilots pressed their machine-guns and never used their cannon at all. They couldn't get around to press that trigger.

In fighting the Japs the ammunition should be loaded: one incendiary, one tracer, and one armor-piercing. The incendiaries, of course, are of the utmost value. They burn very nicely. I think most of the fighters used five armor-piercing, three incendiaries, and two tracers.

Another thing I would like to see on the P-38 is some kind of fire extinguisher for the engine. On one occasion I saw one engine burn out of a plane. If we could get some kind of fire extinguisher with automatic or manual control from the cockpit that would spray around the engine, *I believe it would save some planes and pilots*.

We always flew with a shoulder holster out there. That is much more comfortable. We had difficulty getting them so we had them made on our own hook. We did get a .38 caliber pistol. In my opinion the shoulder holster should be standard issue for all pilots.

My squadron was far from being up to T/O in enlisted men. A twin-engine squadron is supposed to have 278 men, I believe, and I was about fifty men short. The ground crews should be relieved out there in less than eighteen months. Those boys have been doing a wonderful job out there ever since

I have been out there. I have been more than satisfied with the work they were doing. At one time in Guadalcanal we had eight P-38's and they were keeping seven and sometimes eight in commission, with practically no spare parts. If those men stay out there too long their morale is going to go down. If they would bring them back now when they have a little fighting and experience, I think it would be fine to have some as instructors in ground schools.

Each squadron should have some generators, as there are not nearly enough. I think we are allowed one. Considering the number of radios, radio stations, tools, communications, we need at least three or four.

It would be a good idea if each one of the units out in that area had some kind of small water-purification system. I don't know whether such a thing is available or not. If each squadron had one of those it certainly would save a lot of wear and tear on transportation. We had to haul water eight miles in one little tank which held about 300 gallons. We had to haul all the water we drank, washed with, bathed with, and used for every purpose.

I would like to mention one thing about the P-39. They came out just before I came back and were red-lined at 350 miles an hour. That airplane is not any good for altitude work. It is to be used for divebombing and strafing, and that is about all it can be used for. It is a fine airplane for divebombing but if you can't dive it over 350 miles an hour, I don't see how you will be able to use it. I flew one before I left, and when you get over 350 miles an hour, *you get the damnedest tail flutter I have ever seen in any airplane.*

Q: How did you make out in bailing out of the P-38's?

A: We have had two men bail out. One parachute was seen to open, but we never saw the man again. The other boy managed to get out all right and back okay. He got back to Henderson Field without any injury at all. He said he just leaned over the side and slid off the wing. I think we have heard of several other cases where they have bailed out of P-38's, but those are the only two cases I actually know of where they bailed out without any trouble.

Q: Did you have dinghys, sir?

A: Yes. At first we didn't have any but later they gave us dinghys to sit on and we carried them with us all the time.

Captain Lanphier: I originally flew P-39's, and we used to hear all the tales about P-38's—that you couldn't bail out of it, that you couldn't dive it straight down, and many other stories. None of us wanted anything to do with it. We were going to stay with the 39's until we got the 51's or the 47's. Finally they sent some of the 38's.

Major John W. Mitchell was named squadron commander of the P-38's.

He learned P-38 tactics and flew them. He originated tactics which the rest of us now use in that area. When we checked out, about fifty or sixty of us, we had about fifteen or twenty hours. Varied sorts of missions were assigned to us. We were high cover over the field, and had a patrol running constantly in this area, and in the area up to the Russells. We also had escort missions from Munda, to Rekata, to Kahili. We escorted these missions; it was a little bit out of the P-40's range, although the P-40's used to go out there. It was also out of the range of the Vought Corsair, so that we were the sole escort. Quite a few missions were escorted to Munda.

One afternoon the photographic planes came back with some pictures of little floatplanes. There were about forty of them. The Navy decided that Corsairs and the P-38's were to go up and strafe. On the first three or four missions we had been high cover at 30,000 feet. The P-40's were 25,000 and the Grummans at 15,000 or 20,000. Up where we were it was hard to see what was going on down below. The Grummans would be engaged by three or four Zeros and the 38's would never see them. When we would come home they would say, "Did you see the fight?" "No, what fight?" So they got to calling the P-38's "high altitude foxholes." This was an opportunity to scotch that. They gave eight of us and some F-4-U's a chance to go and get the people on the water, who were in a pretty well-fortified little spot in the harbor at Faisi. We took off about three o'clock in the morning. By the time we got to Faisi we ran into a lot of weather and some of the planes turned around and went back home.

It was about dawn when we got there. We had been forewarned there was going to be a lot of opposition, and there was, particularly for the people in the back. It was always okay when you led the strafing missions from the front, for you got the credit and not much of the anti-aircraft. It was the fellow in the back who caught it.

We did a good job of strafing and on the way back we ran into a destroyer. There were six of us. We made a few passes at it and it started to burn and the people started to jump off. The Navy likes to have factual evidence, and by good luck they got a picture of the thing sinking. We reported that we set it on fire and that it was burning. We were right down on the water and we couldn't see very well. Pretty soon the pictures came in and they gave us credit for the destroyer. That scotched the "high altitude foxhole" business for a while.

Meanwhile, there wasn't so much activity for the P-38 versus the Zero. Major Mitchell used to meet them, but always at tremendous disadvantage, and perfected, in those days, the evasive tactics we used. Mitchell got so he would meet the Zeros over Kahili—forty or fifty to our four or five. The bomber men will tell you Mitchell and his men never let them down. There were no bomber losses while the P-38's were escorting them until the one or two sad days when the Navy lost some B-24's. They hadn't the experience the B-17 pilots had and made some tactical errors. We also lost a couple of P-38's. That was the first occasion that I know of that anybody in a fighter of any kind had been seriously and fatally hit by antiaircraft in the Solomons. Our own antiaircraft used to knock out the Jap bombers when they would come over, so there was no real occasion, for quite a long while, to find out what the P-38's could do against the Zeros.

One day they came down about 200-odd strong. Official bulletins said something about 180, but according to the tallies about 280 came over. About eighty of our fighters got into the air. We were sent out over the Russells, and intercepted them there. Incidentally, we expected to intercept high cover Zeros out over the Russells. We met three of them at 30,000 feet. We got those three, turned back toward home again, and then saw eight more. We engaged the eight for some time until there were none left. We only claimed four, because we didn't see what happened to the others. General credit is given for seven out of eleven by these four and I think the people on the Russells said nine or ten planes fell in that vicinity. Since no one actually claimed them they don't count as victories.

The P-38's were on the ground when the alert was called. Eighteen minutes later they were at 30,000 feet—four of them in formation. that is the fastest, I assure you, that you will get four airplanes to 30,000 feet. That is not four or five thousand feet a minute, but a little over 2,000 feet a minute, keeping your formation. With one plane you can go to 30,000 feet at four or five thousand feet a minute, but we had four pilots—four different kinds of pilots handling their engines four different kinds of ways, trying to keep together, looking around, always staying in contact with the ground and doing as told. That is the best we can do, eighteen minutes. I hope we get something that will do it faster, though now we don't need it. We get information on their arrival when they are 150 miles away.

On one mission two or three of us had a chance to abuse our engines. We pushed the Allison engines often and never got any trouble from them at all. The men working in the ground crews do some wonderful jobs of maintenance, and the engines really perform for us. We use them far beyond the Wright Field limitations in the time of fight and so on. Sometimes when we are pressed, we have to go hours beyond the 50- or 100-hour limit and they still give nice performances. We have had occasion to fire both engines sometimes for as much as eight or ten minutes wide open. I have seen them indicating 200 in a climb and climb 2,500 feet a minute, which is pretty fair stepping for a combat airplane out where you are doing the fighting. That is at full load of course, with all the ammunition and a full load of gasoline.

For the most part we used two-ship formations with four-ship sections, each man taking care of the other. On escorting bombers we are given the top position, and the plane being what it is, the visibility isn't too good below. The P-38 is too big to scissors with very much, which is still a good evasive maneuver. If jumped from straight behind you could dive down, spread out and cross over, and pretty soon be in a better position.

The one thing that we all dreamed of in the early months was to come down on the Japs from above. We were flying P-39's and P-40's then and escorting SBD's, and the Grummans. If the Japs didn't outnumber you, they would fly along and tease you, come up on the side and take a roll over the top of you, then follow around and come on the other side. We watched them do that for a long time, and watched some of the boys get hurt. Finally the P-38's came out and we were able to [come] down on them. I don't think they really knew what a P-38 could do. We captured a pilot who said that the Nips feared the P-38's, but they weren't afraid of the men who flew them. It was quite some time ago that they said that. We hope we have revised their opinion somewhat.

In formations of airplanes there were always two or three that wouldn't fly as far or as fast as the rest. We would go to Kahili, which was our most distant target—350 miles—on escort missions and use up a lot of gas. We used two belly tanks which would hold enough gas to get us up there. To do any fighting and get home again we were limited to 350 miles, or at the very most 400 miles. Unless the target was well worth it we didn't care to go that far. 350 miles was the range. 300 was comfortable, and if you didn't fight too long you could get home all right from 350. It didn't make any difference how much gas you carried up there—if you had to fight you had to drop your tank. Fighting, of course, uses up a tremendous lot of gas.

In altitude, they say the P-38 is limited only by the pilot's ability to take it. I have never flown higher than 35,000 feet. Our oxygen equipment worked very well. Most of the people don't like that confined feeling, but I can assure you that you forget all about it as soon as you see the Japs. The equipment, also, is very handy. In the old days we had to keep changing it manually. However, in the P-38's when you keep changing altitude quite a bit, it does it automatically. That is one of the nicest devices on the airplane.

When they sent the new pilots out to us, they would hear all the wild tales about the Zeros and about the P-38's. Some of them had been flying them for eight or nine hours. They are just ordinary kids. All people these days are mostly kids and subject to a little simple encouragement or discouragement—it takes a lot to encourage them but not much to discourage them until they see for themselves. When we got them out there, as Major Mitchell said, we had to start them all over again. They would get in the airplanes as soon as they would learn that it was not the killer it was supposed to be. We would then put them in acrobatics. The P-38 will dive straight down as long as you want to dive. You have to use some discretion when you are going to start pulling out. They had heard about the tail breaking off. The tail will not break off. It will jump and buck, but will not come off. It will stall some until you let it go and ease it out.

Usually we try experimenting. Most of the men we lost were lost during the first two or three combat missions they flew. There are many reasons for that. They were in a funk. They didn't know where they were, or what had happened to them. On several occasions we lost P-38 boys—who didn't stick together in the fight, got lost from their leaders, and didn't know where they were. They were just befuddled. They weren't scared—everybody is frightened a time or two—but they were in a fog and didn't know where they were. They weren't shot down. They just didn't know their way home. So we aimed to give them as much experience as possible flying airplanes with some experienced pilots back of the lines.

The Japanese airplanes just blow up if you get a good burst into them with the P-38's four guns in the nose. When you fire your tentative burst to see how your aim is, you usually get them right then. The new square-tipped wing Zero apparently doesn't burn as easily. They may have the type of tank we have in them. However, they will burn with one burst if you hit them correctly around the wing root or the cockpit. It will either explode or get the pilot. They are just like tissue paper.

Our airplanes come back riddled, but the pilot is still all right. That is a factor these new pilots soon learn, which is most encouraging to us and most unhappy for the Japanese. If you keep your head and keep watching them until they get in range you'll get them. We haven't had more than one or two men out of all the boys out there who really failed. Some were scared when they got started. Some were poor flyers, but turned out to be better combat pilots.

I would like to add a bit to what Major Mitchell had to say. It takes a long time to get supplies. We flew over that water for months before we ever had any dinghys. We finally got two or three and then cut cards for those—assuming that when someone went down, somebody else would circle and throw him the raft. We helped a B-26 out one day, by circling around and throwing a raft out to the crew.

We never did get jungle packs. I have heard of them, but never have seen them. We had to make our own. Also, I wish someone would devise a comfortable flying suit for the Army people. From the time I left the States until the time I arrived back, the only piece of equipment I got from the Army was my parachute and goggles. Later at Caledonia we started to get some stuff in, but that was all out of proportion to what was issued. Pilots who were completely equipped were sent to San Francisco, put on bombers there, and ordered to leave everything behind. They arrived at our station and hadn't a thing on them except their clothes and their orders. The things are shipped out by boat, and it takes two or three months.

While we have little knowledge of the P-51's and the P-47's, as far as we are concerned, the P-38 is a far better airplane. It is faster, and it will go as high, and higher. It will fly almost as far as a Zero, and it will outshoot it. The Zero shoots short, and way out of range. You can see the bullets and there is no actual trajectory. They are sprayed out. Unless you are vitally hit, you just keep on going.

It is nice to have two engines when you are 300 miles from home. If you get one shot out, and you can get it feathered, you can fly all the way home and land your plane with no trouble at all. Probably some of you have read about Barber. When strafing a destroyer he got a little eager and flew right down into it, tearing 42 inches off his wing. He flew home 210 miles and made a normal approach and landing and set it down without any trouble.

Don't you worry about the P-38. It is a good airplane. If we can get more like them we can win this war for you in a hurry.

Appendix E

Letter to Parents from Thomas G. Lanphier

December 1942

Mother and Dad,

Still in the pink and finding the time passes quickly at last. BACK IN—
after we'd attained a certain ability and experience we all felt we were
marking time and wasting time.

Up here we are doing what we've been trained all this while to do—and
in the short week we've been here we've helped the cause no little. You're
doubtless reading of our daily efforts in the line—I've gotten in fourteen
hours of combat in the air—not all of that is fighting of course, most of
it is getting to and fro. We are no longer outnumbered and poorly equipped—
we're well set up and have lots of company.

It's the same old story it has been in other wars—some few of the lads
have too much imagination and aren't of much use but the great majority
go at it hell-for-leather, which is best. Our opposition can't seem to cope
with aggression. We've been quite successful in bulling right into them and
scattering them to the four winds.

Things are much better all around here than they used to be. Living conditions are halfway decent and we get enough rest now that we aren't harassed
the way they used to be.

We are, of course, fighting a different sort of war than are the men in
the trenches—and the effects (whatever they are supposed to be) of battle
don't show on the pilots the way they do on the foot soldiers.

Our flying units are pretty much the same thing a fraternity house used
to be—all young men, few of these the grim and "hard bitten" characters
Time loves to depict. Most of the flyers here have been my cohorts, on and

off, since we left the States—a lot of them I went to school with, back in training days.

We lose a boy now and then but it's rare that a pilot fails to get back to our base, even when shot down. Things move pretty swiftly and we don't seem to feel the concern [we] might feel at other times—when one of them fails to return. Can't afford to, I guess.

The thing that impresses me is the way all of our pilots—the loud ones and the quiet ones, the hard ones and the soft ones—stick together when it gets rough upstairs. That's our saving factor and one the other people don't utilize very much. We stick together and work together and it pays dividends.

I've been flying in front of four and eight men on all my flights—I worried at first about the responsibility but things have worked out so that we've all come back from every flight—and did a lot of damage to the other team while at it—so I don't fret about it much anymore. I destroyed two planes on the ground the other day. They don't count on the "record" as victories—but they'll never fly again which is what counts. All the business about "how many Japs did so and so get" is pretty much nonsense.

There are many men here who'll have hundreds of hours in combat—good men, the best—who only have one or two Nip planes to their credit. But God knows how many guns they've wiped out strafing, how many ships they've sunk dive-bombing—how far and how well they've led their men out and back safely. Some seem to have the good fortune to find opposition and get a crack at them—others fly for hours and never get a shot.

I, and the other people with me, seem to have the knack of finding excitement—two of us have planes shot down to our credit and the whole outfit has played hell on several occasions with the Nip cause.

The types of flying and fighting are myriad—some of it things never dreamed of in training schools or home guard squadrons and a pilot girded for a flight is a sight to see. There is no distinguishing uniform—everyone wears what best suits him—but all wear enough to cover them from head to foot—tropical heat regardless—in case of fire.

A helmet and goggles, a radio headset, an oxygen mask, a throat mike, a life vest, a parachute (in which every kind of first aid and emergency ration is stored somehow), a hunting knife, a gun in a shoulder strap (for comfort in a cramped cockpit), a watch, dog tags, heavy shoes, gloves, pockets full of miscellaneous items and coins (for largesse to natives; in case of emergency the natives will help unbelievably for a shilling or less).

My uniform aground is a fatigue hat—fatigue jacket and trousers and a canteen—we must drink close to a gallon of water per man per day. Baths are scarce but drinking water is everywhere—and has to be. Salt tablets every hour are routine—vitamin and atabrine pills a daily dose and effective too. We all feel better than we did in—, lassitude got us there soon after we arrived. Doing nothing day after day—as we were there—is the hardest thing of all to endure.

We're actually "eager"—as they say here—and are going at the business hard and fast. I don't know how we'll feel a month from now—but along about then we should be pulling out for a rest (that's the policy here and now)—so it shouldn't be so bad.

If Charles gets down here he'll be in rare company—the marine pilots are really good and fine fellows. They're deadly shots—they've had hours of practice the Army somehow hasn't managed to give its pilots. Most start off with a bang and keep it up—most Army pilots have to learn their shooting in combat. They catch on quickly, but they ought to have the practice before they get here—as do the Marines.

I expect a couple of turns up here—an interval of rest between them— and then home!! I don't imagine they'll let us stay in the States forever— when we do get home—but a few months is all any of us ask.

I sometimes wonder if people well established at home fully appreciate what they have. The one thing above all else that every man out here longs for is a sight of home and the ones he loves.

I feel now that I'm earning my chance to go home. However long they keep me out here is all right—things are being accomplished here and there's a feeling of getting a job done throughout.

I want you to know that I'm well and well fortified to fight my little corner of the war.

Capt. Thomas P. Lanphier,
Guad.

Appendix F

Pilot's Combat Report, John W. Mitchell

17 December 1942

GP-347-SU-OPS (FTR)
Sep-Dec 1942
Folder #84581
Group Intelligence Office
Headquarters 347th Fighter Group
APO 502

17 December 1942

SUBJECT: Pilot's Combat Report.
TO: COMGENSOPAC, (Through channels).

1. I was the leader of a flight of 12 P-39's that took off October 4th with Cactus as our destination. We arrived safely at Cactus on October 7th.
2. The first day we were there, things were quiet. Those of us that thought it was going to remain quiet were in for a rude awakening.
3. At daylight on October 9th, I led a flight of 8 P-39's as fighter escort for Navy SBD's that were to acck [attack] a Jap Naval Force of one cruiser and five destroyers. We flew up the middle of the channel and made contact with the force about 150 miles from Guadalcanal. The SBD's started their dive, peeling off one behind the other. After taking a good look around at 12,000 feet, we started to follow the SBD's down over the target. At 10,000 feet my wing man spotted a Jap float plane. I closed

in on him fast and opened up at about 300 yards with machine guns and 37 MM cannon. My third shell hit him directly under the fuselage and he exploded in my face causing parts to fly past my cockpit. I pulled up to look for another and spotted one a thousand feet below. I wend [went] down on him but had trouble with my guns so, I pulled off again. The SBD's had completed their mission and we were low on gas so we headed for home. This was our first brush with the enemy and we had downed one and had two probables. From no in [now on] it was easy pickings. That afternoon, we attacked another force of several destroyers and a cruiser, but there was no air opposition, though the ships' anti-aircraft guns put up a heavy barrage for us and the SBD's.

4. The next morning, October 10th, we again took off before daylight to hit the same force we had contacted the night before. The Japs were putting heavy AA fire and we ran into about 12 float planes. The Marine Fighters were with us this time and when the count was taken after the battle, we found that 10 float planes had been knocked down and one of our pilots was missing. The SBD's had also scored several hits and several ships had been left smoking and burning.

5. For the next few days things were quiet; the lull before the storm. On the night of October 14th, began a siege which was to leave us all practically exhausted but still with the same fighting spirit that the pilots and enlisted men kept throughout. On this night at 2400, we were all awakened by a terrific explosion which to be only a few feet away. Actually it was about 150 yards away. We all made a dive for our foxholes and then all hell broke loose. There were 15 of us crammed into a fox hole built for about 8 men. It was hot and you couldn't move without kicking someone in the face. Star shell and shells with horribly beautiful green and white flares were exploding over our heads. Coconut palms were gashed and completely knocked down. Dirt trickled down our necks and formed little muddy rivulets where it mixed with the sweat. I had only a pair of shorts on and the mosquitos were practicing their dive-bombing on me. For three hours this went on and then suddenly ceased. We gradually emerged but we stuck close to the fox hole that night and there was no sleep.

6. On the fifteenth day we were flying all day and that afternoon, a large force of destroyers and cruisers and six transports was sighted off the south-eastern end of Santa Isabel. SBD's and P-39's loaded with bombs and attacked them. One transport was sunk. The antiaircraft fire was terrific and Lt. E. E. Barr, was shot down, but managed to reach the Russell Islands where he was picked up a few days later and returned to Guadalcanal on October 21st.

7. That night, we were shelled again and the next morning there were five transports beached just east of Kokumbona. We loaded our P-39's and dropped our 500 lb. bombs about 0730. The antiaircraft we had experienced was nothing compared to what we encountered that morning. All the escorting warships and transports seemed to be a single sheet of flame and shrapnel was falling so fast that the water looked as though there was a heavy rain squall going on. Zeros were swarming over the whole area. We dodged them and went down through the AA. Lt. Wallace Dinn dropped one five hundred pounder right in the center of one of the transports. Jap bodies were hurled right and left and the transport caught on fire. On the way back to the field Captain Bill Sharpsteen shot down a zero. Before the day was over, four of the transports were sunk, one was towed away under its own power. Tojo certainly failed on this mission to land troops and supplies.

8. During the next few days we were on many strafing and dive-bombing missions against land troops. Very often the Marines found dead Japs in the woods, their shoes blown off and no outwardly wounds; killed by concussion. Those that weren't dead soon tasted cold US steel as the Marines used their bayonets to finish the job. Several Jap Diaries were taken from Japs by the Marines, told of the yellow men's great fear of the "Long-nosed airplanes."—meaning the P-39's.

9. One morning we decided to pull a surprise raid on Rekata Bay, a Japanese seaplane base on Santa Isabel, about 160 miles from Guadalcanal. We loaded our P-39's with five hundred pound bombs and with a group of SBD's and Marine Fighters took off at such time as to reach Rekata Bay before daylight. It was good daylight when we arrived. We all dropped our bombs just where we wanted them and then commenced to strafe. There were eight seaplanes on the beach and on the water. We destroyed all of these and set a large gasoline dump on fire. Lt. Dinn had his prestons and oil lines shot away and was forced to bail out about five miles from Jap territory. His trip back to Guadalcanal in a native canoe with native paddles and his capture of a Jap Zero pilot on a nearby island is one of the most interesting stories of this war. I returned to Rekata Bay that afternoon with Lt. Jacobson to see if we could see any trace of Lt. Dinn. We destroyed two more planes and set a gasoline dump on fire. I had a large hole shot in my wing which severed my right aileron control, causing me to have to fly home with my stick all the way over to the right side of the cockpit.

10. On October 23d, while on a patrol mission over some small boats enroute to Tulagi, a few Zeros came over the field and I managed to shoot down

one out over the channel. This same day we were out on evening patrol and the weather closed in while we were out. Lt's Jacobson, Dinn, and Purnell, were with me and did a most commendable job of landing in a heavy rain after dark.

11. October 25th was a day long to be remembered. It was Sunday and Zeros were over the field all day. Five dive-bombers bombed us. A Jap destroyer sneaked in and sunk three of our Guadalcanal and Tulagi boats. The Japs lost seventeen Zeros and five bombers this day. We were shelled again that night.

12. About this time a Jap force of one battleship and one light cruiser and six destroyers were spotted just east of Florida Island. The SBD's stuck first and hit the battleship, damaging it slightly. We prepared to strike with 4 P-39's but I was unable to get off due to engine trouble. However, Lt.'s Purnell, Jacobson, and Dinn went ahead and dropped their bombs. Three men and planes against 6 destroyers, one cruisers and one battleship. Later that evening we again attacked with some SBD's. Several hits were made.

13. On November 7th we loaded 8 P-39's with five-hundred pound bombs to strike a Jap Naval Force, one cruiser and 14 destroyers. On our way out, we ran into five Jap float planes. Lt.'s Dinn, Shaw, Purnell, Geyer and I, each got one plane. It was then too late to attack the force, so we returned to Henderson Field. The weather was very bad and it was dark but we managed to land safely.

John W. Mitchell,
Captain, Air Corps,
339th Fighter Squadron.
Home Address
Enid, Mississippi.

Appendix G

"What's Past Is Prologue"

Rear Admiral William C. Mott, USN (Ret.)

The title of this commentary is taken from Shakespeare's *The Tempest*, but it aptly applies to a planned World War II prosecution for treason which, had it not been avoided, *might* well have precluded the shootdown of Admiral Isoroku Yamamoto, the architect of Pearl Harbor. After consultation with Admiral Mac Showers, I decided to write about an important missing link in the chain that led ultimately to the aerial intercept of Admiral Yamamoto over Bougainville on 18 April 1943.

First, let me say a word about ULTRA, or communications intelligence (COMINT), so central to the Yamamoto story. In early 1942, I was ordered to the White House from Naval Intelligence to be in charge of the navy section of the White House Intelligence Center, or Map Room, as it was called. We briefed President Franklin D. Roosevelt everyday, sometimes twice a day on all current intelligence, including ULTRA. Lt Cmdr Alwin Kramer from OP 20G (who we called The Shadow) used to deliver to me a locked briefcase containing translations of the latest Japanese intercepts. He really wanted to deliver them directly to the President, but didn't understand that the time and schedule of the President of the United States permitted few such interruptions. In fact, it frequently fell to me to read the intercepts, underline what I considered important for the President to read, and brief him privately in Admiral Ross McIntire's office. No one else in the White House except Captain John McCrea, the President's naval aide, had access to these intercepts.

*Condensed from the *Naval Intelligence Professional*, January 1990; reprinted with permission.

Captain Pineau had access to COMINT and later served for 10 years as assistant to Samuel Eliot Morison in the writing of the latter's massive 15-volume history of World War II. He couldn't inform Morison that COMINT was the source of some of the victories he was writing about. His exit oath, he wrote, "forbade unauthorized mention of COMINT to anyone." Oddly enough, I have no memory of any such exit oath. But we all knew of the danger of disclosing COMINT and kept the faith without a briefing, an oath, or a debriefing when we left the wartime White House. Samuel Eliot Morison was a Harvard graduate and friend of Roosevelt (also Harvard), and he wanted access to the Map Room and all of its secrets. But the President did not want any historians in the Map Room, including Sam Morison.

After the battle of Midway in June 1942, a reporter for the *Chicago Tribune*, Stanley Johnson, was improperly allowed access to COMINT while in the Pacific Theater. He learned that we had a leg up on victory because we had broken the Japanese codes and knew their battle plans. When he returned to the mainland, Johnson wrote that story and the *Tribune* published it on 7 June 1942! Consternation and subdued rage in the navy codebreaking fraternity was instant and far-reaching. This transgression was brought to the attention of President Roosevelt (an ex-navy man), who sent for the Attorney General to examine the statutes under which Johnson and the *Tribune* might be prosecuted (hopefully in secret). Colonel McCormick, who owned the *Tribune*, got wind of the possible prosecution and vowed to spend every dime of his considerable fortune to defend "freedom of the press."

While the President and the Attorney General were conferring, I received a call in the White House Map Room from the guard at the northwest gate. "You have a visitor, Lieutenant." "Who is it?" I asked. "A Captain Safford," was the reply. "Fine, send him in. I will meet him outside the door to the Map Room." There, another guard was stationed to monitor entrance.

Captain Safford was well known to me from my days in Naval Intelligence where I first gained access to ULTRA. Where he came from or who sent him I'll never know. He had been the head of OP 20G in Naval Communications, the Washington DC code breaking center (NEGAT), which would later have a leading role in translating the raw message giving Yamamoto's itinerary. He was a genius, but apt to be excitable in time of crisis, when his voice had a tendency to break in the high registers. With no social preliminaries, he opened the conversation by saying, "Lieutenant, you've got to stop this lawsuit against Stanley Johnson and the *Tribune*." "Who, me?" I replied. "You don't know how the President feels about the whole *Tribune* staff beginning at the top with Colonel McCormick, and besides, I'm only a Lieutenant, what reason could I possibly give the President, assuming I can get access, which would cause him to drop the suit?"

Captain Safford, as we walked outside to maintain secrecy, explained in his still agitated manner that OP 20G and its message-processing units in Pearl Harbor and Melbourne, Australia, were making steady progress in deciphering the Japanese Navy operational codes, including working on their flag officer codes. (We were already deciphering the diplomatic codes.) Suddenly he stopped and turned to me saying, "You're a lawyer aren't you, and President Roosevelt is a lawyer also—right?" "Well, yes, but . . . " "Then you ought to know that you can't possibly have a suit against the press without leaks—they'll push their perceived First Amendment right to the limit."

The result of such a trial and its possible leaks, Safford continued, would cause the Japanese to make substantial changes in their codes, which so far they hadn't. "Apparently, they don't read the *Chicago Tribune!* But, if we are put back to square one, the cost may be thousands of American lives in the Pacific." That prospect galvanized me like an electric shock, and I resolved to try my hand at persuading the President to drop the suit. After all, I had two brothers in the Pacific, one the gunnery officer of *Enterprise*, which had a key role in the victory at Midway, and the other, a submariner, who had been captured by the Japanese at Cavite and was a prisoner of war. Moreover, my own orders to the Pacific were not far distant.

That night, when President Roosevelt came into Dr. Ross McIntire's office for his nightly sinus treatment and leg massage, I told him about my visitor and cited all the reasons he had given me, adding some of my own from the legal standpoint. The President's initial reaction was negative, "but this was a traitorous act and should be punished," he exploded. I felt I was losing, when suddenly the President sat up and asked, "Who was your visitor?" "A Captain Safford from the Navy Code Breaking Establishment, OP 20G." "You mean Sappho—I know Sappho." (Midshipmen acquire outrageous nicknames. Sappho was a Greek poetess.)

"Why didn't you bring Sappho in to see me?" he demanded. "Well, Mr. President, I did call Grace (Tully), and she said you were terribly busy with the Attorney General and others, and she didn't think I should intrude." After a few moments of silent thought, President Roosevelt turned to me and said, "Okay. You tell Sappho there will be no lawsuit." It thus seems likely that the shootdown of Admiral Yamamoto in 1943 might very well not have happened without Captain Safford's passionate plea and President Roosevelt's acquiescence.

Appendix H

1985 Victory Credit Board of Review

22 March 1985

Members

CHAIRMAN: Lt Col Frederick E. Zoes, Commander, USAFHRC
RECORDER: Mr. R. Cargill Hall, Chief, Research Division
Major Lester A. Sliter, Chief, Inquiries Branch
Dr. Benjamin B. Williams, Col, USAFR (Ret)
Dr. Donald B. Dodd, Lt Col, USAFR
Dr. Daniel L. Haulman, Historian

Board members convened at 1330 hours on 22 March at the USAF Historical Research Center, Maxwell Air Force Base, Alabama. With all members present, Lt Col Frederick E. Zoes, Board Chairman, charged the board to reconsider the awarding of victory credits for the destruction of Admiral Yamamoto's aircraft on 18 April 1943.

Background

The Victory Credit Board of Review convened in response to an official request from Dr. Richard H. Kohn, Chief, Office of Air Force History, to review the credit awarded in the 18 April 1943 mission that destroyed the Betty Bomber carrying Admiral Isoroku Yamamoto on a flight from Rabaul to Ballale Island. Verifying this particular victory credit was made more difficult because of the scarcity of primary source materials, the conflicting accounts of the engagement in a key source, and the large amount of publicity that occurred in the years following the mission. For the purposes of this review and determination, the board considered only primary sources: The mission planning documents, the post-engagement intelligence debriefing, and the eyewitness account of a Japanese survivor, Vice-Admiral Matome Ugaki, Chief of Staff of the Combined Fleet, who recorded an account of the engagement in his diary. Secondary sources such as newspaper articles and citations for awards, were excluded from consideration. Personal recollections of the participants offered over 40 years later, were also excluded because of the passage of time.

The board convened for the purpose of reconsidering the award of original victory credits made by the USAF Historical Division (predecessor of the USAF Historical Research Center) in the late 1960s and published in the official listing of USAF World War II victory credits in 1978.* At that time, historians assigned to the original victory credit team judged that the destruction of Admiral Yamamoto's Betty bomber resulted from the gunfire of two P-38s piloted by Capt Thomas C. Lanphier and 1st Lt Rex T. Barber. The victory credit was thus shared under the XIII Fighter Command practice for awarding fractional aerial victory credits; that is, if two or more fighter pilots fired on and hit the same aircraft, which crashed, the credit was equally shared. (In the same engagement, for example, 1st Lt Barber and 1st Lt Besby T. Holmes both fired on and destroyed another Betty bomber, and that victory credit is likewise shared.)

Findings

Because of the security surrounding this particular World War II mission, XIII Fighter Command did not assay claims and issue general orders officially confirming these singular victory credits. Historians are thus left with only two primary sources: The eyewitness account of a Japanese survivor, and the post-mission intelligence debriefing that appears to have helped generate the dispute in question. The crux of the dispute hinges on the true number of Betty bombers involved in the engagement. Were there only two bombers, a determination made by the original victory credit team, or actually three bombers, as implied in the narrative of the Army intelligence debriefing after the mission?

The three-page Army intelligence debriefing of 18 April 1943 is flawed on two counts: First, it did not identify statements contained in the narrative with any particular pilot (though identities can be inferred), and second, it presented conflicting evidence regarding the number of bombers involved. In the excitement and elation of the moment, what appears as an obvious discrepancy was not identified and addressed, at least not until many years

---

*Office of Air Force History, *USAF Credits,* p. 17 (Barber) and p. 111 (Lanphier).

later. Meantime, the debriefing precipitated disparate accounts of the action in Air Force histories and the open literature. Accounts from the available primary sources appear below:

According to Japanese sources, on the morning of 18 April 1943, Admiral Isoroku Yamamoto left Rabaul, New Britain Island, on a flight to Ballale Island, with a final destination of Buin, on Bougainville Island. The flight, consisting of two Type I Betty bombers with an escort of nine fighter aircraft, proceeded directly on a southeasterly heading. "Our bombers flew a tight formation, their wings almost touching, and my plane [Betty] remained slightly behind and to the left of the lead ship." (Diary of Vice-Admiral Matome Ugaki)*

Having broken the Japanese code sometime earlier, a flight of 16 P-38s led by Major John W. Mitchell was dispatched from Henderson Field, on Guadalcanal, to intercept the Japanese Admiral as his airplane proceeded along the southwestern coast of Bougainville Island, 15 minutes before his scheduled arrival at Ballale Island. Four P-38s piloted by Lanphier, Barber, Holmes, and 1st Lt Raymond K. Hine, were designated the attacking section, while the remainder were to fly cover at altitude.

Proceeding on an easterly course, the P-38s approached the coast of Bougainville at the designated time of 0935 (Guadalcanal local time) and made a right quartering intercept of the Japanese formation. "The picture was this: The Lightnings [P-38s] were at 30 feet [above the ocean], heading in toward the coast, and just about to begin to get their altitude for the presumed attack. The enemy was sighted in a 'V,' about 3 miles distant, proceeding down the southern coastline toward Kihili [Kahili]. The two bombers were together, flying at 4500 feet, with two sections—3 Zeros each—1500 feet above them and slightly to the rear." (U.S. Army Intelligence Debriefing)†

In the words of the intelligence debriefing, "when Lanphier and Barber were within one mile of contact, their attack was observed by the enemy. The bombers nosed down, one started a 360° turn dive, the other going [turning] out and away toward the shoreline; the Zeros dropped their belly tanks and three peeled down in a string to intercept Lanphier. When he saw that he could not reach the bomber he turned up and into the Zeros, exploding the first, and firing into the others as they passed. . . . " Barber, meantime, "went for one of the bombers but its maneuvers caused him to overshoot a little. He whipped back, however, and although pursued by Zeros,

---

*Ugaki diary as reprinted in Okumiya and Horikoshi, *Zero!*, 246-47.

†Report, XIII Fighter Command Daily Mission Summaries, p. 2.

caught the bomber and destroyed it. When he fired, the tail section flew off, the bomber turned over on its back and plummeted to earth. . . . " "By this time he [Lanphier] had reached 6000 feet, so he nosed over and went down to the tree tops after his escaping objective. He came into it broadside— fired his bursts—a wing flew off and the plane went flaming to earth. Zeros were now pursuing him and had the benefit of altitude. His mission accomplished, he [Lanphier] hedgehopped the tree tops and made desperate maneuvers to escape."*

Holmes, Hine, and Barber, meantime, were engaged in a dogfight with the pursuing Zeros, and "many shots were exchanged, but results were not observed. The flight was on its way out of the combat area . . . when Holmes noticed a stray bomber near Moila Point flying low over the water. He dove on it, his bursts setting it smoking in the left engine; Hine also shot at it, and Barber polished it off with a burst in the fuselage. The bomber exploded 'right in my face'; a piece of the plane flew off, cut through his left wing and knocked out his left inner cooler and other chunks left paint streaks on his wing, so close was his attack driven home."†

The intelligence debriefing thus counted the Japanese losses at three Type 1M/B Betty bombers and, after more dogfights on the way out, three Type O SSF Zeke fighters. But these results are at variance with Vice-Admiral Ugaki's eyewitness account.

"Without warning the motors roared and the bomber plunged toward the jungle, close behind the lead plane, leveling off at less than two hundred feet. . . . For a few moments I lost sight of Yamamoto's plane and finally located the Betty far to the right. I was horrified to see the airplane flying slowly just above the jungle, headed to the south, with bright orange flames rapidly enveloping the wings and fuselage. About four miles away from us, the bomber trailed thick, black smoke, dropping lower and lower. . . . Tracers flashed by our wings, and the pilot desperately maneuvered to evade the pursuing fighter plane. . . . As our plane snapped out of its turn I scanned the jungle. Yamamoto's plane was no longer in sight. Black smoke boiled from the dense jungle into the air."‡

Still proceeding southeasterly at full speed in a vain attempt to reach Ballale, Vice-Admiral Ugaki's aircraft reached Moila Point where it was raked

---

*Ibid.

†Ibid., 2-3.

‡Ugaki diary, as reprinted in Okumiya and Horikoshi, *Zero!*, 247-48.

repeatedly by machine gun and cannon fire, killing most of the crew and passengers. "Another cannon shell suddenly tore open the right wing. The chief pilot, directly in front of me, pushed the control column forward. Our only chance of survival was to make a crash landing at sea. . . . Almost to the water, the pilot pulled back on the controls to bring the airplane out of its dive, but he could no longer control the aircraft. Enemy bullets had shattered the cables. . . . At full speed the bomber smashed into the water. . . . "*

Conclusions

Based on the available evidence, including the maps attached, board members reached the following conclusions:

1. Clearly, only two Betty bombers were involved in this six- to ten-minute engagement, not three as at first supposed by Army intelligence.
2. Capt Lanphier and 1st Lt Barber therefore did not destroy one bomber each over the jungle.
3. The evidence points to 1st Lt Barber as the first to fire on Admiral Yamamoto's lead bomber, setting it afire and causing a portion of the tail empennage to fly off. But the burning bomber, in the words of Admiral Ugaki, continued to fly under power just above the jungle, losing altitude. Barber's wingman, Capt Lanphier, once disengaged from the Zeros, next struck Yamamoto's bomber broadside, severing a wing. The bomber turned over on its back and plummetted to earth. Barber, on looking back after his pass, saw the airplane fall and understandably presumed it to be the result of his attack.
4. During the heat of ensuing dogfights, 1st Lt Holmes observed Admiral Ugaki's Betty proceeding southeasterly near Moila Point. Holmes attacked the second bomber "setting it smoking in the left engine." Barber "polished it off," pieces of the bomber exploded outward from the impact of the 20mm cannon shells, some of them striking his fighter. Admiral Ugaki's bomber, however, did not explode in the air as Barber supposed, but rather dove out of control into the sea.
5. Based on the guidelines established by XIII Fighter Command for the awarding of victory credits (cited above at page 2), credit for the destruction of both bombers is properly shared; the findings of the original USAF Historical Division victory credit team are judged to be accurate

---

*Ibid., 249-50.

and confirmed; the official USAF shared credits will remain unaltered for this engagement.

Having considered and debated the evidence, members of the Board agreed unanimously in these findings and conclusions. It was noted that *any speculation* about the ability of Admiral Yamamoto's crippled bomber to continue another ten minutes in flight just above the jungle to its destination on Ballale, if Lanphier had not attacked, had no bearing whatsoever on these deliberations and must remain always—speculation.

There being neither dissenting opinion expressed nor minority reports proposed, at 1510 hours the Chairman dismissed the Board.

R. Cargill Hall
Recorder

Certified True and Complete

Frederick E. Zoes, Lt Col, USAF
Chairman

Other Sources Consulted

1. Daily Mission Reports, XIII Fighter Command, April-June 1943.

2. Extract from Air Command Solomon Islands Intelligence Bulletin, 18 April 1943.

3. Cpl. Tommie Moore, Story of 339th Fighter Squadron, Public Relations Office, 13th AAF. Report of Action, 18 April 1943 (March or April 1944), pp. 14-15.

4. 70th Fighter Squadron, History, 1 Jan-30 Jun 1943.

5. Operations Letters, Ltr, Harmon to Arnold, 1 May 1943.

6. History of the Thirteenth Air Force, March-October 1943, AAFRH-20, AAF Historical Office, Sept. 1946.

Appendix I

Memorandum for Commander Aircraft, South Pacific Force

30 May 1943

SUBJECT: Investigation concerning leakage of information concerning the fighter sweep of the Kihili [Kahili] area on April 18, 1943.

1. Upon receipt of information that an important Japanese naval officer was flying into the Kihili-Ballale area about 1000 Love, April 18th, a conference was held in the Admiral's cabin with the Admiral, General Harris and Commander Ring present. These two officers were told the contents of the dispatch just received and all present agreed that a conference should be held immediately with Fighter Command representatives to discuss possible means of interception.

2. This conference was held later [on 17 April] in the morning, again in the Admiral's cabin. Present were:
   General F. Harris, USMC, Chief of Staff
   Commander S. C. Ring, USN, Ass't Chief of Staff for Operations
   Commander W. A. Read, USNR, Ass't Chief of Staff for Administration
   Lt. Col. E. L. Pugh, USMC, Fighter Command OIC
   Lt. Col. H. Viccellio, AAF, Fighter Command Ass't OIC
   Major J. P. Condon, USMC, Fighter Command Operations Officer
   Major J. W. Mitchell, AAF, Proposed Strike Group Commander
   Capt. T. G. Lanphier, AAF, Attack Section Leader of Strike Group

3. All present were informed of the fact that a MOST SECRET dispatch had been received concerning the flight of an important Japanese naval officer into the Kihili area the following day and asked for comments on possible means on interception. It was obvious from the beginning of the discussion that all officers present considered the mission a most hazardous

one and the chances of interception very slight indeed. In order to impress all concerned with the importance of a successful interception and to provide an additional incentive of the flight, disclosure was made of the Japanese naval officer involved. No mention whatsoever was made of the source of information contained in the dispatch. A plan was formulated and presented by General Harris to Admiral Mitscher who approved it in the presence of Admiral Fitch.

4. Upon completion of the conference in the Admiral's cabin the Fighter Command representatives adjourned to the Fighter Command dug-out where the mechanics of the strike were laid out. Present were:

      Lt. Col. E. L. Pugh, USMC
    #Lt. Col. L. S. Moore, USMC, Fighter Command Ass't OIC
      Lt. Col. H. Viccellio, AAF
      Major J. P. Condon, USMC
      Major J. W. Mitchell, AAF
      Capt. T. G. Lanphier, AAF
    #Lt. P. Lewis, (A-V(S)), USNR, Fighter Command Intelligence Officer
    (# Additional officers informed of the particulars of the strike)

Plans were laid out concerning course, speed and altitude to the Kihili area, point of anticipated interception, and return flight to Henderson. The discussion took place around the map table of the dug-out and no other people were present.

5. Later in the evening a conference was held in Major Mitchell's tent of all the pilots who were to take part in the following day's operations. Present were:

Attacking Section:	Capt. T. G. Lanphier, AAF
	1st Lt. R. T. Barber, AAf
	1st Lt. B. T. Holmes, AAF
	1st Lt. R. K. Hine, AAF
Covering Section:	Major J. W. Mitchell, AAF
	Major L. R. Kittel, AAF
	1st Lt. J. Jacobson, AAF
	1st Lt. D. S. Canning, AAF
	1st Lt. D. C. Goerke, AAF
	1st Lt. R. J. Ames, AAF
	1st Lt. L. A. Graebner, AAf
	1st Lt. E. H. Anglin, AAF
	1st Lt. W. E. Smith, AAF
	1st Lt. A. R. Long, AAF

1st Lt. E. E. Stratton, AAF

2nd Lt. G. Whittaker, AAF

In addition to the pilots above, Lt. (jg) J. E. McGuigan, A-V(S), USNR, Air Combat Intelligence Officer, was present to brief the pilots on location of friendly coastwatchers and natives. Admiral Yamamoto's name was mentioned in this conference.

The following morning the strike group took off on schedule and made a successful interception. The officers returning were briefed in a routine manner with only Lt. Col. E. L. Pugh, USMC, Lt. Col. H. Viccellio, AAF, Major J. P. Condon, USMC, and Capt. W. Morrison, AAF, a USAFISPA representative present. According to Capt. Morrison, the only reference made concerning the enemy naval officer concerned was a remark, believed to have come from Capt. Lanphier, that, "That son of a bitch won't dictate any peace terms in the White House".

6. In accordance with instructions from Headquarters, Air Command, the action report was prepared and submitted treating the strike as a routine fighter sweep.

7. No evidence has been unearthed which would indicate that any information concerning this strike was passed to newspapermen directly or indirectly.

M. A. Mitscher

Appendix J

Memorandum on Admiral Yamamoto, the Death of

23 May 1945

The following is a chronology of events associated with the death of Admiral Isoroku Yamamoto:

April 14, 1943

1. At 140108Z, FRUPAC sent out a dispatch to COMINCH, CINCPAC, COM-SOPAC, and COM7thFLT containing a fragmentary translation of a Japanese message, dated 1755/I 13 April 1943, from CINC SOUTHEASTERN AREA FLEET to several addressees, including COMDR. BALLALE GARRISON: A paraphrased version of this message follows:

    On 18 April CINC COMBINED FLEET will — — — as follows: Ballale Island — — — — — — — — — — — —.

    Comment by FRUPAC: This is probably a schedule of inspection by CINC COMBINED FLEET. The message lacks additives, but work will be continued on it.

2. At 141910 and 142157Z, FRUPAC and Op-20-G, respectively, sent out more complete translations of the same message. Op-20-G's paraphrased version read as follows:

    In accordance with the following schedule CINC COMBINED FLEET will be at Ballale and Buin on 18 April:

    1. In a medium attack plane escorted by six fighters depart Rabaul at 0600. At 0800 (1000 "L" time) arrive Ballale. Proceed by mine-sweeper to — — —, arriving at 0840. At #1 Base have minesweeper ready to proceed to — — — arriving at 0840. At 0945 depart

——— in minesweeper and arrive at 1030 at Ballale. In a medium attack plane depart Buin at 1400 and arrive at 1540 at Rabaul.

2. The Commander in Chief will make a short tour of inspection at each of the above-mentioned places and will visit the sick and wounded, but current operations should continue. Each Force Commander ———.

3. In case of bad weather the trip will be postponed one day.

April 15, 1943

1. At 150249Z CINCPAC issued a daily ULTRA Bulletin to all Task Force Commanders in the Pacific. The following is a paraphrased extract:

At 1000 on 18 April YAMAMOTO himself, via bomber escorted by six fighters, will arrive from Rabaul in the Ballale-Shortland area. He will leave Kahili at 1600 the same day and return to Rabaul. All dates and times are "L". In case of bad weather the trip will be postponed until 19 April.

2. At 150653Z, FRUMEL disseminated to COMINCH, CINCPAC, COMSO-PAC and COM7thFLT the translation of another Japanese message, dated 122/I April 14, from RABAUL BASE FORCE to an unidentified addressee, wherein reference was made to "the special visit of Yamamoto", and "in view of the situation regarding air attacks on the post", certain precautionary arrangements were requested, including the moving of the "post" to a new location.

April 18, 1943

1. At 0505 and 9535/I April 18th, a Jap plane was noted by FRUPAC originating encoded weather reports. FRUPAC commented (in his 181926) that this was an "unusual time for Nip plane weather mission".

2. At 180229Z a paraphrased message of COMAIRSOLS reported as follows: "Major J. William Mitchell, USAAF, led P-38's into Kahili area. Two bombers, escorted by six Zero's flying in close formation, were shot down about 0930L. One other bomber shot down was believed to be on test flight."

May 21, 1943

1. At 1500 I May 21st, the Japanese Navy Department originated an Alnav, in plain text, reading in part as follows:

"The Commander-in-Chief of the COMBINED FLEET, Admiral Isoroku Yamamoto, died a heroic death in April of this year in air combat
with the enemy while directing operations from a forward position."

2. Chungking reported on May 21st that, according to a Domei radio broadcast of that date, Admiral Yamamoto had been killed in April in an air
combat somewhere in the Southwest Pacific area, and that he had been
shot down by U.S. fliers.

The following report was contained in the intelligence summary of Headquarters Allied Air Forces, Southwest Pacific Area, Serial No. 101, May 8,
1943, Page 8:

P-38s Fly 410 miles to Intercept—BETTYS, ZEKES

28a. Sixteen P-38s took off from Guadalcanal on April 18 at 0725 to intercept
3 Type 1 M/B BETTYS and 6 Type O SSF ZEKES. Four P-38s were designated the attacking section, the balance as their protective cover. From
the take-off the flight went 410 miles over the circuitous all-water route,
flying all the way at an altitude of 10 to 30 feet above the water. The
course had been figured and timed so that the interception most probably
would take place upon the approach of the P-38s to the Southwestern
coast of Bougainville at the designated time of 0935. As this point was
reached the enemy was sighted!

29. The Lightnings were at 30 feet, heading in toward the coast and just
about to climb for altitude. The enemy aircraft were in a "V", about
three miles distant, proceeding down the southern coastline towards
Kahili.

30. Two bombers were together, flying at 4,500 feet, with the ZEKES in
two sections of three each, 1500 feet above them and slightly to the
rear.

31. As the enemy, apparently unaware of opposition, pursued his course,
the covering group of P-38s climbed for altitude, ultimately reaching
15000 to 18000 feet.

32. The attacking section of four P-38s flew nearly parallel to the course
of the enemy, flying in toward them a bit and indicating 200 m.p.h. in
a 35° climb. Actual rate of climb was 2,200 feet per minute. When level
with the enemy bombers and about 2 miles away two of the P-38s dropped
their belly tanks and swung into the attack at 280 m.p.h. indicated. One
P-38 had difficulty in releasing his tank and another remained with him
until he could do so.

33. When the two attacking P-38s were within one mile of their objective, their attack was observed by the enemy. The BETTYS nosed down. One started a 360° turn dive; the other retreated toward the shore line. The escorting ZEKES dropped their belly tanks and three of them peeled down in a string to intercept one of the P-38s. When our pilot saw this and realized that he could not reach the BETTY he turned up and into the ZEKES, exploding the first and firing into the others as they passed. By this time he had reached 6000 feet, so he nosed over and went down to the tree tops after the escaping BETTY. He came into her broadside and fired. The BETTY burst into flames, lost a wing, and crashed to earth.

34. The P-38 was then forced to out-run and out-manoeuvre the pursuing ZEKES who had the advantage of altitude. Meanwhile, the second of the two attacking P-38s had destroyed the other BETTY. The other two P-38s now had jettisoned their belly tanks and came into help ward off the ZEKES. Many shots were then exchanged but results were not observed. The flight was leaving the combat area and in the neighborhood of enemy bases at Kahili, Ballale and Shortland-Faisi when a stray bomber was noticed near Moila Point flying low over the water. One P-38 dived on it, his bursts setting it smoking in the left engine; a second P-38 shot at it and a third P-38 finished it off with a burst in the fuselage. A piece of the enemy bomber flew off, cut through the left wing of the P-38 and knocked out the left inner cooler, and other chunks left paint streaks on the left wing, so closely was the attack driven home.

The remaining ZEKES attacked and three more were destroyed.

Respectfully submitted,
J. N. Wenger
Captain, USN
Op-20-G

Appendix K

War Plans, CINCPAC Secret Files, Captain Steele's "Running Estimate and Summary"

16 and 17 April 1943

April 16. (Oahu Date)

Eleven TBF, five B-17s, nine B-24s attacked the KAHILI area between 2004 and 2130 (-11) April 17 [Guadalcanal date]. Two enemy planes attacked GUADALCANAL the night of the 16th (-11). Only slight damage was reported.

12 SBD escorted by 13 VF attacked MUNDA at 1415 (-11) the 17th.

Admiral Halsey in BRISBANE to discuss plans for the continuation of the NEW GUINEA—SOLOMONS offensive with General MacArthur. There is considerable newspaper discussion now appearing regarding reenforcements for General MacArthur.

CTF 16 reports 11 VF attacks on KISKA from AMCHITKA on 15th (+10). A total of 91 tons of bombs were dropped on KISKA that day in 13 attacks. The first report of attacks [illegible] on 16th (+10) shows that 49 planes attacked KISKA. Considerable damage was inflicted but will not be assessed until the photo interpretation is completed.

An attempt will be made to intercept an enemy high commander when he makes a projected visit to the BUIN area the 18th (-11).

April 17th. (Oahu date)

Com 3rd Fleet 180611 is an operation summary for his area. Major SOPAC task forces continue in port. It seems probable that CinC Combined was shot down in a plane over the BUIN area today by Army P-38s.

It is possible that a Jap sub is being towed toward the MARSHALLS by a DD and is now roughly half way between CANTON and FUNAFUTI. If the contact can be developed air attacks will be made.

Large scale air attacks continue on KISKA from both AMCHITKA and ADAK. There are beginning to be signs of enemy distress from these attacks. The NEVADA and IDAHO are standing to the westward from ADAK to patrol to the Northwest of ATTU. In view of possible stepping up of Jap sub operations in the ALEUTIANS the use of BBs in this kind of an operation is not without risk.

Appendix L

Naval Messages

18 and 24 April 1943

FROM COMAIRSOLS

ACTION COMSOPAC
INFO CINCPAC
COMAIRSOPAC ADMIN
COMINCH

DATE 18 April 43
TOR CODEROOM 0707/0735
DECODED BY DAYTON/DAYTON
[Time of transmission, Greenwich Mean Time] 180229   NCR 8838

COMAIRSOLS SENDS TO COMSOPAC. INFO CINCPAC AND COMAIRSOPAC

P-38s LED BY MAJOR J WILLIAM MITCHELL USAAF VISITED KAHILI AREA.
ABOUT 0930L SHOT DOWN 2 BOMBERS ESCORTED BY 6 ZEROS FLYING
CLOSE FORMATION. 1 OTHER BOMBER SHOT DOWN BELIEVED ON TEST
FLIGHT. 3 ZEROS ADDED TO THE SCORE SUMS TOTAL 6. 1 P-38 FAILED
RETURN. APRIL 18 SEEMS TO BE OUR DAY.

PASSED TO COMINCH FOR INFO BY RDO HONOLULU AS 180701
3 COPIES TO 20G

FROM COMSOPAC   ACTION CINCPAC
                                         INFO COMINCH

DATE 24 April 43
TOR CODEROOM 0948/0828
DECODED BY NICHOLS/NICHOLS
[Time of transmission, Greenwich Mean Time] 240315   NCR 2800

COM THIRD FLEET SENDS ACTION CINCPAC INFO COMINCH.
THIS IS ULTRA.

HIGHLIGHTS OF REPORT MAILED ON BUIN ACTION OF 18TH. 12 P-38'S
WERE COVER FOR 4 P-38'S WHICH DID ALL ATTACKING. 33 MILES NORTH-
WEST KIHILI [Kahili] SIGHTED 2 BOMBERS TOGETHER AT 4500 FEET. 6
ZEROS 1500-2000 FEET ABOVE SLIGHTLY TO REAR. BOMBERS PARTED
AND DIVED WHILE ZEROS STRUCK AT P-38'S. 1 ENEMY BOMBER WAS
ATTACKED JUST ABOVE TREE TOPS. WING FLEW OFF AND BOMBER WENT
FLAMING TO EARTH. SECOND BOMBER QUOTE TAIL SECTION FLEW OFF
BOMBER TURNED ON ITS BACK AND PLUMMETED TO EARTH. [end quote]
A THIRD BOMBER ENCOUNTERED WHEN P-38'S WITHDRAWING EX-
PLODED IN AIR.

Bibliography

Compiled by Captain George W. Cully, USAF
Chief, Inquiries Division
USAF Historical Research Center

Primary Sources in USAFHRC Collections

Briefing, Air Command Solomon Islands Intelligence, 18 April 1943 (extract). USAFHRC# 751.331.

History, 339th Fighter Squadron, October 1942-June 1943 (COMAIRSOLS letter of 17 July 1943—award of Navy Cross to Lanphier). USAFHRC# SQFI-339-HI.

History, 339th Fighter Squadron, 3 October 1942-December 1943. Dated 15 June 1944. Pages 8-10 describe mission based on "special information"; reports one Betty for each for Lanphier and Barber. No mention of Yamamoto. USAFHRC# SQ-FI-339-HI.

History, "Story of 339th Fighter Squadron," Cpl. Tommie Moore, XIII Fighter Command (see 13AF Report of Action, 18 April 1943, pp. 14-15). USAFHRC# SQ-FI-339-SU-RE-D March-April 1944.

History, 70th Fighter Squadron, 1 January-30 June 1943 (see p. 4: confirms Lanphier with 1 Zero and 1 MB for 18 April 1943). USAFHRC# SQ-FI-70-HI.

History, 70th Fighter Squadron, October-31 December 1943 (letter to accompany Distinguished Flying Cross awarded on 17 February 1943). USAFHRC# SQ-FI-70-HI.

Interview, AC/AS Intelligence (original notes of interviews with Mitchell and Lanphier). USAFHRC# 142.052-128, 15 June 1943.

Letter, Air Adjutant General Operations Letter, Harmon to Arnold, 1 May 1943. (Harmon says Mitscher had proposed Medal of Honor for Lanphier and others. Award later downgraded to Navy Cross.) USAFHRC #168.491, vol. 2.

Letter, Lanphier to parents, December 1942, 13AF Mission Reports, 1942. 3 pp. USAFHRC# 750.332.

Press release, "Two Outstanding Pilots of AAF Tell of South Pacific Air Battles," 13AF PAO, 17 June 1943 (Mitchell and Lanphier interviews). 3 pp. USAFHRC# 750.309.

Report, Historical Office, 13AF, March-October 1943. USAFHRC# 101-120.

Report, USAFISPA Air Information Bulletin No. 8, 29 April 1943 (see Tactics I, "A Polished Performance," 18 April 1943). 2 pp. USAFHRC# 705.607.

Report, XIII Fighter Command Daily Mission Summaries, April-June 1943 (see Fighter Interception Report to CG, USAFISPA, 18 April 1943). 4 pp. USAFHRC# 751.331.

S.O., 347th FG, 3 January 1944 (Lanphier transfer order). USAFHRC# 751.308.

Books and Monographs

Adams, Bruce. 1975. *Rust in Peace: South Pacific Battlegrounds Revisited,* pp. 168-69, 201-6. Sydney, Australia: Antipodean Publishers. Map, photos of wreckage, including Yamamoto's supposed seat, fact data plate, and control column "now held by 183rd Recon Flt, Pacific Islands Flight, Lae."

Agawa, Hiroyuki. 1979. *The Reluctant Admiral.* New York: Harper and Row. Translation of Japanese language original. Considered one of the most authoritative biographical sources regarding Yamamoto.

Albright, Harry. 1988. *Pearl Harbor: Japan's Fatal Blunder,* pp. 369-72. New York: Hippocene Books. Says the mission was called "Operation Vengeance"; claims Secretary of the Navy Knox and General Arnold concurred; presents text of alleged message from Knox.

Brown, Anthony Cave. 1987. *"C," The Secret Life of Sir Stewart Graham Menzies,* p. 469. New York: Macmillan. British intelligence chief thought Yamamoto mission "irresponsible"; feared Japanese code inquiry would result.

Christie, Joe, and Jeff Ethell. 1978. *P-38 Lightning at War,* pp. 73-76. New York: Scribner's. Gives Yamamoto Betty credit to Lanphier, shared credit for Ugaki Betty to Barber and Holmes. P-38 technical data.

Closterman, Pierre. 1952. *Flames in the Sky,* chap. 4. London: Chatto and Windus. Journalist-style account of mission; claims code break was result of windfall capture of Japanese code book. Numerous factual errors.

Craven, Wesley F., and James L. Cate, eds. 1950. *The Pacific: Guadalcanal to Saipan,* pp. 213-14. Vol. 4 of *The Army Air Forces in World War II.* Chicago: University of Chicago Press. Says Yamamoto was "victim apparently of Captain Lanphier."

Davis, Burke. 1969. *Get Yamamoto*. New York: Random House. Chapter notes (p. 228) report, "though there is no truly clarifying and definitive document on the Yamamoto mission, official sources (all in Aerospace Studies Institute, Maxwell AFB, AL,) are plentiful."

Donovan, Robert J. 1961. *PT-109: John F. Kennedy in World War II*, p. 58. New York: McGraw-Hill. Claims JFK saw Lanphier do victory rolls; disputed by Burke Davis (above). No source notes.

Famous Airplanes of the World, No. 155: Mitsubishi Type 1 Attack Bomber. May 1986. Japanese language publication. Contains structural drawings and marking data for Betty Type 11 (G4M1).

Ferguson, Robert Lawrence. 1987. *Guadalcanal, The Island of Fire: Reflections of the 347th Fighter Group,* pp. 200-204. Blue Ridge Summit, Pa.: Aero, Tab Books. Mission "has been subject of numerous controversial analyses . . . surviving Japanese pilot's account [on videotape at Fredericksburg, Tex.] lends credence to Barber . . . There is much support for [Mitchell's] position [in favor of] dual credit" for Lanphier and Barber.

Frey, Royal D. 1975. "P-38 Lightning." In *Flying Combat Aircraft of the USAAF-USAF,* ed. Robin Higham and Abigail T. Siddall, pp. 131-39. Ames: Iowa State University Press. Flying characteristics of the P38.

Glines, Carroll V. 1990. *Attack on Yamamoto*. New York: Orion Books. Makes a case for sole credit in favor of Rex Barber, with the evidence arranged accordingly.

Gurney, Gene. 1958. *Five Down and Glory: A History of the American Air Ace,* ed. Mark P. Friedlander, Jr., pp. 131-35. New York: Putnam. Lengthy Lanphier statement; no source cited. Extract in USAFHRC case file.

———. 1969. *The P-38 Lightning,* pp. 38-46. New York: Arco. Lengthy but standard account.

Halsey, William F., and J. Bryan III. 1947. *Admiral Halsey's Story,* pp. 155-57. New York: McGraw-Hill. Halsey's reaction to shootdown. Map of "The Slot."

Hattori, Takushiro. 1953. *The Complete History of the Greater East Asia War,* vol. 2, pt. 5, pp. 10-11. Tokyo: Masu. Original in Japanese; four-volume manuscript translation in the archives of the Office of the Chief of Military History, Washington, D.C. Brief mention.

Hess, William N., ed. 1978. *The American Fighter Aces Album*. Dallas: Taylor. Published by the American Fighter Aces Association; contains brief biographical sketches of U.S. aces, including Barber (p. 22), Lanphier (p. 126), and Mitchell (p. 160).

Holmes, W. J. 1979. *Double-Edged Secrets,* pp. 135-36. Annapolis, Md.: Naval Institute Press. Identifies intelligence team at FRUPAC; says "it became an item of widespread interservice gossip" that Yamamoto mission was result of codebreaking—a "minor miracle" that story did not break in papers.

Hoyt, Edwin P. 1990. *Yamamoto: The Man Who Planned Pearl Harbor.* New York: McGraw-Hill. A valuable biography of the admiral and description of the fight for Guadalcanal and New Guinea, told from the Japanese side. Contains no additional information on the mission that claimed the admiral's life, which the author terms an "assassination."

Jablonski, Edward. 1982. *America in the Air War,* pp. 153-55. Time-Life Epic of Flight Series. Alexandria, Va.: Time-Life Books. Says Lanphier and Barber were "within two miles of Yamamoto's plane" when they saw the escorts drop their belly tanks. Color photo of crash site, formal portrait of Yamamoto.

Kahn, David. 1967. *The Codebreakers: The Story of Secret Writing,* pp. 595-602. New York: Macmillan. Has text of intercepted itinerary message, map of route.

Layton, Edwin T., Roger Pineau, and John Costello. 1985. *"And I Was There,"* pp. 473-76. New York: William Morrow. Suggests Admiral Nimitz authorized mission, not Secretary of the Navy Knox. Action report quoted, says two bombers shot down.

Lewin, Ronald. 1983. *The American Magic,* pp. 187-91. New York: Penguin. Includes text of original decrypted message, but cites only secondary sources in describing the Yamamoto mission.

Loomis, Robert D. 1961. *Great American Fighter Pilots of World War II,* pp. 99-102. Landmark Books, No. 96. New York: Random House. Names Mitscher's planner. Lanphier credited with Yamamoto, Barber with second Betty; says "for weeks afterwards P-38s flew patrols near area" to protect code break.

Lord, Walter. 1977. *Lonely Vigil: Coastwatchers of the Solomons,* pp. 145-46. New York: Viking. Says "just about everybody" on Guadalcanal knew of shootdown by nightfall; confirms coastwatchers had no role other than as cover for code work.

MacArthur, Douglas. 1964. *Reminiscences,* pp. 174-75. New York: McGraw-Hill. Colorful but inaccurate mission description; claims there had been "much skepticism that the [travel] message was a hoax."

Melhorn, Charles M. 1974. *Two-Block Fox: The Rise of the Aircraft Carrier, 1911-1929.* Annapolis, Md.: Naval Institute Press.

Miller, Thomas G., Jr. 1969. *The Cactus Air Force,* pp. 206-7. New York: Harper and Row. Limited coverage of Yamamoto mission, but excellent background on 1942-43 airwar in Solomons.

Morison, Samuel Eliot. 1950. *Breaking the Bismarcks Barrier,* pp. 128-29.

Vol. 6 of *History of United States Naval Operations in World War II*. Boston: Little, Brown. Gives sole credit to Lanphier; Barber credited with second Betty.

Morton, Louis. 1962. *Strategy and Command: The First Two Years*, p. 415. The United States Army in World War II: The War in the Pacific Series. Washington, D.C.: Office of the Chief of Military History, Department of the Army. Brief mention. Cites four-volume Japanese-language history of Pacific War by Takushiro Hattori; translation on file at U.S. Army Center of Military History, Washington, D.C.

Office of Air Force History. 1978. *USAF Credits for the Destruction of Enemy Aircraft, World War II*. Washington, D.C.: U.S. Government Printing Office.

Okumiya, Masatake, and Jiro Horikoshi, with Martin Caidin. 1956. *Zero!*, chap. 20. New York: E. P. Dutton. Eyewitness account of Vice Admiral Ugaki, Chief of Staff, Combined Fleet, Imperial Japanese Navy. Was in second bomber, saw Yamamoto's plane "flying slowly just above the jungle, headed to the south, with bright orange flames rapidly enveloping *the wings* and fuselage" (p. 248). [Emphasis added; implies aircraft went down with wings intact.]

Pineau, Roger. 1976. "Admiral Isoroku Yamamoto." In *The War Lords: Military Commanders of the Twentieth Century*, ed. Field Marshal Sir Michael Carver. Boston: Little, Brown. Next to Agawa, probably the most authoritative short biography of Yamamoto.

Potter, E. B. 1976. *Nimitz*, pp. 232-34. Annapolis, Md.: Naval Institute Press. Discusses factors leading to order from CINCPAC. Says Nimitz got go-ahead from Knox.

Potter, John Deane. 1965. *Yamamoto: The Man Who Menaced America*, 301-13. New York: Viking. Quotes Ugaki. Says Lanphier selected Betty #323 because of "olive green stripes."

Reel, A. Frank. 1949. *The Case of General Yamashita*. Chicago: University of Chicago Press.

Spector, Ronald H. 1985. *Eagle against the Sun*, pp. 229-30, 453-54. New York: Free Press. Brief treatment, but excellent bibliographic notes suggest possible leads for further research on Yamamoto in Japanese sources.

Spector, Ronald H. 1988. *Listening to the Enemy: Key Documents on the Role of Communications Intelligence in the War with Japan*. SRH-127. Wilmington DE: Scholarly Resources Inc. "Narrative, Combat Intelligence Center, Joint Intelligence Center, Pacific Ocean Area" (p. 158) describes consternation when nature of the Yamamoto mission was known all over Guadalcanal by day's end, 18 April 1943; also, "History of the Operations of Special Security Officers Attached to Field Commands, 1943-1945: On

Rapid and Secure Dissemination of ULTRA Intelligence to Operating Commands" (p. 201) covers steps taken in Pacific in summer of 1943 to control dissemination and improve security of ULTRA traffic.

Taylor, Theodore. 1954. *The Magnificent Mitscher,* pp. 149-55. New York: Norton. Good detail on mission planning.

Thorpe, Donald W. 1977. *Japanese Naval Air Force Camouflage and Markings, World War II.* Fallbrook, Calif.: Aero Publishers. Paint and marking data on Betty.

Toland, John. 1970. *The Rising Sun: The Decline and Fall of the Japanese Empire, 1936–1945,* pp. 554-58. New York: Random House. Reports Lieutenant General Imamura (CG, Imperial Japanese Army on Guadalcanal) warned Yamamoto not to fly to front, based on his own near-fatal encounter with U.S. fighters near Bougainville. Says Mitchell radioed emphatic "get the bombers" message to Lanphier during initial moment of attack. "Both [Barber] and Lanphier were sure they had shot down the first bomber, Yamamoto's."

Wible, John T. 1988. *The Yamamoto Mission.* Fredericksburg, Tex.: Admiral Nimitz Foundation. Published to commemorate Yamamoto Retrospective held on 18 April 1988. Says of Barber's 1950 request to AU for correction: "there clearly was no official interest from the start . . . nor would either be afforded such courtesy in later years" (p. 30). "The Air Force [in its 1985 Board decision] has conspicuously washed its hands of the matter" (p. 38).

Winterbotham, F. W. 1974. *The Ultra Secret,* p. 252. New York: Dell. Recaps British outrage over use of Ultra to kill an admiral, without any cover story prepared for it.

Periodicals and Readers' Correspondence

Aiken, David, ed. 1983. "The Admiral's Last Flight." *Japanese Information Clearinghouse Bulletin* 1, no. 1. Entire issue dedicated to mission reportage: includes analysis, copies of mission notes, photos and drawings, Japanese investigators' comments re: crash site details.

Alsop, Joseph. 1959. "The Major's Friend." *New York Herald Tribune* (26 January), p. 18. Apparently based on 1945 interview with Barber in China; Alsop says Barber credited Lanphier with Yamamoto victory. According to Wible, Barber attempted to demand Alsop print correction; no success.

Bechtel, Paul S. 1985. Letter. *Air Force Magazine* (July): 14. 12th Fighter Squadron C.O.; says he was present at debrief; "it was agreed that Barber and Lanphier would share credit." Rebuts Gwynn-Jones article (see below).

Boghosian, S. Samuel. 1985. "The Yamamoto Ambush." *Air Classics* 21, no. 5 (May): 44-47, 62-63. "No one will ever know" who shot Yamamoto down. 1980 photos of wreckage clearly show tail-gun mount, but no gun. Mention of post-attack comment by Lanphier: "*We* got the son-of-a-bitch." Emphasis added; differs from other quotes, which are in first-person singular.

Chandler, George T. 1987. "Who Really Did Shoot Down Admiral Isoroku Yamamoto?" *King's Cliffe Remembered* 5, no. 3 (Winter): 2-8. Somewhat partisan account; suggests entire credit should be given to Barber.

Closterman, Pierre. 1953. "Target Yamamoto." *Royal Air Force Flying Review* 8, no. 4 (January): 37, 43. Repetition of *Flames in the Sky,* chap. 4 (see above); journalist-style piece with numerous errors.

Condon, Maj. Gen. John P., USMC (Ret.). 1990. "Yamamoto Post-Mortem." *U.S. Naval Institute Proceedings* 116/No. 11/1053 (November). The COMAIRSOLS' Fighter Command operations officer recalls the mission and the controversy that followed it; includes references to the Hayashi interview (in this volume).

Davenport, Manuel. 1990. "False Reports: Misperceptions, Self-Deceptions, or Lies?" *Southwest Philosophy Review* 6, no. 1 (January): 113-21. An attempt to explain why Lanphier recollected the mission in terms of support for his own claim to sole credit—but based on the presumed accuracy of other mission participants' recollections and partisan accounts that favor Barber's claim to sole credit.

Falk, Stanley L. 1963. "The Ambush of Admiral Yamamoto." *Navy* 6, no. 4 (April): 32-34. Journalist-style narrative; credits Lanphier with Yamamoto, Barber with other Betty.

Field, James A., Jr. 1949. "Admiral Yamamoto," *U.S. Naval Institute Proceedings* 75, no. 10 (October): 1105-1113. Good thumbnail sketch; discusses U.S. press reaction to announcement of Yamamoto's death in 1943.

Green, Murray. 1980. Letter. *The Retired Officer* (January): 56. "Special Projects" officer who reviewed Mitchell's opposition to sole claim for Lanphier, apparently in 1946-47; was working for Stuart Symington; supports joint claim. Rebuts Robert Vote article (see below).

Gurney, Gene. 1959. "How They Got Yamamoto." *American Legion Magazine* 66, no. 1 (January): 12-13, 36-38. Journalist-style narrative; scant mention of Barber.

Gwynn-Jones, Terry. 1985. "In Search of Yamamoto." *Air Force Magazine* (April): 120-25. Argues for shared credit; "no doubt Barber hit tail . . . Lanphier finished off." Visit to crash site: photo of starboard wing. See rebuttal letter by Bechtel, above.

———. 1981? "On the Trail of Yamamoto." *Geo* 3, no. 3, pp. 5-19. Visit to crash site; photos.

Harris, Roy. 1989. "Yamamoto: Rendezvous over Bougainville." *Confeder-*

ate Air Force Dispatch 14, no. 2 (March/April): 40. Synopsis of symposium at San Antonio and request for funds for SYMA New Guinea trip. No mention of Lanphier; photo caption says Barber made "first and perhaps only firing pass."

Heppenheimer, T. A. 1989. "Yamamoto and the Hijackers." *Defense World* 1, no. 2 (August-September): 46, 50. Claims Col. Oliver North derived idea of forcing down fleeing Achille Lauro hijackers in Italy from Yamamoto events.

Holmes, Besby F. 1967. "Who Really Shot Down Yamamoto?" *Popular Aviation* 1, no. 1 (March/April): 56-64. Photos. First-person account-implies that Holmes saw Yamamoto's Betty go down.

"Japanese Admiral Killed in Combat." *New York Times,* 21 May 1943, pp. 1, 5. First announcement of Yamamoto's death. No mention of possible USAAF involvement.

Lanphier, Thomas G., Jr. 1945. "Flier Who Shot Down Yamamoto Says White House Baited the Trap," *New York Times,* 12 September, p. 2; "Yamamoto's Killer Arrived on the Dot," *New York Times,* 13 September, p. 5; "Yamamoto Died in Flaming Crash," *New York Times,* 14 September, p. 7. Three-part article distributed by North American Newspaper Alliance. No mention of Barber taking part in the actual interception, or Barber's Betty credit.

———. 1966. "I Shot Down Yamamoto." *Reader's Digest* 89, no. 536 (December): 82-87. Lanphier cites telegram from Secretary of the Navy Knox as authority for mission.

McNally, Richard. 1989. "Aerial Ambush!" *Airman* 33, no. 6 (June): 14-19. Based on March 1989 interview. Quotes Mitchell and Barber; Barber claims Yamamoto credit. "Controversy has raged for 46 years." Sidebar announces expedition, says results will be presented to AF credit review board.

Michel, Marshall. 1966. "To Kill an Admiral." *Aerospace Historian* 13, no. 1 (Spring): 25-29. Narrative account, no notes.

Mitchell, John. 1988. "The Yamamoto Mission." *King's Cliffe Remembered* 5, no. 4 (Winter): 10-12. "Debrief was very shoddy and inconclusive"; implies Barber should get sole credit.

Radimey, Walter. 1989. "Yamamoto Incident." *Guadalcanal Echoes* (April): 11. Second-hand account in Guadalcanal veterans' newsletter of Australian commando unit member's report of finding the body of Raymond K. Hine on Bougainville Island, with dogtags. But dogtags never turned in to authorities, because Total Army Personnel Center, Casualty and Mortuary Affairs Division, still carries Hine MIA; report appears to be spurious.

Smith, Dale O. 1967. "Who Shot Down Yamamoto?" *Aerospace Historian* 14, no. 1 (Spring): 9. Editorial comment on letters sent in reply to Marshall Michel article (see above); only letter printed came from Lt. Col. Ken Barber in *Aerospace Historian* 13, no. 2 (Summer 1966): 79, praising Michel treatment.

Taylor, Blaine. 1988. "Ambush in Hostile Skies." *Military History* (August): 42-49. Interview with Rex Barber.

———. 1989. "The Plot to Kill Yamamoto." *Air Classics* 25, no. 4 (April): 18-28, 68-75; 25, no. 5 (May): 24-31, 75-78. Includes Barber and Mitchell interview material.

"Thank You, Mr. Yamamoto," *Time* 41, no. 22 (31 May 1943): 28. Announcement of Yamamoto's death. Contains masked reference to Lanphier: ". . . the U.S. will have a new hero"; same issue features veiled reference to shootdown in biographical sketch of Lanphier on p. 66.

"Thirteenth [AF] Was the 'Jungle Bunny' of Pacific." *Army Times* (AF Ed.) 6, no. 39 (4 May 1946): 16. Weekly series describing numbered AF WWII accomplishments "prepared from official records." Gives Lanphier sole credit; Mitchell complained to General Spaatz, received "noncommittal answer," according to Wible monograph, p. 27.

Toliver, Raymond. 1988. Letter, *King's Cliffe Remembered* 6, no. 1 (Spring): 11. Supports Barber's claim; believes in third bomber scenario.

"Tom Lanphier: New President Is 31-Year-Old Newspaperman, Former Fighter Pilot." *Air Force Magazine* 30, no. 11 (November 1947): 17, 45. Biographical sketch of Lanphier as of assumption of presidency of Air Force Association, apparently based upon speech delivered by Lanphier at AFA National Convention; contains brief mission account.

Vote, Robert. 1979. "The Death of Admiral Yamamoto." *The Retired Officer* 35, no. 11 (November): 27-30. See rebuttal letter by Green, above.

"Who Shot Down Yamamoto Is Still in Question." *CAF Dispatch* 14, no. 6 (November/December 1989): 38. Announcement of traveling Yamamoto shootdown exhibit sponsored by Nimitz Museum.

Wible, John T. 1967. "The Yamamoto Mission." *Journal of the American Aviation Historical Society* 15, no. 3 (Fall): 159-67. Supports Barber credit, but includes written rebuttal by Lanphier. In a letter to Wible, quoted in this article, Barber described the post-mission debriefing and claimed the bomber he attacked lost "his rudder and a good portion of his vertical fin . . ." (p. 163). But Barber remembered it differently in 1988; see Wible, above.

"Yamamoto's Killer Identified by Army." *New York Times,* 12 September 1945, pp. 1-2. Gives Lanphier sole credit for kill; credits Barber with second Betty.

"The Younger Generation," *Time* 41, no. 22 (31 May 1943): 66. Biographical sketch of Lanphier; contains veiled reference to shootdown, which is also reported in same issue on p. 28.

Index